SOCIAL WORK AND HUMAN RIGHTS

SOCIALWORK AND HUMAN RIGHTS

A FOUNDATION FOR POLICY AND PRACTICE

ELISABETH REICHERT

COLUMBIA UNIVERSITY PRESS ■ NEW YORK

Columbia University Press
Publishers Since 1893
New York   Chichester, West Sussex
Copyright © 2003 Elisabeth Reichert

Library of Congress Cataloging-in-Publication Data

Reichert, Elisabeth.
    Social work and human rights : a foundation for policy and practice /
Elisabeth Reichert.
       p. cm.
    Includes bibliographical references and index.
    ISBN 0–231–12308–6 (cloth : alk. paper) — ISBN 0–231–12309–4
(paper : alk. paper)
      1. Social service.   2. Human rights.   I. Title.

  HV41 .R433 2003
  361.2—dc21

2002190835

Columbia University Press books are printed on permanent and durable acid-
free paper.

Printed in the United States of America

c 10 9 8 7 6 5 4 3 2 1
p 10 9 8 7 6 5 4 3 2 1

For the figures in this book, Columbia University Press gratefully acknowledges permission to use material from *Women's Human Rights Step by Step: A
Practical Guide to Using International Human Rights Law and Mechanisms to Defend Women's Human Rights* by Women's Law and Development International
and Human Rights Watch (Washington, D.C.: Women's Law and Development
International, 1997).

To all who have helped build the road
toward a more just and fair world

CONTENTS

Foreword by Katherine van Wormer ix

Introduction 1

1   Development and History of Human Rights 18

2   Universal Declaration of Human Rights 44

3   Building on the Universal Declaration: The International Covenant
    on Civil and Political Rights
    Robert J. McCormick and Elisabeth Reichert 83

4   The International Covenant on Economic, Social,
    and Cultural Rights
    Robert J. McCormick and Elisabeth Reichert 112

5   Vulnerable Groups: Women 133

6   Vulnerable Groups: Children, Persons with Disabilities
    and/or HIV-AIDS, Gays and Lesbians, Older Persons,
    and Victims of Racism 162

7 International Aspects of Human Rights 196

8 Applying Human Rights to the Social Work Profession 224

Conclusion 249

Appendices 251

  Appendix A: Universal Declaration of Human Rights 251
  Appendix B: International Covenant on Civil and
    Political Rights 257
  Appendix C: Optional Protocol to the International Covenant
    on Civil and Political Rights 275
  Appendix D: International Covenant on Economic, Social,
    and Cultural Rights 279

Credits and Permissions 289
Index 291

FOREWORD

*Where, after all, do universal human rights begin? In small places, close
to home—so close and so small that they can't be seen on any map of the
world. Yet they are the world of the individual person.*

—Eleanor Roosevelt (1958)

Last year (2001) at a national social work conference I attended, the
presenter reported on a survey she had taken of her American and Al-
banian students of social work. How many had read the Universal Declaration of Human Rights? Only a minority had read the document,
and twice as many of the Albanians as American students had done
so. Upon my return I posed the question to my advanced graduate
class. A few had heard of the document but none had read it. I then
proceeded to pass out copies of the document that could be considered the foundation for human rights.

As we enter the global age, an age characterized by ethnic cleansing,
suicide bombings, air strikes, the war on terrorism, suppression of
civil liberties, and the decline of the welfare state to comply with the
dictates of the free market economy, there is a need for new under-
standings, new approaches. Many problems that seem endemic to one
state or one country can only be understood internationally, as common problems with common solutions.

Social welfare, in the sense of the well-being of a people, and
human rights are inextricably linked. People cannot enjoy a sense of
security and well-being if their rights are systematically violated by

the very state representatives from whom they would seek protection. Nor can they enjoy the benefits of human rights such as exist in a democracy if their social welfare need for such things as food, shelter, and clothing are not met. Hence the reasons for *Social Work and Human Rights: A Foundation for Social Work Policy and Practice*. Its publication is timely. The rationale of this book is consistent with the 2000 NASW policy statement, "International Policy on Human Rights." This statement strongly endorses the Universal Declaration, conventions, and treaties that, according to NASW, provide a human rights template for social work.

Three categories of rights are provided in the declaration: economic and cultural rights; protection against discrimination based on race, color, sex, language, religion, and political opinion; and civil and political rights against the arbitrary powers of the state. Those articles of the declaration concerned with economic, social, and cultural rights range from the less urgent, but also important, rights of "rest, leisure, and reasonable limitation of working hours and periodic holidays with pay" (art. 24) to the more fundamental rights of food, housing, health care, work, and social security (art. 25). The fact that these rights are included nowhere in the U.S. Constitution (but in many European constitutions) has hindered the American people in their claims to basic social and economic benefits.

The principles of social and economic justice as enunciated in the Universal Declaration closely parallel the values practiced by the founding mothers of social work since the earliest days and those more recently spelled out in the NASW's 1996 *Code of Ethics*. Unique to social work among helping professions is the emphasis on social justice in the social environment. Merely putting Band-Aids on clients is never, can never be, enough. Because the personal is political, and the political personal, the artificial split between macro and micro is just that—artificial. American social work education has been remiss in its failure to integrate human rights content into the curriculum and to prepare students for the kind of ethical dilemmas they may face when a client's rights are being violated. Only in 1996, in fact, had the word *global* even been included in our social work code of ethics. This inclusion is most striking in Standard 6:01: "Social workers should promote the general welfare of society from local to global levels."

Elisabeth Reichert's *Social Work and Human Rights* aims to remedy the relative neglect of human rights issues in American social work and to bring human rights concepts to the forefront of the discussion. Reichert's aim is achieved and achieved magnificently. Drawing on international law as presented in United Nations documents, this book successfully presents the unifying and systematic conceptualization of human rights for the profession that we sorely needed. However, do not think this is your usual dreary theoretical treatise. The presentation is as dynamic as the content. Consider some of the questions addressed in this book:

- Is the social work profession a human rights profession?
- To what extent are economic rights human rights?
- Why does the United States vehemently oppose ratification of the U.N. Convention on the Rights of the Child?
- Which highly vulnerable group found in every country is not included in any human rights document?
- How do we reconcile the value of cultural relativism with the recognition that some truths are universal?
- On what occasion and to what extent did governments acknowledge that poverty was a form of violence against women?
- What is the role of social workers with regard to human rights?
- In what way does the Universal Declaration of Human Rights go beyond the limits of the U.S. Constitution?
- How can the social work code of ethics be regarded as a mini-Universal Declaration?
- Does America's war on terrorism violate human rights?

There is much to learn here. This is a book not to be merely read or skimmed, in fact, but to be pored over. The human rights framework as presented in this volume provides a prism through which to view the hidden assumptions and values of the social work profession.

"Where is the human rights compass to guide social workers?" asks Elisabeth Reichert (in the last, climactic chapter). I have found it, and it is here— in the pages that follow.

Katherine van Wormer
Professor of Social Work
University of Northern Iowa
Cedar Falls, Iowa

SOCIAL WORK AND HUMAN RIGHTS

Introduction

Human Rights belong to everyone, or they are guaranteed to no one.
                                                    —*Amnesty International*

The concept of human rights has occupied social workers, educators, philosophers, lawyers, and politicians for ages. The proposition that all individuals who inhabit planet Earth share inherent privileges and rights has great attraction. This commonality among all who reside on the planet, regardless of country or nationality, aims to bring individuals closer together than might otherwise be the case. After all, if someone who lives in the United States acknowledges that someone living in Russia or China has the same right to a safe, nonviolent environment, this link can lead to better cooperation in resolving key issues affecting human existence.

Of course, human rights cover domestic, as well as international, circumstances. Unless individuals, communities, corporations, governments, and other groups recognize human rights at home, promotion of human rights on a broader level appears meaningless or, at best, superficial. The most appropriate place to begin the study and application of human rights lies within a person's own environment. Only after the individual, entity, or group thoroughly understands human rights in a local sense can human rights be expanded to a broader spectrum of circumstances.

THE DRED SCOTT CASE

The United States often leads the charge against violations of human rights. However, while the United States has some justification in presenting itself as a model for promoting human rights, history has not always been so kind to this beacon of liberty. Only after the Civil War in 1865 did the country definitively prohibit slavery and grant citizenship to all persons born within the United States by enacting amendments to the Constitution (U.S. Constitution, amend. 13 and 14).

Before those amendments, a decision by the U.S. Supreme Court had ruled that African-Americans were not citizens of the United States: slavery was legal unless banned by a particular state, and slaves were property protected by the Constitution (*Scott v. Sandford*, 1857). This decision is known as the Dred Scott case and can only be viewed as an abomination of political, social, and cultural thought. Dred Scott had been a slave in the state of Missouri, which allowed slavery. Scott's owner then moved with Scott to the free state of Illinois and free territory of Wisconsin, areas that prohibited slavery. By residing in a free state and free territory, Scott gained his freedom. However, after having gained his freedom, Scott returned to Missouri. At the time Scott initially returned to Missouri, the prevailing law in Missouri stated that if a slave returned to Missouri after having resided in a free state or territory, that slave could then retain his or her freedom (*Rachael v. Walker*, 1837). To obtain his freedom, Scott began legal proceedings in Missouri. As Scott's case wound its way to the Missouri Supreme Court, the debate over slavery became increasingly heated. Instead of following previous legal precedents, the Missouri Supreme Court overturned those principles and refused to grant Scott his freedom.

Scott's plea for freedom then went to the U.S. Supreme Court, which rendered its decision that Scott, as an African Negro, could never be a citizen of the United States and, further, was considered to be a piece of property protected by the Constitution. Outrage followed this decision, but not until after the Civil War did Congress begin overturning the legal principles established by the Dred Scott case. In reality, decades passed before Congress removed all the legal residue of the Dred Scott decision. Segregation in many southern states legally allowed separation of races in schools, eating facilities, public transport, and other institutions until prohibited by court decisions in the 1950s and 1960s. Even today, though, ghosts from the Dred Scott case remain, a reminder that a society must always be diligent in the protection of basic human rights and freedoms.

WHAT ARE HUMAN RIGHTS?

To begin any study of human rights, the initial and obvious question arises: What are human rights? Without a coherent response to this question, no further study or understanding of human rights can occur. Unfortunately, many individuals (especially, it seems, politicians) blithely employ the words *human rights* as if automatic comprehension necessarily follows. Nothing could be further from reality. For instance, American politicians frequently criticize China for its human rights violations, with little explanation as to the nature of those violations. One may wonder: What violations? What specific acts perpetrated by China run afoul of human rights? Why are those acts violations of human rights? Who defines human rights? Do violations of human rights occur only in China and other countries outside the United States? General statements alleging that a country violates human rights creates confusion because such generalizations usually provide scant insight into the true concept of human rights. This does not mean that China or some other country is *not* violating human rights. However, before a politician, social worker, or other individual accuses another individual or entity of violating human rights, he or she needs to have at least a basic grounding in the concept of human rights. Unfortunately, this does not appear to be the case in many instances.

As this book will explain, human rights are not limited to political ideals, meaning democratic elections, freedom of speech and religion, and other rights typically associated with the American political system. Human rights encompass a wide variety of political, economic, and social areas. For example, a specific human right includes the right to adequate health care, which the United States does not legally recognize. Does this mean that in

---

Forty-two million U.S. citizens and residents have no medical coverage with which to help pay the costs of medical care (Krutsinger 2001). U.S. politicians talk about human rights violations in China—lack of freedom of speech and religion in particular. Which set of human rights is more important? Does an individual who refuses to seek medical attention because he or she cannot pay for it suffer a human rights violation? Under human rights principles, this would be the case.

this regard the United States violates the human rights of its citizens? This book will address this issue in later chapters. Clearly, though, a selective recognition of human rights by U.S. politicians and other individuals indicates a lack of understanding about the overall concept of human rights.

Human rights define needs but also present a set of rights for each individual, no matter where that individual resides. The concept of human rights can generally be defined as "*those rights, which are inherent in our nature and without which we cannot live as human beings. Human rights and fundamental freedoms allow us to fully develop and use our human qualities, our intelligence, our talents and our conscience and to satisfy our spiritual and other needs*" (United Nations 1987; emphasis added).

Of course, this definition immediately raises questions about whose "nature" is being defined. A U.S. citizen might feel that having access to running water, electricity, and other similar resources is inherent in her or his nature and therefore necessary to fully develop as a human being. On the other hand, a citizen of Afghanistan might feel that simply having enough to eat and possessing warm clothing is enough to live with dignity as a human being. Whose version of human rights should prevail? Are some people entitled to greater human rights than others because they possess the means with which to obtain or purchase valuable resources? From a purist's viewpoint, certainly not. Every individual is entitled to the same human rights. The difficulty arises in allocating resources to achieve human rights. A fundamental issue concerning human rights lies in constructing policies by which human rights apply to all, not simply select individuals and groups.

Clearly human rights principles require cultural understanding and attention to existing resources. Certainly, a social work practice based on human rights is no panacea for discrimination, inequality, poverty, and other social problems. Yet knowledge of human rights can help the social work profession better understand its role as a helping profession. By integrating human rights into the profession, social workers will obtain unique insight into issues central to the profession.

UNIVERSALITY AND INDIVISIBILITY

When beginning to study human rights, a social worker needs to understand two basic concepts relating to those rights: universality and indivisibility. The concept of *universality* underpins human rights. Every individual has a claim to enjoyment of human rights, wherever the individual resides.

For example, human rights include adequate health care and nutrition for everyone. Perhaps a country's resources are insufficient to provide universal health care and food and, therefore, not everyone receives adequate care and nutrition. However, because health care and food are integral to human rights, governments have an obligation to provide a framework for ensuring the delivery of these rights. Lack of resources may actually be a subterfuge for ignoring these human rights. By classifying certain rights and freedoms as human rights, all governments recognize a common goal of creating conditions to guarantee those rights and freedoms.

Not all human rights are so clear-cut as the above examples, which can result in reluctance to promote a particular human right. The notion of universality may clash with particular cultures, laws, policies, morals, and other regimes that fail to recognize the human right in question. In some countries, discrimination against gays and lesbians is allowed because cultural or religious norms permit this type of discrimination. Yet such discrimination appears to violate human rights principles even though human rights require sensitivity to culture and religion. Which should prevail, the cultural or religious norm or the human right? If human rights apply to everyone, then the human rights doctrine must prevail. Of course, the issue is not so simple. Who defines a human right? Who benefits from the definition? Who loses from the definition? Whose voices are being heard in enforcing human rights? Who defines culture? Does one government have the right to tell another government that its policies violate a human right? In the case of disagreement over interpretation of a human right, who decides? Obviously, the issue of universality can lead to bumps along the way in exercising human rights.

This principle of universality places a unique stamp upon the body of laws and other guidelines commonly known as human rights. "Human rights doctrine is now so powerful, but also so unthinkingly imperialist in its claim to universality, that it has exposed itself to serious intellectual attack. These challenges have raised important questions about whether human rights norms deserve the authority they have acquired: whether their claims to universality are justified, or whether they are just another cunning exercise in Western moral imperialism" (Ignatieff 2001:102). In later chapters, this book will address in more detail issues surrounding the universality principle.

Social workers may find the notion of universality difficult to fit within other social work principles, especially those of cultural diversity and self-determination. However, universality does not mean that everyone is alike or should develop in the same manner. Universality allows all types of diversity and differences among individuals and groups. The key to understanding universality is to accept that the goal is not to create sameness among different cultures. Universality aims to ensure that individuals and peoples everywhere have basic rights in their existence, but makes no pretense that everyone will exist in the same manner.

In addition to universality, the other concept important to human rights is that of *indivisibility*. The concept of indivisibility refers to the necessity that governments and individuals recognize *each* human right and not to selectively promote some rights over others. The fact that U.S. policy does not guarantee health care to all its citizens highlights the importance of indivisibility among human rights. Without adequate health care, an individual may fail to attend to an illness that becomes life-threatening or debilitating. Impaired health reduces an individual's enjoyment of other human rights, such as the promotion of family or employment. Impaired health could even affect the will or ability of an individual to participate in an election or other activities viewed as human rights. Consequently, the denial of one human right can easily impact the enjoyment of other human rights and directly or indirectly deny other human rights. For this reason, the notion of indivisibility plays a key role in the exercise of human rights.

Indivisibility does not come without a certain degree of controversy. Admittedly, not every country can afford to provide all the economic rights defined as human rights. Should not this excuse the provision of that right? And what if a country views a particular human right as unsuitable for its citizens? Can that country refuse to acknowledge that human right? While indivisibility occupies a key position within human rights, no simple answers apply to issues surrounding this basic concept.

Many of the concepts about human rights may appear impractical, strange, or merely utopian. Yet by analyzing specific human rights and the justification for a particular human right, social workers can better understand how human rights naturally connect to their profession. This book aims to fill in perceived gaps about the nature of human rights and what they really mean for the social work profession.

RELUCTANCE TO INTEGRATE HUMAN RIGHTS INTO U.S. SOCIAL WORK

On an international level, social workers have embraced the concept of human rights as a key component in their profession (Staub-Bernasconi

1998; Ife 2001; IFSW 2000). However, social workers in the United States have lagged behind their counterparts from other countries in connecting human rights to social work policies and practices (Reichert 2001). The U.S.-based National Association of Social Workers does not even mention the term *human rights* in its *Code of Ethics* (NASW 1996). Yet the concept of human rights has equal importance to U.S. social workers. Social workers in the United States follow many of the concepts contained within the Universal Declaration of Human Rights (see appendix A) and other human rights instruments.

Why has there been so little discussion by the social work profession in the United States concerning human rights? The current reluctance of U.S. social workers to join their international counterparts in promoting human rights appears to be the result of three primary factors:

1. *A focus in the United States on social justice instead of human rights.* U.S. social workers continue to adhere to the concept of social justice as the dominant theme in their profession, with little mention of human rights (Pelton 2001). The promotion of social justice as the central theme in the profession originates from historical and philosophical theories that frequently appear confusing and outdated. For example, no clear definition of social justice even exists. Social work academics describe various types of social justice with little explanation as to what kind of social justice applies to the circumstances at hand (Hartman 1990; Tyson 1995). By focusing on social justice, U.S. social workers might believe they are also addressing human rights. However, human rights encompass a more comprehensive set of guidelines for the social work profession.

2. *The inclination of U.S. social workers to view human rights as only political rights.* Aside from using as its ideal an amorphous concept of social justice, the social work profession in the United States often equates human rights with constitutional and legal issues. An equating of human rights with purely legalistic notions sidesteps any apparent importance of human rights for the nonlawyer. The liberal U.S. political tradition, as reflected in early documents like the Declaration of Independence and Bill of Rights in the Constitution, emphasizes individual political and civil rights (Roche and Dewees 2001). However, these documents reflect relative indifference to economic and social rights (Charlesworth 1994). Civil and political rights such as freedom of

speech, press, and religion are officially protected cornerstones of U.S. public policy. But economic, social, and cultural components of human well-being, such as food, shelter, health care, and cultural identity, tend to be relegated to individual initiative and personal achievement (Flowers 1998). Social workers may discount the importance of human rights by viewing the Constitution and other basic documents as encompassing the entire gamut of human rights, thus assuming that it is unnecessary to explore the topic further. Therefore, when U.S. social workers encounter the term *human rights*, they may view those rights as only indirectly related to the social work profession.

3. *A more local view of the world by U.S. social workers.* Another factor inhibiting U.S. social workers from embracing human rights lies in the international nature of human rights. Social workers in the United States have shown themselves to be rather myopic in their worldview of social work (Sanders and Pedersen 1984). This narrow view of social work possibly contributes to the reluctance of social workers in the United States to embrace human rights to the extent of their international counterparts (Reichert 1998). Human rights embrace cross-cultural concepts, which transcend national boundaries. Therefore, unless U.S. social workers adopt a more worldly outlook, they most likely will continue to view human rights as foreign to the profession.

This reluctance to promote human rights does not mean U.S. social workers are less competent than their international counterparts. However, because human rights occupy a central role in the social work profession, both in the United States and elsewhere, social workers could benefit from a better understanding of human rights and the relationship of those rights to the profession.

In a recent policy statement, the National Association of Social Workers (NASW) supported efforts to link human rights with the social work profession: "*Human rights and social work are natural allies. Social workers need to be aware of this conceptual link and the power of working in concert with human rights organizations and activists throughout the world*" (NASW 2000:181; emphasis added). Yet even with this NASW policy statement, current attention to human rights and their application to the profession seems inadequate to help social workers understand this important link.

Certainly, as indicated by the NASW policy statement, not all U.S. social workers ignore the strong connection between human rights and their profession. Social workers have expressed the need to establish social work as a human rights profession and integrate human rights into social work teaching, research, and practice (Witkin 1993, 1998; Mayadas and Elliot 1997). Social work educators have developed a teaching model for human rights (Roche, Dewees, Trailweaver et al. 1999; Roche and Dewees 2001). Social work literature exists on connecting women's rights to human rights (Wetzel 1993; Reichert 1996, 1998; Roche 1996). The literature also impugns the federal U.S. welfare act enacted in 1996 as a violation of immigrants' human rights (Reichert and McCormick 1998). However, these voices in the social work profession are few. Usually, human rights simply become merged into a vague but ubiquitous classification of social and economic justice.

SOCIAL JUSTICE—AN OUTDATED CONCEPT?

Social workers in the United States generally have encountered a guiding principle in their training known as social justice, which tends to concentrate on the needs of a client, rather than on the rights of the client. In the education of social workers, the National Association of Social Workers' *Code of Ethics* (NASW 1996) and the handbook of the Council on Social Work Education (CSWE 1994) reflect this strong commitment to social justice.

While the social work profession couches all types of goals beneath the umbrella of social justice, close scrutiny of this concept reveals shortcomings, primarily in the precise contours of social justice itself. The satisfying sound of this term clearly lends support to the continued use of the term in the profession. However, the use of a term simply because it evokes a desirable resonance defies logic if the term itself lacks a clear definition and ready application to social work practice. An attempt to define social justice indicates that three main theories of social justice exist: libertarian, utilitarian, and egalitarian. Each theory has its followers and adherents, though the egalitarian theory is apparently the most relevant to social work practice.

Libertarian Theory The libertarian theory of social justice proposes that each individual is entitled to any material possession he or she has legally acquired (Nozik 1974). Under this theory, the individual has autonomy and has no obligation to share resources with others. This autonomy militates against any forced redistribution of resources from the haves to the have-nots. Charity, or service to others, occurs from the largess of the benefactor, rather than through any right of the recipient to obtain what the benefactor possesses.

As an entitlement-based form of social justice, the libertarian theory rejects distributive justice. For this reason, social workers may not readily subscribe to this theory of social justice. Yet in reality, many of the basic principles in the organization and sentiment of government structures within the United States follow a libertarian theory, with frequently only limited attention to the redistribution of resources.

Utilitarian Theory A second theory of social justice evaluates actions on the basis of whether they provide the greatest happiness for the individual or the greatest number. This utilitarian theory holds that, although an individual has the right to be free from coercion, at times a redistribution of scarce resources meets the interest of the common good and should occur (van Soest 1994). For example, under this theory, conditions should be promoted that encourage the greatest production of food for all, regardless of an individual's circumstances.

Essentially, providing the greatest good for the greatest number forms the primary principle under utilitarian theory. In contrast to the libertarian theory, a utilitarian will not hesitate to infringe upon an individual's right to resources if the sharing or redistributing of those resources would benefit the greatest number within a defined region. Obviously, the inherent conflict with this theory of social justice lies in determining what benefits the greatest number.

Egalitarian Theory The egalitarian theory of social justice corresponds most closely to what the social work profession appears to mean when it portrays social justice (Reisch and Taylor 1983). Under this theory, the needs of all must be considered (Rawls 1971). Redistribution of scarce resources becomes a moral imperative, and any redistribution should benefit, or at least not harm, the most vulnerable in society. This distributive theory of social justice holds that the disadvantaged have a right to basic resources for living.

Clearly, the egalitarian theory of social justice rebuts the libertarian and utilitarian theories when equality becomes a defining value (Rawls 1971). In an egalitarian society, citizens must have equal rights, equality of opportunity, and equal access to social resources. Inequalities in resources should be allowed only when those within the lowest margin of society benefit (van Soest 1992). Social resources generally refer to economic benefits, but the egalitarian theory can also be applied to noneconomic goods. Alleviating noneconomic "deprivations" can be a form of social justice (Rawls 1971; Wakefield 1998).

Summary of the Three Theories Even based on the above three theories, the term *social justice* remains elusive for it defies a single, relatively concrete definition. Under the libertarian theory, social justice protects the rights of the individual. The utilitarian theory tempers the libertarian theory to provide for the greatest good of the people, while the egalitarian theory forms the basis for redistributing resources to the less endowed in society. In other words, depending on the theory, social justice means different things to different people.

In a social work context, social justice appears to be used to reflect the egalitarian theory more than the other theories. The social work profession uses social justice to encompass fairness in the distribution of resources, rights, opportunities, and duties (Rose-Miller 1994). Social policy concerns the allocation of resources, while social justice is about ensuring that all people have the same access to those resources. Social work is about addressing the way injustices are structured into the allocation of resources and the disadvantages that accrue from such injustices (Benn 1991).

In attempting to illuminate social justice for the profession, a debate over whether justice should be focused on individuals, as opposed to groups, has emerged (Longres and Scanlon 2001; Pelton 2001). The notion that needs of individuals are often subordinate to those of the community or group forms the basis for this debate. For example, "Advocates of recent welfare reform claimed that, *in general*, denying welfare benefits to women in need and children would contribute to the growth of the economy and reduce child poverty by motivating impoverished mothers to find jobs" (Pelton 2001: 433). The greater good here is the "growth of the economy" with its alleged spill-over effect of "motivating impoverished mothers to find jobs." While social workers may question this sacrificing of individuals to the much larger community in the name of social justice, at times attention to group associations can promote access to resources. "Without studying group inequalities and generating appropriate policies and practice models, we would be inadvertently fostering the relative exclusion of some groups from social and human services (e.g., education, health, and mental health) and their overall inclusion in others (e.g., public welfare, criminal justice, and employment)" (Longres and Scanlon 2001:443). By focusing on the group, rather than individuals, social workers may discover dynamics that impact on the group.

In summary, though, while academics may debate concepts of social justice, even they must admit that a social work definition of social justice "remains an open question" (Longres and Scanlon 2001:444). "Our case study of researchers and research instructors in a School of Social Work indicated that social workers appear to lack a coherent sense of what constitutes social justice, sometimes equating it with Rawls's fairness model of individual rights, at other times sounding a call for equality between social groups" (444).

The *Encyclopedia of Social Work* (Edwards 1995) lists three components of social justice: (1) legal justice, which is concerned with what a person owes to society; 2) commutative justice, which is concerned with what people owe each other; and (3) distributive justice, which is "what society owes a person" (van Soest 1995:1811). This three-pronged definition seems of little help in ferreting out specific details relating to social justice. Minds will inevitably differ on what society owes a person or what a person owes society. For instance, does society owe a person a job? Health care? Depending on the definition of social justice, answers to those questions could be either "yes" or "no."

Curiously, while the NASW has numerous policy statements on all types of social issues, the only policy statement that specifically mentions social justice is within the context of peace. This policy statement, entitled "Peace and Social Justice," focuses on peace and reduction in military spending, which emphasizes that people have a need to live without violence (NASW 2000:238–43). No definition of social justice appears within that six-page statement, although reference to the promotion of "social and economic development and protection of the environment" seems to fall within the vague contours of social justice (242).

While NASW policy statements do little to define or explain social justice, their statement on human rights presents a view that could be interpreted as ranking social justice below the importance of human rights:

Social work can be proud of its heritage. It is the only profession imbued with social justice as its fundamental value and concern. But social justice is a fairness doctrine that provides civil and political leeway in deciding what is just and unjust. Human rights, on the other hand, encompasses social justice, but transcends civil and political customs, in consideration of the basic life-sustaining needs of all human beings, without distinction. (NASW 2000:180)

Even with the above attempts to explain the term *social justice*, the current use of the concept is elusive and misleading (Rose-Miller 1994). No theory fully explains the concept of social justice, and definitions simply beg more questions about the meaning. In light of these difficulties, social workers should view current usage of the term critically (Rose-Miller 1994). The dilemma with regard to social justice is that social workers are somehow supposed to know what social justice actually means, even though no satisfactory definition exists.

Like social justice, definitions of human rights can also present open-ended responses. However, human rights encompass a more comprehensive and defined set of guidelines for social work practice than social justice. Human rights focus on what must be given to a client, which elevates the discussion into one not simply of recognizing the needs of a client but also of effectively satisfying those needs. While social workers may perceive human rights as being overly legalistic and a topic more appropriate for lawyers, this belief should not prevent the study of human rights. By learning more about human rights, social workers can then understand why this idea should play an important role in the profession.

Human rights do not replace principles of social justice, no matter how amorphous the definition of those principles may seem. The study of human rights complements and broadens the perspective of social workers when carrying out policies and practices. By recognizing the importance of human rights, social workers can only enhance the profession. A foundation in human rights can provide a much clearer framework and structure with which to connect the social work profession to economic, political, and social aims.

OUTLINE AND PURPOSE OF THIS BOOK

This book dissects various aspects of human rights as they relate to the social work profession and presents each of those parts in an understandable form. The purpose of this book is to present the groundwork for understanding human rights. By no means does this book pretend to be anything more than an elementary or beginning text on linking the social work profession to human rights. For those persons who wish to deepen their knowledge about human rights, further study will be required.

Chapter 1 traces the development and history of human rights to the present. Much of what we now call human rights has evolved since 1945. However, the underlying themes within human rights draw upon historical traditions existing well before then. This chapter also explains the specialized language commonly encountered within human rights documents, such as *declaration, covenant, ratification*, and other key terms.

Chapter 2 focuses on the Universal Declaration of Human Rights, first presented in 1948. The Universal Declaration forms the basis for contemporary human rights principles. This chapter lists and analyzes each human right contained in the declaration. Issues related to concepts of universality and indivisibility receive additional attention.

The third chapter introduces instruments drafted by the United Nations to supplement the Universal Declaration of Human Rights. These combined documents are known as the International Bill of Human Rights. To begin the discussion of UN articles drafted after the Universal Declaration, this chapter provides a detailed explanation of the International Covenant on Civil and Political Rights. This covenant addresses numerous political rights that countries must provide their citizens.

Chapter 4 details the United Nations document known as the International Covenant on Economic, Social, and Cultural Rights, which addresses numerous economic, social, and cultural rights that countries should provide their citizens. Chapter 5 looks at human rights issues relating to vulnerable populations, with a focus on women. This chapter draws upon various declarations and conventions that specifically concern the human rights of women. The sixth chapter continues the discussion of human rights issues relating to vulnerable populations and draws upon various declarations and conventions that specifically address the human rights of those groups.

Chapter 7 examines human rights in an international framework and centers on international perspectives as they relate to human rights and social work. Chapter 8 addresses social work policy and practice in the context of human rights. To integrate human rights into policy and practice, the social worker must develop a connection between human rights and ethics. This last chapter also provides case studies that illustrate the application of human rights to social work practice. Finally, the appendices include the Universal Declaration of Human Rights and other major documents relating to human rights.

QUESTIONS AND EXERCISES

1. Distinguish the concepts of social justice and human rights.
2. How would you define human rights at this time?
3. Do you believe that it is possible for everyone in every country to enjoy the same basic rights?
4. How would you respond to the following statements?
    (a) Social justice has served the social work profession well for many years.
    (b) The profession has no need to introduce human rights into the social work curriculum.
5. What human rights issues do you believe you have encountered personally, academically, or professionally?
6. What do you see as the greatest hurdle to universal human rights?
7. How large a role should culture play in determining the validity of a human right?
8. Should some human rights be more important than others?
9. Which theory of social justice do you feel is most compatible with human rights?
10. Why has there been reluctance on the part of the social work profession to embrace human rights specifically?

REFERENCES

Benn, C. 1991. Social justice, social policy, and social work. *Australian Social Work* 44.4: 33–39.
Charlesworth, H. 1994. What are "women's international human rights"? In R. J. Cook, ed., *Human Rights of Women: National and International Perspectives.* Philadelphia: University of Pennsylvania Press.
Council on Social Work Education (CSWE). 1994. *Handbook of Accreditation Standards and Procedures.* Alexandria, Va.: CSWE.
Edwards, R., ed. 1995. *Encyclopedia of Social Work.* 19th ed. Washington, D.C.: National Association of Social Workers.

Flowers, N., ed. 1998. *Human Rights Here and Now*. Minneapolis, Minn.: Human Rights Educators Network, Amnesty International USA.

Hartman, A. 1990. Many ways of knowing (editorial). *Social Work: Journal of the National Association of Social Workers* 35: 3–4.

Ife, J. 2001. *Human Rights and Social Work: Towards Rights-based Practice*. Cambridge: Cambridge University Press.

Ignatieff, M. 2001. The attack on human rights. *Foreign Affairs* 80.6 (November-December): 102–16.

International Federation of Social Workers (IFSW). 2000. *See* www.ifsw.org/4.5.6.pub.html.

Krutsinger, L. 2001. Lack of health care a costly problem. *Southern Illinoisan* (July 19): A3.

Longres, J. and E. Scalon. 2001. Social work and social justice: A reply to Leroy Pelton. *Journal of Social Work Education* 37.3: 441–44.

Mayadas, N. and D. Elliot. 1997. Lessons from international social work. In M. Reisch and E. Gombrill, eds., *Policies and Practices in Social Work in the 21st Century*, 175–97. London: Pine Forge.

National Association of Social Workers (NASW). 1996. *Code of Ethics*. Washington, D.C: NASW Press.

——. 2000. *Social Work Speaks: National Association of Social Workers Policy Statements, 2000–2003*. 5th ed. Washington, D.C.: NASW Press.

Nozik, R. 1974. *Anarchy, State, and Utopia*. New York: Basic Books.

Pelton, L. 2001. Social justice and social work. *Journal of Social Work Education* 37.2: 433–39.

Rachael v. Walker, 4 Mo 350 (1837).

Rawls, J. 1971. *A Theory of Justice*. Cambridge: Harvard University Press.

Reichert, E. 1996. Keep on moving forward: NGO Forum on Women [4th UN World Conference on Women], Beijing, China [1995]. *Social Development Issues* 18.1: 61–71.

——. 1998. Women's rights are human rights: A platform for action. *International Social Work* 15.3: 177–85.

——. 2001. Placing human rights at the center of the social work profession. *Journal of Intergroup Relations* 28.1 (Spring): 43–50.

Reichert, E. and R. McCormick. 1998. U.S. welfare law violates human rights of immigrants. *Migration World* 26: 15–18.

Reisch, M. and C. Taylor. 1983. Ethical guidelines for cutback management: A preliminary approach. *Administration in Social Work* 9.4: 59–71.

Roche, S. 1996. Messages from the NGO Forum on Women, Beijing, 1995. *Affilia: Journal of Women and Social Work* 11: 484–94.

Roche, S. and M. Dewees. 2001. Teaching about human rights in social work. *Journal of Teaching Social Work* 21.1–2: 137–55.

Roche, S., M. Dewees, R. Trailweaver, S. Alexander, C. Cuddy, and M. Handy. 1999. *Contesting Boundaries in Social Work Education: A Liberatory Approach to Coop-*

erative Learning and Teaching. Alexandria, Va.: Council on Social Work Education.

Rose-Miller, M. 1994. Evaluation, social justice, and social work. *Australian Social Work* 47.4: 21–26.

Sanders, D. and P. Pedersen. 1984. Developing a graduate social work curriculum with an international cross-cultural perspective. In Sanders and Pedersen, eds., *Education for International Social Welfare*, 15–26. Honolulu: University of Hawaii Press.

Scott v. Sandford, 60 US 393 (1857).

Staub-Bernasconi, S. 1998. Soziale Arbeit als Menschenrechtsprofession. In A. Woehrle, ed., *Profession und Wissenschaft Sozialer Arbeit: Positionen in einer Phase der generellen Neuverortnung und Spezifika*, 305–32. Pfaffenweiler, Ger.: Cenaurus.

Tyson, K. 1995. *New Foundations for Scientific Social and Behavioral Research: The Heuristic Paradigm*. Boston: Allyn and Bacon.

United Nations. 1987. *Human Rights: Questions and Answers*. New York: UN.

Van Soest, D. 1992. Peace and social justice as an integral part of the social work curriculum: A North American perspective. *Australian Social Work* 45.10: 29–38.

——. 1994. Strange bedfellows: A call for reordering national priorities from three social justice perspectives. *Social Work: Journal of the National Association of Social Workers* 39.6: 710–17.

——. 1995. Peace and social justice. In Edwards, ed., *Encyclopedia of Social Work* 3:1810–17.

Wakefield, C. 1988. Psychotherapy, distributive justice, and social work. *Social Service Review* (September): 353–82.

Wetzel, J. 1993. *The World of Women: In Pursuit of Human Rights*. London: Macmillan.

Witkin, S. 1993. A human rights approach to social work research and evaluation. *Journal of Teaching Social Work* 8.1–2: 239–53.

——. 1998. Human rights and social work. *Social Work: Journal of the National Association of Social Workers* 43: 197–201.

1

Development and History of Human Rights

Human rights is a relatively new term, with its initial use occurring in 1945, after the end of World War II (Morsink 1999). This enormous catastrophic conflict reached into almost every corner of the globe, leaving few countries unscathed, but it provided the catalyst for peoples and governments everywhere to create a mechanism by which to prevent such a vast and destructive event from ever happening again, at least on a worldwide scale. The result of this effort to create a more stable and peaceful world order culminated in 1948 with the Universal Declaration of Human Rights (Morsink 1999)

The Universal Declaration was nothing short of a revolution in thought: instead of each nation being the master of its own domain, incumbent universal principles or rules now appeared. A higher authority—in this case, the United Nations—issued a set of guidelines which, at least in theory, was meant to inhibit its member nations from violating these agreed-upon human rights. No longer could a nation treat its own citizens or those of other nations simply as it wanted. The Universal Declaration set minimum standards of conduct for governments all over the world (*Economist* 1998; Press 2000).

In spite of efforts before the Universal Declaration to establish a model standard of conduct applicable to every individual and government, no prior document could match the Universal Declaration in scope or participation. The development and eventual fruition of the Universal Declaration exemplifies how individuals and groups from diverse backgrounds mutually produced an extraordinary document that transcends customary borders. While many nations still do of course violate human rights as contained in the declaration, international pressure for countries to adhere to the declaration does exist. Governments or individuals who ignore or violate human rights often face diminished reputation, scorn, or harsh criticism (*Economist* 1998). Even with its shortcomings, the Universal Declaration of Human Rights must rank as one of the most esteemed accomplishments in political, social, economic, and cultural history.

THREE GENERATIONS OF HUMAN RIGHTS

While chapter 2 will cover the Universal Declaration in detail, a brief summary of that document reveals three distinct sets (or generations) of human rights. The first set or generation lists political and individual freedoms (Reichert 2001). The right to a fair trial, freedom of speech and religion, freedom of movement and assembly, and guarantees against discrimination, slavery, and torture fall within these political and civil human rights (United Nations 1948: art. 2–15). These rights are often referred to as *negative rights* in that they restrict the role of government. In other words, any government (or other authority) shall refrain from doing a certain act. This "shall not" set of guidelines emphasizes noninterference by government, or a negative position.

Another set of human rights in the declaration embodies so-called *positive rights* (Reichert 2001). This set of rights attempts to ensure each resident of a country an adequate standard of living based on the resources of that country. Under this second set of human rights, everyone "has the right to a standard of living adequate for the health and well-being of himself and of his family, including food, clothing, housing and medical care, and necessary social services." In addition, "motherhood and childhood are entitled to special care and assistance" and everyone has the right to a free education at the elementary level (United Nations 1948: art. 25 and 26). These rights are termed positive in that governments and individuals must take action to preserve them. In other words, governments "shall" provide these rights.

Of course, the distinction between negative and positive human rights can be viewed as contrived. If government shall not restrict free speech or discriminate against gender or race, who monitors whether government satisfies these negative rights? Obviously, government must affirmatively act to prevent violations of free speech and discrimination. That requires positive acts on the part of government. Still, contrived or not, in discussions about human rights a distinction between negative and positive human rights continues to exist.

A third and final set of human rights involves *collective rights* among nations. This set of rights is the least developed among the three types of human rights. Under the 1948 declaration, everyone "is entitled to a social and international order in which the rights and freedoms" listed in the document can be fully realized (art. 28). Essentially, the promotion of collective human rights requires intergovernmental cooperation on world issues (e.g., environmental protection and economic development). One group of countries should not dictate conditions to another group when these conditions would inhibit the growth or prosperity of the other group. Industrialized countries should not take advantage of less economically developed countries by exploiting resources. The third set of human rights indicates that solidarity among nations and individuals forms a core value of the declaration.

Paradoxically, reference to three generations or sets of human rights may actually inhibit understanding of those rights as well as the concept of indivisibility. With three different sets of rights, an issue can easily arise as to priority of rights. Are political and civil rights more important than economic, social, and cultural rights or international solidarity? Can human rights even be logically separated into different sets? Unfortunately, the notion of different sets of human rights continues to exist. A better approach is to avoid reference to different sets and acknowledge that all human rights are equally important.

HISTORICAL BEGINNINGS OF HUMAN RIGHTS

The Universal Declaration of Human Rights did not arise from a vacuum. Early civilizations produced religious codes that established standards of conduct for fairly homogeneous groups within limited territorial jurisdictions (National Coordinating Committee 1998). By requiring people to treat fellow humans with dignity and help provide for each other's needs, many religions are precursors to human rights (1). In varying degrees, Judaism, Christianity, Buddhism, Confucianism, and Islam all stress what would now be called human rights. These religions emphasize the necessity of fairness from political authorities and in the distribution of economic resources to those in need (Laqueur and Rubin 1979; Wronka 1998; van Wormer 1996; McKinney and Park-Cunningham 1997; Ife 2001).

Since ancient times, philosophers have written about equality and justice. These great thinkers, including Plato and Socrates, more than two thousand years ago explored the realm of basic, inalienable rights of man, which in those times literally meant "man" (Wronka 1998). Women's rights *as* human rights came much, much later (Reichert 1996, 1998). The Greek philosopher Aristotle wrote that an unjust man is a man who is not content to have an equal share with others (Wronka 1998:43). Since the unjust thing is the unequal thing, it is obvious that there must be a mean between greater and less inequality. If then the unjust is the unequal, the just is the equal. The Romans developed the "Twelve Tables," which stress the necessity for a proper trial, the presentation of evidence and proof, and the illegality of bribery in judicial proceedings (Wronka 1998:46).

In the year 1215, a cornerstone of human rights came into existence when English nobles, bishops, and archbishops forced the then reigning King John to end the abuses against his subjects. The subjects drafted a document known as the Magna Carta, which King John signed. The Magna Carta prohibited a sovereign from taking property without due process and from the detention of his subjects without a legal judgment by their peers—the forerunner of trial by jury. The document also highlighted the importance of family and provided for safety from abusive treatment.

Another concept behind the development of human rights is *natural law*, which holds that a certain order in nature provides norms for human conduct. Saint Thomas Aquinas wrote that natural law was humanity's "participation" in the comprehensive eternal law (Hall 1992:581). People could grasp certain self-evident principles of practical reason, which corresponded to the various goods toward which human nature inclined. Natural law was a standard for human laws: unjust laws in principle did not bind in conscience. During the seventeenth century, European philosophers advocated for what they viewed as the natural rights of the citizens—the idea that people by their nature have certain basic rights that precede the establishment of any government (590). Two early modern political philosophers, Thomas Hobbes and John Locke, explored the theme of natural rights. Hobbes and Locke stated that the source of natural law was not a set of naturally ordered ends of human well-being and fulfillment but an innate desire for self-preservation (581). From this idea, Hobbes and Locke erected a new doctrine known as *natural rights*. The desire for self-preservation in a state of nature led to the establishment of a social contract, the foundation of civil society. The fundamental duty of government, according to Locke, became the protection of rights to life, liberty, and property. This concept of natural rights went beyond theoretical views of man and society and aimed to establish actual rules of conduct. Initially, these natural rights focused on freedom of the press, with subsequent attention to freedom of thought in politics and religion. Abolition of slavery and a more humane treatment of criminals also formed part of the natural rights movement (Rawls 1993)

Uprisings in the late eighteenth century against government and royalty in France and the American colonies engendered considerable discussion as to how nations should treat its citizens. Until this period, privileged males occupied center stage in the discussion about concepts of human rights, with most if not all such rights understood as being solely for men. However, in 1787 the French philosopher Condorcet published a treatise on the rights of women, holding that women had the same "natural rights" as men (Staub-Bernasconi 1998). During the French Revolution (1789), women were extremely active in the fight against an old feudal regime. Women led demonstrations that forced the king from his palace at Versailles. Women's groups in Paris demanded the same political rights as men, as well as change in marriage laws and women's social conditions. One of the most outspoken advocates for women's rights during the French Revolution was Olympe de Gouges. Two years after the revolution began, she published a declaration on the rights of women and demanded the same rights for women as men. In 1793 a backlash occurred, and the French government beheaded Olympe de Gouges and banned further political activity for women. The tragic irony in the beheading of de Gouges becomes evident when reading the French Declaration of the Rights of Man and Citizen, adopted by the French government in 1789 (Staub-Bernasconi 1998). That declaration referred only to men and specified numerous negative rights, including freedom from excessive punishment, freedom of thought and religion, and freedom to speak, write, and print. Only later would women be specifically recognized as entitled to basic human rights and freedoms.

While the French Revolution was gearing up, American colonists instigated their own uprising against the British. Out of this revolt came various documents expounding on the rights of man, including the Declaration of Independence (1776) and, later, the U.S. Constitution (1787, as amended). The Declaration of Independence held certain rights—notably, life, liberty, and the pursuit of happiness—as being "self-evident." And a key part of the U.S. Constitution, placed immediately after articles defining the mechanical functioning of the newly formed U.S. government, became known as the Bill of Rights. The Bill of Rights consists of the first ten amendments to the body of the Constitution and specifies certain civil and political rights. For instance, in the First Amendment, government shall make no law respecting an establishment of religion or prohibiting the free exercise of religion. Government may not abridge the freedom of speech, or of the press; or the right of the people peaceably to assemble. The people also have the right to petition the government for a redress of grievances. Other amendments guarantee the right of the people not to be subjected to unreasonable searches (amend. 4) or to cruel and unusual punishment (amend. 8). Nobody has to testify against herself or himself, and government may not take "life, liberty, or property, without due process of law" (amend. 5).

The Bill of Rights took a major step in defining and limiting government action in political and civil matters. However, what the Bill of Rights and the U.S. Constitution omitted were guarantees of economic and social needs. It took another revolution of sorts to focus on these aspects of human existence.

In the late eighteenth and early nineteenth centuries, the age of industrialization began in England, Europe, and the United States. In these parts of the world, people left their agricultural-based activities to find work in factories, often working long hours in unsanitary conditions. Factory owners frequently exploited their workers, paying them little for their efforts. Children, too, would work at an early age in the factories. Of course, in those days many people accepted these circumstances as the normal course of events. However, opposition to the exploitation of labor in the industrialized world began to emerge in the middle of the nineteenth century. Karl Marx and Friedrich Engels produced the *Communist Manifesto* (1848) in op-

As noted earlier, *human rights* as a term did not exist until around 1945. However, human rights activists have always existed throughout history— for example, Ida B. Wells-Barnett, an African-American woman. Born in 1862, Wells-Barnett became active in fighting against discrimination of blacks. In 1883, Wells-Barnett refused to move from a coach reserved for white women and was then evicted from the coach (Peebles-Wilkins and Francis 1990). From that day on, she attacked all types of discrimination against blacks through writings and actual participation in campaigns.

In 1892, Wells-Barnett began an antilynching campaign. She viewed lynching as a direct result of the gains blacks were making in the South and as an attempt to stop that progress. Her attacks against lynching infuriated whites, who then destroyed her printing press while she was on a speaking tour. However, Wells-Barnett continued her campaign against lynching and even traveled overseas to raise consciousness against what was happening in the United States.

On her return to the United States in 1893, Wells-Barnett continued her activism against exclusion of African-Americans from society. Her campaign for human rights lasted until 1931, the year she died (Peebles-Wilkins and Francis 1990).

position to what they saw as exploitation of the working class by owners of factories and other means of production (Wronka 1998). The manifesto outlined the class struggle against capitalists and the eventual takeover of the means of production by workers. While many of the predictions of Marx and Engels never came about, the underlying theme of their writings resulted in greater attention to the less economically fortunate of the world.

Toward the latter part of the nineteenth century, governments in Europe began to support the development of social welfare as social activists recognized the inadequacy of individual responses to broad economic problems such as massive poverty (Wronka 1998). At this time, social workers began to join together to share ideas and experience, to develop their practice, and to express a collective response to the issues they encountered.

In the early twentieth century, World War I and its aftermath brought greater attention to humankind's interdependence. A shared desire to condemn warfare and develop institutional frameworks for international cooperation took form. Establishment of the League of Nations and the Interna-

Alice Salomon has been called the Jane Addams of Germany (Healy 2001:29). The reference to Jane Addams stems from the social work activism carried out by Salomon. Another forerunner of human rights promoters before the term became prevalent, Salomon fought for the equal rights of women as well as other human rights.

Born in 1872 in Berlin, Germany, Salomon developed an early interest in the plight of women, especially in the workplace. She experienced women working in "sweat shops" and women suffering from hunger and disease (Wieler 1988). Salomon promoted adult education for women and wrote a controversial paper entitled, "Unequal Payment of Men's and Women's Work." In 1908, Salomon founded the first school of social work in Germany.

Salomon traveled and lectured extensively in Europe and the United States and devoted herself in about equal parts to social work and work with councils of women (Kendall 1989:28). She became active in an international peace movement with Jane Addams. When Hitler came to power in Germany in 1933, he targeted Salomon as an enemy, since she was Jewish. Salomon's work in peace and disarmament as well as women's rights conflicted with Nazi doctrines. In 1937, Hitler's National Socialist government forced Salomon to leave Germany or be put into a concentration camp. She moved to the United States, where she died in 1948.

tional Labor Organization and the inception of social welfare organizations such as the International Conference of Social Welfare reflected this new mood of international, regional, and national collaboration. Among social workers, the establishment of intergovernmental organizations such as the International Committee of Schools of Social Work and the International Permanent Secretariat of Social Workers paralleled this collaboration. During this period, social work organizations began to establish the basis for a social work profession and create social work values for their practice. This international promotion of social work formed a key concept that social work values could transcend borders, a notion that would manifest itself in the drafting of the Universal Declaration a few years later. However, while concepts of human rights underpinned the value base of social work, no formal teaching on human rights issues occurred (Center for Human Rights 1994).

Despite recognizing the dangers of war, especially after the immense destruction caused by World War I, Europe became almost immediately embroiled once again in armed battle. Budding international organizations faltered owing to limited support and no real enforcement powers. For instance, the League of Nations encountered obstacles from the start, mainly because the United States withdrew its membership (Alexander 1996). The league became little more than a forum in which European countries could discuss world issues. Enforcement of decisions remained absent.

In 1939, with Hitler's invasion into Poland, World War II began, involving even more countries and areas of the world than in the first global conflict. But before the end of this second conflagration in 1945, many groups would devote attention to notions of human rights (Wronka 1998; Morsink 1999). Wartime conferences in London, Moscow, the United States, and Yalta by major countries aligned against Germany issued declarations in regard to the failure of the League of Nations. They emphasized the need to develop a "United Nations" to maintain international peace and security. In 1941, U.S. President Franklin D. Roosevelt enunciated four freedoms: freedom of speech and expression, freedom of worship, freedom from want (i.e., economic security), and freedom from fear (e.g., international peace). Three years later, President Roosevelt asked Congress to explore the means for implementing an Economic Bill of Rights, including the rights to a useful and remunerative job; sufficient income to provide adequate food, clothing, and recreation; a decent home; medical care; retirement, disability, and unemployment security; and a good education. All of these concepts contributed to ideas cited in the soon-to-be-formulated Universal Declaration of Human Rights.

While construction of the Universal Declaration might appear to have been primarily a project of Europe and the United States, this was not the case. Other regions of the world had developed their own laws, principles, and religions that in many ways had much in common with concepts eventually included in the Universal Declaration. For instance, in China elements of classical Confucian thought formed a basis for modern human rights doctrines (Gangjian and Gang 1995:36). In South America, nineteenth-century movements led by Simon Bolivar and others provided later impetus for contributions to human rights principles. In the Soviet Union, the Soviet constitution of 1936 contained numerous references to civil and political rights and stressed economic and social rights (Wronka 1998).

Indigenous peoples such as Native Americans also contributed concepts of freedom, peace, and democracy to the development of human rights (Wronka 1998:70). However, during the nineteenth century, European countries and, to a lesser extent, the United States began massive colonial exploitation ("colonization") of indigenous peoples in Africa and parts of Asia. Depending on the colonizer, the degree of political and civil freedoms varied. The "new" citizens of Australia and the United States instigated a massive decimation of their own respective indigenous populations, the idea being that these populations were inferior and had little to contribute to the needs of a modern country (Brown 1970; Hughes 1987; Alexander 1996). Unfortunately, colonization and expulsion of indigenous peoples did much to silence the voices of these groups.

DEVELOPMENTS AFTER 1945

World War II ended in Europe in May 1945 with the defeat of Germany and in the Pacific arena in August 1945 with the defeat of Japan. Devastation from the war was so horrendous that, at its end, individuals and governments from every corner of the globe realized another such global catastrophe would probably spell the end of humankind. The search for universal principles of conduct now began in earnest.

Until 1945, the notion of state sovereignty dominated international relations (*Economist* 1998). Within its borders, a State controlled its own affairs. A State generally did not interfere in the affairs of another State; whatever States did to their own nationals was their business. Of course, this respect for noninterference in the affairs of other States did not prevent the colonization and destruction of those peoples who had no defined national boundaries. African, American, Australian, and other aborigines generally found themselves on the losing end of better-armed Europeans who had arrived to expand their own nation's sovereign reach.

After World War II, however, the concept that a state or nation should have total control over its own affairs mellowed somewhat. Extreme nationalism gave way to a more global consciousness where the international community would not remain silent when egregious abuses occurred within a particular country. The primary issue then became one of defining rights, abuses, and other universal principles by which every country would subscribe.

In June 1945, in San Francisco, the United States, Soviet Union, France,

Cuba, Chile, Panama, and many other countries laid the groundwork for the creation of a United Nations (Morsink 1999). The UN Charter pledges the organization to reaffirm faith in fundamental human rights, and article I of the charter cites "promoting and encouraging respect for human rights and for fundamental freedoms for all without distinction as to race, sex, language or religion" (*Economist* 1998). As part of this charter, participants agreed to establish a Commission on Human Rights. Before the creation of this commission in 1946, the term *human rights*, as previously noted, had not been a commonly used expression, while the development of human rights principles had been occurring for centuries.

A universal declaration of rights ranked high on the agenda of this new organization known as the United Nations. However, many governments were reluctant to accept detailed provisions concerning human rights. The Soviet Union had its Gulags, or labor camps, for those who spoke against the government; the United States had its numerous racial problems; and the Europeans had their colonial empires (Buergenthal 1988). All these circumstances could be viewed as contrary to human rights principles. Consequently, establishing a strong international mechanism for protecting human rights could work against the interests of these major blocs. Certainly the Soviets did not want human rights inspectors examining their labor camps and talking with dissidents inhabiting the camps. The United States did not want human rights examiners questioning what could be considered near-apartheid conditions, especially in the South. And European countries had no interest in allowing human rights monitors to look into the exploitative activities surrounding their African and Asian colonies.

Fortunately, the impetus for a more detailed and comprehensive set of rights than desired by the major blocs existed in the form of private institutions now commonly known as nongovernmental organizations (NGOs) (Farer 1989:195). According to John Humphrey, the first director of the Division of Human Rights at the United Nations, without the efforts of a few deeply committed delegates and representatives of forty-two private organizations serving as consultants, human rights would have received only a passing reference. With the promotion of human rights by NGOs and dedicated countries making headway, by 1947 the international consensus for human rights became aggressive.

The Commission on Human Rights held its first session in early 1947, electing Eleanor Roosevelt as president and Rene Cassin from France as vice

NONGOVERNMENTAL ORGANIZATIONS (NGOS)

As organizations formed by people outside of government, NGOs monitor the proceedings of human rights bodies such as the Commission on Human Rights and are the "watchdogs" of the human rights that fall within their mandate. Some are large and international (e.g., the Red Cross, Amnesty International, the Girl Scouts); others may be small and local (e.g., an organization to advocate for people with disabilities in a particular city; a coalition to promote women's rights in one refugee camp). NGOs play a major role in influencing UN policy, and many of them have consultative status at the UN (United Nations and Human Rights 2001).

president. The member commission included representatives from Australia, Belgium, the Byelorussian (Belorussian) Soviet Socialist Republic, Chile, China, Egypt, France, India, Iran, Lebanon, Panama, the Philippine Republic, United Kingdom, United States of America, Union of Soviet Socialist Republics, Uruguay, and Yugoslavia. The commission drafted an initial document on human rights containing numerous articles on the rights and duties of individuals. The document covered political, social, and economic rights, with differing viewpoints on how much influence should be extended to each set of rights. In June 1948 the commission completed its draft declaration and the entire General Assembly of the United Nations began debating the draft (Morsink 1999).

At the time the commission submitted its draft declaration on human rights to the General Assembly, the United Nations consisted of fifty-six countries. Most of these countries were located in North and South America, Europe, and the Soviet Union. A few Arabic countries were also members, but Africa and Asia had little representation because of colonization by European countries. Only later, beginning in the late 1950s, did colonized territories begin the path to independence and membership in the United Nations.

In spite of this limited membership within the United Nations in 1948, a spirited debate surrounded the draft declaration. Many countries agreed to the necessity for enforcement provisions that would ensure compliance with human rights principles. Countries did not want an organization that would be as impotent as the League of Nations had been. Obtaining agreement that countries should give human rights more than just lip service was perhaps the easiest point to discuss. The U.S. contingent focused on political and civil rights, desiring no guarantee to economic and social rights. This viewpoint simply matched common U.S. strains of thought about government and society. Nobody owes anybody a job, unemployment benefits, or medical care. Why should governments be responsible for those items? Yet government should stay out of religion, refrain from censorship, and ensure numerous other safeguards against governmental interference in the liberty of its citizens. On the other hand, the Soviet Union viewed free speech and other political rights, American-style, as anathema to their society. Instead, the distribution of economic and social benefits to all citizens was a priority. Other countries, such as Saudi Arabia, weighed in with objections to provisions on the right to change religions and equal rights concerning marriage, believing this would conflict with marriage laws in most Muslim countries. The Union of South Africa objected to numerous provisions in the draft document that could be used to attack its apartheid system of segregation. Chile, often taking the lead for the Latin American contingent of the commission, believed that economic and social rights had to be assured, thereby making a return to fascism impossible.

The final draft of the document that would become the Universal Declaration of Human Rights bore the unmistakable stamp of the horrific experiences of the recent war. Rene Cassin, the French delegate, stated that "the last war had taken on the character of a crusade for human rights" and that the declaration was most urgently needed as a protest against oppression (Morsink 1999:37).

On December 10, 1948, the General Assembly of the United Nations adopted the Universal Declaration of Human Rights. The declaration passed unopposed, but the entire Soviet bloc, Saudi Arabia, and South Africa abstained from voting because of objections to certain provisions within the declaration (Morsink 1999).

While the Universal Declaration of Human Rights was not a legally binding document—who could have enforced it anyway against powerful countries like the United States and the Soviet Union?—a common precedent for universal human rights now existed. The significance of this step cannot be underestimated. From this point forward, human rights have made astonishing inroads into the vocabularies of social workers, philosophers, educators, political leaders, lawyers, and many other groups.

One of the more well-known human rights activists from a non-Western country is Mohandas "Mahatma" Gandhi, who was born in India in 1869. As a young man, Gandhi studied law in London and in the early 1900s moved to South Africa, where he worked as a lawyer. In South Africa, Gandhi encountered the inhumane racial laws propagated by the South African government. Those racial laws divided nonwhites into various categories and restricted nonwhites in all types of endeavors. Gandhi protested against those discriminatory laws, especially as they related to Indian immigrants in South Africa, and so frequently served time in jail for his human rights activities.

In 1915, Gandhi returned to India where he became active in the struggle for independence from Britain. Eventually, in 1947, Britain granted India its independence but split the territory it (Britain) had held into two states: India and Pakistan. As in many other countries at this time, where the transition from colonial territory to newly formed, independent nation proved to be quite difficult, the resulting partition of India and Pakistan led to violent clashes among different groups. Gandhi spent the remaining months of his life preaching against this violence, but in 1948 he was assassinated.

Gandhi never preached violence as a means to achieve goals. Gandhian principles were based on carefully considered philosophical beliefs—cooperation over competition, interdependence over rugged individualism, and compassion for others over the pursuit of self-interest (Walz and Ritchie 2000:213). These principles of nonviolent civil disobedience, or *satyagraha*, still have great importance in the contemporary pursuit for human rights.

HISTORICAL ROLE OF SOCIAL WORKERS IN HUMAN RIGHTS

During the historical development of human rights, social workers have played a key role. For instance, social workers have been involved with the League of Nations, the Red Cross, the Women's International League for Peace and Freedom, and Save the Children, all organizations aimed at promoting human rights (Ife 2001). Social workers were active in international and social justice issues that correlated with human rights issues. Milestones in social work that relate to human rights include:

- In 1915, Jane Addams attended the Women's Peace Conference at The Hague and then traveled to Berlin to meet with the German chancellor in an attempt to convince him to end World War I hostilities.

Eglantyne Jebb was clearly a forerunner to the contemporary human rights scene. Born in 1876 in England, Jebb trained as a teacher but subsequently became involved in social work with the Charity Organization Society (Healy 2001:49). In 1913, Jebb did relief work after the Balkan Wars and observed appalling conditions of refugees displaced by war. That experience led Jebb to her life's work: helping children (49). After World War I, Jebb helped establish the Save the Children Fund, which still exists today. Two principles of the fund were that aid should be based on need and that children should not suffer due to wars they had no part in (50). In addition to helping found Save the Children, in 1923 Jebb also drafted a Declaration on the Rights of the Child, which formed the basis for the 1989 Convention on the Rights of the Child.

Jebb suffered from chronic poor health and died in 1928 at the age of 52. However, the work Jebb did during her lifetime helped shape the human rights movement today.

- In 1919 social worker Eglantyne Jebb founded the Save the Children Fund in England. Jebb contributed extensively to promoting children's rights, and in 1924 the League of Nations adopted a declaration on the Rights of the Child, authored by Jebb.
- In 1929 social workers formed the International Association of Schools of Social Work (IASSW) with forty-six member schools in ten countries. Goals of this association included development of an improved approach to humanitarian work and closer international cooperation among social workers.
- In 1931, Jane Addams received the Nobel Peace Prize.
- During the 1930s, social workers became more active in economic and social justice issues (Healy 2001).

Unfortunately, with events in the late 1930s leading to international armed conflict, much of the human rights activities of social workers halted. International connections among social workers became increasingly difficult and eventually impossible in the wartime environment. In Germany the Nazis forced Alice Salomon, founder of the German schools of social work and activist in the international peace movement, to leave the country because she was Jewish (Wieler 1988). Salomon had worked closely with Jane

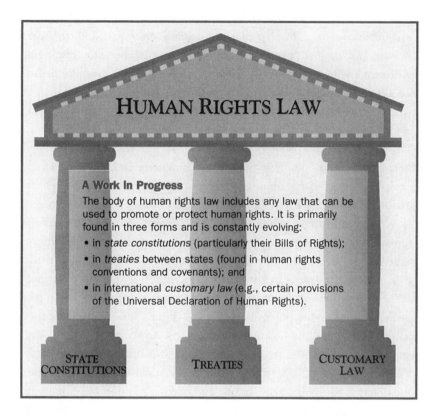

HUMAN RIGHTS LAW

A Work In Progress

The body of human rights law includes any law that can be used to promote or protect human rights. It is primarily found in three forms and is constantly evolving:

- in *state constitutions* (particularly their Bills of Rights);
- in *treaties* between states (found in human rights conventions and covenants); and
- in international *customary law* (e.g., certain provisions of the Universal Declaration of Human Rights).

STATE CONSTITUTIONS   TREATIES   CUSTOMARY LAW

FIGURE 1.1

Addams in social work issues and was prominent in the social work profession in Europe.

Social workers played a large part in creating the foundation of the current human rights movement. Involvement of social workers in human rights issues becomes clear when examining goals of the profession. Many of those goals stem from human rights concepts even though, in the United States, the social work profession rarely refers to the term *human rights*.

TERMINOLOGY OF HUMAN RIGHTS DOCUMENTS

To understand the significance of documents relating to human rights, social workers must become familiar with the terminology assigned to various documents. Significant terms in the area of human rights include *declaration*, *covenant*, *convention*, *treaty*, *platform*, *accession*, *ratification*, and *customary international law*. For purposes of this book and the general understanding of human rights documents, social workers do not need to study the fine points of international law regarding the terms. A brief introduction to these terms suffices for understanding the significance of a particular document and the legal standing of provisions contained in the document.

Declaration   In respect to human rights documents, a declaration presents a formal and solemn nonbinding statement listing general principles and broad obligations (Center for Human Rights 1994:14). For instance, the Universal Declaration of Human Rights contains many statements on human rights with the goal of encouraging countries to recognize human rights. However, the declaration does not impose any specific requirement on a particular country or nation to actually comply with the declaration.

The nonbinding nature of a declaration may appear detrimental in promoting human rights. After all, words are cheap. However, a declaration does indicate a position on human rights issues. Any country signing a declaration definitely states to other countries that it intends to abide by the declaration and make efforts to put principles contained in the declaration into practice. By signing a declaration and making no effort to comply with that declaration, a country is, at a minimum, showing bad faith and running a risk of losing respect within the international community. The country of Afghanistan provides a recent example of the loss of respect resulting from a blind eye to human rights principles. Afghanistan belongs to the United Nations and has accepted principles contained in the Universal Declaration of Human Rights. Yet among other human rights abuses, the Taliban government of that country openly placed restrictions on women that inhibited their education, employment, and other benefits. Even after allowing for a culturally specific interpretation of human rights principles, Afghanistan clearly violated many provisions of the Universal Declaration. A direct consequence of those violations was a lack of international respect for the ruling government of Afghanistan. The vast majority of countries had no diplomatic relations with Afghanistan and entertained little contact with the country. This isolation and failure to at least acknowledge some provisions within the Universal Declaration worked to the detriment of most Afghan citizens.

Declarations commonly address human rights issues and allow countries the opportunity to gather and discuss current areas of concern. Countries within the United Nations often schedule conferences on human rights topics with the goal of presenting a declaration on the various topics. These conferences can often be controversial, as conflict frequently arises among participants over particular language within the declaration. For instance, in a recent conference on racism, the United States objected to positions taken concerning Israel and walked out of the conference (Swarns 2001).

The importance of declarations should not be underestimated, even if countries pay no more than lip service to statements within the declarations. By merely signing on to a specific position concerning human rights issues, a country and its government does indicate intent to follow that position. Individuals and groups can at least point to the declaration in shaping policies their government should be pursuing.

Covenant, Convention, and Treaty   In contrast to the nonbinding nature of a declaration, the United Nations has adopted the use of various instruments that do impose specific obligations on those countries signing and ratifying the instruments. Those instruments are known as covenants, conventions, and treaties.

Generally, a covenant on human rights principles serves as a promise between two or more countries that they will enforce provisions of the covenants with specific laws (Campbell Black 1968). A convention is an international agreement that contains provisions to promote or protect specific human rights or fundamental provisions (Center for Human Rights 1994:14). Both covenants and conventions relating to human rights documents generally require a specified number of countries to agree to the document before the document becomes effective. A treaty is much like a covenant or convention but may not require any specific number of signatures before becoming effective. Other than a declaration, human rights instruments generally are classified as a covenant or convention but would also fall within the definition of treaty.

A key distinction between a covenant, convention, or treaty and a declaration is that of obligation. Countries signing a covenant, convention, or treaty intend to bind themselves to provisions within the document, while countries signing a declaration merely indicate their intent to follow provisions within the declaration. The language of a covenant, convention, or treaty generally imposes obligations upon a State or country to ensure and undertake certain human rights, while the language of a declaration focuses more on the need to recognize particular human rights.

Accession and Ratification When a country signs a human rights covenant or convention, that country must either "accede to" or "ratify" the covenant or convention before provisions within the document become a legally binding instrument in that country. The terms *accession* and *ratification* relate to the means by which a country expresses consent to be bound by the document, with technical distinctions between those terms best left to international lawyers.

In the United States, a treaty, including a covenant or convention, becomes legally binding upon its ratification, as opposed to accession. Under the U.S. Constitution, the president has the power, with the advice and consent of the Senate, to make treaties, provided two-thirds of the Senate concur with the treaty (U.S. Constitution, art. 2). As noted, a covenant or convention on human rights would be viewed as a treaty. Therefore, in the United States, before any human rights covenant or convention can become legally binding, a two-thirds majority of the U.S. Senate must vote for the covenant or convention. This required approval by the Senate can result in a president's signing a human rights covenant or convention for consideration by the Senate, which might then delay approval of, or even refuse to approve, the document. For instance, in 1978, President Jimmy Carter submitted the human rights document known as the International Covenant on Civil and Political Rights to the Senate (see appendix B). Yet the Senate did not ratify the covenant until 1992 (Newman and Weisbrodt 1996). In some cases, a U.S. president may sign a treaty without the Senate ever ratifying it. At the time President Carter submitted the Covenant on Civil and Political Rights to the Senate, he also submitted the International Covenant on Economic, Social, and Cultural Rights (see appendix D). However, the Senate has never ratified that covenant nor does ratification of that instrument by the Senate appear likely at this time.

Another point to note concerning a State's acceptance of a covenant or convention involves the practice of some countries to place "reservations" on particular provisions within the document. A *reservation* expresses the intent of a State to modify or use a different standard from a particular provision of a covenant or convention. Under commonly accepted laws regarding treaties, a State may place a reservation on a treaty unless the treaty specifically prohibits or limits reservations (Vienna Convention 1969, art. 19). Where the treaty does not prohibit or limit reservations, a State may place a reservation on the treaty provided the reservation is not incompatible with the object and purpose of the treaty.

Customary International Law   In addition to a State's acceding to or ratifying a covenant or convention on human rights, another process exists by which a country can be legally bound to follow human rights principles. That process is known as customary international law and essentially means that a particular rule has become so matter-of-fact or commonplace all over the world that all countries should enforce the rule. Certain human rights, particularly some of those listed in the Universal Declaration, probably qualify as customary international law and therefore could be enforceable in all countries. In the United States, a federal court has held that a foreign national may sue in a U.S. court for civil damages allegedly caused from torture perpetrated by a Paraguayan national (*Filartiga v. Pena-Irala* 1980). The court considered the human right to be free from torture as binding on all countries:

> For although there is no universal agreement as to the precise extent of the "human rights and fundamental freedoms" guaranteed to all by the [United Nations] Charter, there is at present no dissent from the view that the guaranties include, at a bare minimum, the right to be free from torture. This prohibition has become part of customary international law, as evidenced and defined by the Universal Declaration of Human Rights." (*Filartiga v. Pena-Irala* 1980:882)

The court did not indicate that all human rights contained in the Universal Declaration met the standard of customary international law. Rather, courts would need to examine the particular right at issue and then determine whether that right qualified as part of customary international law.

While the intricacies of international law obviously exceed the scope of this book, social workers should understand the concept of customary international law and how that concept applies to human rights principles. If virtually every country accepts a particular human right as being fundamental to human existence, then that right could become part of customary

Because international law can play a significant role in the application of human rights to local situations, it seems logical that courts should look beyond the confines of domestic law and embrace legal principles contained within international law. After all, U.S. courts have recognized that customary international law should apply to domestic circumstances. However, U.S. courts have been reluctant to consider international principles within their rulings.

In an essay appearing in the *Christian Science Monitor*, a law professor at Albany Law School argues that U.S. courts should incorporate international law into their rulings:

> During its current term, which started last week [October 2000], the Supreme Court will consider issues such as disability rights, treatment of pregnant women, and restrictions on legal services. In so doing, it would serve the court to consult not only U.S. precedents, but international law.
>
> A growing body of lawyers and judges worldwide look to international human rights norms when addressing domestic legal issues. European nations such as Germany, Commonwealth countries such as Canada, India, and Australia, and developing nations such as South Africa and Namibia, routinely look to international law in establishing and interpreting domestic laws. This approach will rapidly gain momentum with England's Oct. 1 [2000] accession to the European Convention on Human Rights. U.S. courts, however, are largely insular in their practices. This isolationist stance is bad for U.S. laws and counterproductive for a country that seeks to promote human rights in other nations.
>
> Ironically, U.S. courts are playing a growing role in bringing foreign wrongdoers to justice. In August, a New York City jury relied on the Alien Tort Claims Act to award $745 million to 12 Bosnian women victimized by soldiers controlled by Radovan Karadzic, the political leader of the Bosnian Serbs. Similar cases are pending around the country.
>
> Yet U.S. judges have rarely looked at the broader implications of international law within our own borders. International treaties and customary law address a range of individual rights and protections, from child care to housing to affirmative action. However, as Justice Ruth Bader Ginsburg recently noted, the last time the U.S. Supreme Court cited the UN Universal Declaration of Human Rights was 35 years ago. Similarly, when Justice Stephen Breyer referred to European federal systems in a 1997 dissenting opinion, he was roundly criticized by the majority. And in deciding a 1998 case involving the right of a citizen father to sponsor his out-of-wedlock child for citizenship, the U.S. Supreme Court failed even to cite a 1997 Canadian Supreme Court case dealing with the same issue but reaching the opposite conclusion.

(continued)

Such legal isolationism is antithetical to the increasing international contact that marks American life. It forces the U.S. into an uncomfortable "do as I say, not as I do" posture when urging rogue nations to abide by international human rights laws. It deprives U.S. judges of perspectives and ideas that would enhance their decision-making. And in an era where the balance of power is increasingly shifting from the federal government to the states, it denies American citizens a counterweight that might shore up critical individual and civil rights.

Granted, U.S. law carefully cabins the internal impact of international agreements, ensuring that they typically are not enforceable until implemented by Congress. But even if litigants can't sue directly under the UN Convention on the Rights of the Child, for example, U.S. courts should not render decisions in a domestic vacuum. In last term's challenge to the Violence Against Women Act, for instance, the Supreme Court concluded that Congress exceeded its authority under both the equal protection and commerce clauses of the Constitution when it enacted a civil rights remedy targeting perpetrators of gender-based violence. However, the Supreme Court ignored an amicus brief submitted by 36 distinguished international law scholars and human rights experts, who argued that the U.S. ratification of the International Covenant on Civil and Political Rights (ICCPR) in 1992 created an obligation to address gender-based violence in this country. Since Congress has primary responsibility for implementing international treaties ratified by the U.S., the experts argued, Congress's authority to enact the women's civil rights remedy arose directly from this international obligation.

Accepting this position would have changed the outcome of the case. But by wholly failing to address U.S. obligations under the ICCPR, whether to uphold or distinguish them, the Supreme Court tacitly took the position that international law—even when ratified by the U.S.—is irrelevant within its own borders. Our courts have ceded leadership in shaping the world's jurisprudence by their singular refusal to examine the interplay between domestic law and the law of nations. The U.S., with its highly respected judiciary, should be a leader in charting the new territory of international law (Davis 2000:9).

international law and enforceable. From a social work perspective, going to court to enforce a human right may appear distasteful. However, the point here is to recognize the importance of human rights within the social work profession and to understand how some of those rights are basic to the human condition.

SUMMARY

Clearly, the process of drafting and obtaining acceptance of a covenant or convention on human rights involves numerous factors. The initial wording of the document contains its own set of challenges, with some countries or groups wanting a particular wording to satisfy their own political or social agenda. After the inevitable tug-of-war over language of a covenant or convention comes the vote on the document. Will enough countries in the General Assembly of the United Nations vote to adopt the instrument? If so, then comes the subsequent process of putting the instrument into effect, which requires a specific number of countries accepting the instrument as the law of their lands. Even acceptance of the document as law does not prevent a country from placing reservations on the treaty. If a country wants to accept the treaty generally but does not like a particular provision, then that country may reserve enforcement of that provision.

Finally, after ratification of the treaty, a country has to decide whether the treaty is self-implementing or requires specific legislation to implement the terms of the treaty. The United States has usually viewed UN treaties as requiring specific legislation to implement. In other words, an individual who might be affected by the treaty could not simply refer to the treaty in a court of law but would need to refer to specific legislation indicating that the treaty applies. If such legislation does not exist, the individual could not rely on the treaty for legal support.

With all the ins and outs relating to human rights documents, social workers might wonder how any document ever sees the light of day. Yet substantial efforts in drafting new documents and revising existing documents continue as a means of improving political, social, economic, and cultural situations around the world. This dedication by many individuals, groups, and governments reveals the importance of human rights principles to social workers and their profession.

QUESTIONS

1. How would you respond to the claim that "human rights" is a Western concept?
2. What is the Universal Declaration of Human Rights?
3. List religious, spiritual, and philosophical values that are incorporated into the Universal Declaration of Human Rights.
4. What reasons existed for the creation of the Universal Declaration in 1948?
5. The Universal Declaration consists of three generations of rights. What are those three generations? Discuss how each generation relates to social work.
6. What objections did some countries have to the Universal Declaration?
7. Does the Universal Declaration relate to indigenous peoples?
8. How are voices of women heard in the Universal Declaration?
9. What is the significance of Nongovernmental organizations (NGOs)?
10. Is the Universal Declaration of Human Rights legally binding on countries adopting the declaration? Explain your response.
11. How can provisions of the Universal Declaration be enforced?
12. What is customary international law? How does this concept relate to human rights?

REFERENCES

Alexander, T. 1996. *Unravelling Global Apartheid. An Overview of World Politics.* Cambridge, Eng.: Polity Press.

Black, H. Campbell. 1968. *Black's Law Dictionary, Abridged: Definitions of the Terms and Phrases of American and English Jurisprudence, Ancient and Modern.* Rev. 4th ed. St. Paul, Minn.: West Publishing.

Brown, D. 1970. *Bury My Heart at Wounded Knee: An Indian History of the American West.* New York: Holt Rinehart and Winston.

Buergenthal, T. 1988. *International Human Rights Law.* St. Paul, Minn.: West Publishing.

Boulding, E. 1992. *The Underside of History.* Vol 2. Newbury Park, Calif.: Sage.

Center for Human Rights. 1994. *Human Rights and Social Work: A Manual for Schools of Social Work and the Social Work Profession.* Training Series no. 1. Geneva: United Nations.

Davis, M. 2000. Bring international law into domestic courtrooms. *Christian Science Monitor*, October 11: 9.

Gangjian, D. and S. Gang. 1995. Relating human rights to Chinese culture: The four paths of the Confucian *Analects* and the four principles of a new theory of benevolence. In F. Davis, ed., *Human Rights and Chinese Values*, 35–55. Hong Kong: Oxford University Press.

Economist, The. 1998. Human-rights law. (December 15): 4–16.

———. 2001. Special report on human rights: Righting wrongs. (August 18–24): 18–20.

Farer, T. 1989. The United Nations and human rights: More than a whimper. In R. P. Claude and B. H. Weston, eds., *Human Rights in the World Community*, 194–208. Philadelphia: University of Pennsylvania Press.

Filartiga v. Pena-Irala, 630 F. 2d 876 (1980).

Gandhi, M. 2002. *See* www.engagedpage.com/gan1.html.

Hall, K., ed. 1992. *The Oxford Companion to the Supreme Court of the United States*. Oxford and New York: Oxford University Press.

Healy, L. 2001. *International Social Work: Professional Action in an Interdependent World*. New York: Oxford University Press.

Hughes, R. 1987. *The Fatal Shore: The Epic of Australia's Founding*. New York: Knopf.

Ife, J. 2001. *Human Rights and Social Work: Towards Rights-based Practice*. Cambridge: Cambridge University Press.

Kendall, K. 1989. Women at the helm: Three extraordinary leaders. *Affilia: Journal of Women and Social Work* 4.1: 23–32.

Laqueur, W. and B. Rubin, eds. 1979. *The Human Rights Reader*. Philadelphia: Temple University Press.

McKinney, C. M. and R. Park-Cunningham. 1997. Evolution of the social work profession: An historical review of the U.S. and selected countries, 1995. In *Proceedings of the 28th Annual Conference, New York State Social Work Education Association*, 3–9. Syracuse: New York State Social Work Education Association.

Morsink, J. 1999. *The Universal Declaration of Human Rights: Origins, Drafting, and Intent*. Philadelphia: University of Pennsylvania Press.

National Coordinating Committee for UDHR50. 1998. Franklin and Eleanor Roosevelt Institute home page (online). *See* www.udhr50.org/history imeline.htm.

National Association of Social Workers. 2000. *Social Work Speaks: National Association of Social Workers Policy Statements, 2000–2003*. 5th ed. Washington, D.C.: NASW Press.

Newman, F. and D. Weisbrodt, eds. 1996. *International Human Rights: Law, Policy, and Process*. 2d ed. Cincinnati, Ohio: Anderson.

Peebles-Wilkins, W. and E. Francis. 1990. Two outstanding black women in social welfare history: Mary Church Terrell and Ida B. Wells-Barnett. *Affilia: Journal of Women and Social Work* 5.4: 87–100.

Press, E. 2000. Human rights–the next step. *The Nation* (December 25): 13–18.

Rawls, J. 1993. *Political Liberalsim*. New York: Columbia University Press.

Reichert E. 1996. Keep on moving forward: NGO Forum on Women, Beijing, China. *Social Development Issues* 18.1: 61–71.

——. 1998. Women's rights are human rights: A platform for action. *International Social Work* 15.3: 177–85.

——. 2001. Placing human rights at the center of the social work profession. *Journal of Intergroup Relations* 28.1 (Spring): 43–50.

Staub-Bernasconi, S. 1998. Soziale Arbeit als Menschenrechtsprofession. In A. Woehrle, ed., *Profession und Wissenschaft Sozialer Arbeit: Positionen in einer Phase der generellen Neuverortnung und Spezifika*, 305–32. Pfaffenweilerm, Ger.: Cenaurus.

Swarns, R. 2001. Conference calls for reversing consequences of slavery: UN meeting on racism ends in controversy. New York Times News Service in *St. Louis Post-Dispatch*, September 9, 2001.

United Nations. 1948. *Universal Declaration of Human Rights.* Adopted December 10, 1948. GA. Res. 217 AIII. United Nations Document a/810. New York: UN.

——. 1987. *Human Rights: Questions and Answers.* New York: UN.

——. 1994. *Human Rights and Social Work: A Manual for Schools of Social Work and the Social Work Profession.* Professional Training Series no. 4. New York and Geneva: UN.

United Nations and Human Rights. 2001. *See* www.hrusa.org/hrh.

Van Wormer, K. 1997. *Social Welfare: A World View.* Chicago: Nelson-Hall.

Vienna Convention on the Law of Treaties (1969).

Walz, H. 1999. *Soziale Arbeit–Menschenrechte-Nachhaltige Entwicklung*, 3–7. Essen: Deutscher Berufsverband fuer Sozialarbeit, Sozialpaedagogik und Heilpaedagogik.

Walz, T. and H. Ritchie. 2000. Gandhian principles in social work practice: Ethics revisited. *Social Work: Journal of the National Association of Social Workers* 45.3: 213–22.

Wieler, J. 1988. Alice Salomon. *Journal of Teaching in Social Work* 2.2: 165–71.

——. 1989. The impact of Alice Salomon on social work education. In *60 Jahre IASSW* (60th anniversary of IASSW), 15–26. Berlin: Fachhochschule fur Sozialarbeit und Sozialpadagogik.

Wronka, J. 1998. *Human Rights and Social Policy in the 21st Century: A History of the Idea of Human Rights and Comparison of the United Nations Universal Declaration of Human Rights with United States Federal and State Constitutions.* Rev. ed. Lanham, Md.: University Press of America.

2

Universal Declaration of Human Rights

*Where, after all, do universal human rights begin? In small places, close
to home—so close and so small they cannot be seen on any maps of the
world. Yet they are the world of the individual person; the neighborhood he
lives in, the school or college he attends, the factory, farm, or office where he
works. Such are the places where every man, woman, and child seeks equal
justice, equal opportunity, and equal dignity without discrimination.
Unless these rights have meaning there, they have little meaning anywhere.
Without concerted citizen action to uphold them close to home, we shall
look in vain for progress in the larger world.*
   —Eleanor Roosevelt (as cited in National Coordinating Committee 1998)

When politicians and others discuss human rights, a question frequently arises as to the actual depth of knowledge those individuals
have concerning human rights. Do they have in mind a specific document, such as the Universal Declaration of Human Rights? If so, to
which provision(s) are they referring? Many people simply throw out
the term with no real understanding of what human rights means. Yet
specific information exists concerning the nature of human rights
and what those rights encompass.

To begin a detailed study of human rights, the inevitable starting
point is the Universal Declaration of Human Rights, adopted by the
United Nations in 1948 and applicable to all countries joining that
body. With the UN's adoption of the Universal Declaration of Human
Rights, a new historical era emerged in how nations viewed circumstances within and outside their borders. While nothing immediately
changed because of the Universal Declaration, as time has passed,

precepts contained in the declaration have frequently affected governmental policies and individual acts.

Like any basic law or constitution, the Universal Declaration is a living document, subject to interpretations that continually change with the passage of time. However, many of the provisions within the declaration contain fundamental freedoms and rights that would clearly apply to any set of circumstances.

PURPOSE OF THE UNIVERSAL DECLARATION

The direct impetus for the Universal Declaration of Human Rights emanated from the horrors perpetrated in Nazi Germany in the name of racial purity and superiority. Laws in Nazi Germany labeled numerous individuals and groups as non-Germans, undeserving of rights and the benefits of citizens. The intent behind these racial purity laws was to exclude those who did not have the "proper" ethnic or religious background from participating in German society. Individuals or groups who spoke out against this discriminatory treatment encountered the wrath of the Nazi government, which tortured and executed many dissidents. Eventually, the Nazi government rounded up Jews and other individuals—including Gypsies, communists, homosexuals, dissidents, and "asoziale" (persons on welfare)—for transport to concentration camps, where many died under German extermination policies. People with mental illnesses or other disabilities were often killed at hospitals (Hansen 1991; Otto and Sunker 1991; Schnurr 1997). The horrors of Nazi Germany seemed unimaginable. People from all over the world wondered how they could prevent those horrors from ever occurring again?

While Nazi Germany and its genocidal policies against Jews and other groups provided the most immediate rationale for universal rules that would protect vulnerable populations, other factors also played a role. Poverty and unemployment had afflicted many individuals throughout the world during the Great Depression of the 1930s. Should individuals everywhere be entitled to a social security net to help them during hard times? The colonization of African and Asian countries by Europeans also provided fuel for a universal rule against exploitation of peoples by the more powerful. Should not the colonized have a right to self-determination? The list of issues concerning the human condition never seemed to end after

World War II. Discussion about these issues led inexorably to the idea that some underlying document should exist that defines the essence of a human being's existence. Given the vast cultural and other differences among individuals, what common needs and freedoms should everyone share? The outcome of this intensive soul-searching was the Universal Declaration of Human Rights. While certainly not perfect, the principles contained within the declaration provide a worthy foundation for advancing political and social rights that everyone should enjoy.

The Universal Declaration itself does not legally bind any nation to enforce the human rights contained in the declaration. Nor do formal penalties exist for nations violating those human rights. However, many countries have integrated human rights specified in the declaration into their own laws. Also, some of the rights in the declaration have become enforceable through customary international law. In this respect, the declaration has been successful in setting the standard for acceptable conduct in the area of human rights.

One point of contemporary interest concerning the Universal Declaration involves its alleged sexist nature (Prigoff 2000). Some references in the declaration refer to "man" and not "woman." However, in a review of the declaration's history, the issue of gender has received significant attention (Morsink 1999). Thus, women delegates involved in drafting the declaration, especially those from Denmark and the Soviet bloc, lobbied strongly for the inclusion of a woman's perspective in all areas of human rights. The outcome of this discussion led to the frequent use of words like "everyone," "all," and "no one" to avoid sexist implications. While framers of the declaration let stand the occasional use of "man" to refer to all individuals, the intent of the provisions contained in the declaration clearly denotes the inclusion of women. The inclusiveness of the overall language indicates that the declaration applies to everyone, without regard to gender. Nonetheless, where it occurs, male-oriented language in the Universal Declaration would not be acceptable today. And in spite of efforts by drafters of the declaration to avoid a sexist document, the subsequent defining of human rights has often become a male-oriented process. This male orientation eventually led to a movement to state emphatically that women's rights are also human rights (see chapter 5 for a discussion of this movement).

MONITORING HUMAN RIGHTS PRACTICES

Various international organizations monitor a nation's compliance with human rights, including those contained in the Universal Declaration of Human Rights. A well-known nongovernmental organization, Human Rights Watch, conducts regular investigations of human rights abuses around the world. Founded in 1978, Human Rights Watch states the following as its mission:

> We address the human rights practices of governments of all political stripes, of all geopolitical alignments, and of all ethnic and religious persuasions. Human Rights Watch defends freedom of thought and expression, due process and equal protection of the law, and a vigorous civil society; we document and denounce murders, disappearances, torture, arbitrary imprisonment, discrimination, and other abuses of internationally recognized human rights. Our goal is to hold governments accountable if they transgress the rights of their people. (Human Rights Watch World Report 2001)

Human Rights Watch includes divisions on Europe and Central Asia, Africa, the Americas, Asia, and the Middle East. In addition, the organization includes three thematic divisions on arms, children's rights, and women's rights. It maintains offices in New York, Washington, Los Angeles, London, Brussels, Moscow, Dushanbe, and Bangkok. Financial support for Human Rights Watch comes from private individuals and foundations. Human Rights Watch does not accept any government funds, directly or indirectly.

In a recent annual report, Human Rights Watch stated the following about the United States: "As the Clinton Administration's second term ended in 2000, evidence of its domestic human rights legacy was scant. The country made little progress in embracing international human rights standards at home. Most public officials remained either unaware of their human rights obligations or content to ignore them" (Human Rights Watch World Report 2001:427). What prompted such criticism?: "As in previous years, serious human rights violations were most apparent in the criminal justice system—including police brutality, discriminatory racial disparities in incarceration, abusive conditions of confinement, and state-sponsored executions, even of juvenile offenders and the mentally handicapped. But extensively documented human rights violations also included violations of workers' rights, discrimination against gay men and lesbians in the military, and the abuse of migrant child farmworkers" (427).

(continued)

Specific discussion in the report about the status of human rights in the United States criticized the failure of the United States to become party to important human rights treaties, including the International Covenant on Economic, Social, and Cultural Rights and the Convention on the Elimination of All Forms of Discrimination Against Women (CEDAW). The United States was one of only two countries in the world—with Somalia, which has no internationally recognized government—that had not ratified the Convention on the Rights of the Child (428).

Human Rights Watch also challenged the treatment of asylum seekers in the United States by the Immigration and Naturalization Service (INS). In September 2000, on a daily average, INS was detaining 20,000 individuals, while in 1995 the daily average had been only 6,700 (437–38). The increasing numbers of detainees "strained the ability of the INS to provide humane and safe conditions in its detention facilities, and the influx of detainees led to a space crisis. More than half of all INS detainees were held in prisons or local jails intended for criminal inmates, exposing them to treatment and conditions inappropriate to their administrative detainee status and hampering their access to legal assistance. Asylum-seekers continued to be detained as the rule, rather than the exception, as the INS continued to ignore international standards relating to the treatment of asylum-seekers" (438).

Of course, the Human Rights Watch report on the United States appears mild when compared with many other countries. In Colombia, human rights defenders, community leaders, government investigators, and journalists continued to face "threats, attacks, and death throughout the year. Four human rights defenders were killed and three 'disappeared' during the first ten months of 2000" (Human Rights Watch World Report 2001:117). The African country of Sierra Leone experienced all types of atrocities by soldiers fighting an ongoing civil war. Some soldiers carried out "rape, murder, torture, abduction, massive looting, forced labor, and indiscriminate ambushes along a major highway" (69).

The continued monitoring of human rights abuses by Human Rights Watch indicates the importance of publicizing those abuses. While governments may choose to ignore reports by Human Rights Watch, the publicity from being exposed as violating human rights can serve to reduce future human rights abuses.

SPECIFIC PROVISIONS OF THE
UNIVERSAL DECLARATION

The Universal Declaration of Human Rights is not a lengthy document. It contains a preamble and thirty relatively concise articles. The language used in the declaration tends to be legalistic, which can detract from its acceptance by social workers. However, social workers continually encounter laws regulating many aspects of their profession. The field of human rights, while based on laws, also incorporates many ideals of the social work profession. The following discussion of the Universal Declaration shows an obvious connection between human rights and social work.

Preamble to the Universal Declaration The preamble of the Universal Declaration of Human Rights states general reasons for the declaration. Subsequent articles then list specific rights for "all members of the human family." The preamble begins with the following statement:

> *Whereas* recognition of the inherent dignity and of the equal and inalienable rights of all members of the human family is the foundation of freedom, justice, and peace in the world,

Every human being is entitled to an inherent dignity, one of the foundations of freedom, justice, and peace. An inherent dignity exists merely by virtue of being human. The other foundation is the equal and inalienable rights of all members of the human family. Inalienable rights refer to rights incapable of being surrendered or transferred. These rights exist for everyone. Without these rights, freedom, justice, and peace in the world could be much more difficult to secure.

> *Whereas* disregard and contempt for human rights have resulted in barbarous acts which have outraged the conscience of mankind, and the advent of a world in which human beings shall enjoy freedom of speech and belief and freedom from fear and want has been proclaimed as the highest aspiration of the common people,

This phrase acknowledges that the horrific experiences of World War II and other "barbarous acts" resulted from "disregard and contempt" of human rights. In a desire never to repeat those experiences, drafters of the declaration proclaim that the highest aspiration of the common people is to create a world tolerant of different views, respectful of individual freedoms and mindful of economic security.

> *Whereas* it is essential, if man is not to be compelled to have recourse, as a last resort, to rebellion against tyranny and oppression, that human rights should be protected by the rule of law,

Without legal enforcement of human rights, the world could again be tossed into tumultuous circumstances. This phrase contemplates respect for human rights by governments through legal frameworks. Reflection in regard to the weakness of the League of Nations and that organization's ineffective enforcement structure prompted concern over how nations would treat human rights. While this provision envisions legal enforcement, the use of the word *should* in "should be protected by the rule of law" indicates the nonbinding nature of the declaration.

> *Whereas* it is essential to promote the development of friendly relations between nations,

This provision highlights the importance of international relations and the necessity of getting along. The concept of human rights would promote amicable dealings between countries and, by extension, individuals from differing countries.

> *Whereas* the peoples of the United Nations have in the Charter reaffirmed their faith in fundamental human rights, in the dignity and worth of the human person and in the equal rights of men and women and have determined to promote social progress and better standards of life in larger freedom,

A somewhat tortuous phrase, this provision states that, regardless of what has happened in the past, all members of the United Nations agree to the need for human rights. Moreover, they believe in human dignity and the equal rights of men and women. The last part of this phrase denotes a desire to improve overall living standards in the context of greater individual freedom. This wording indicates the vagueness of certain concepts, such as freedom. Defining terms like *freedom* always becomes difficult when different cultures and political systems are involved. Therefore, in this context the declaration does not necessarily mean a U.S. system where individual freedoms tend to be greater in many respects than in many other countries. The term "larger freedom" could easily refer to both the United States and Saudi Arabia, with the goal being better social and economic conditions within their respective political systems. In other countries a collective or group-oriented society might be prevalent. In the United States, for instance, individualism is highly valued.

Whereas Member States have pledged themselves to achieve, in cooperation with the United Nations, the promotion of universal respect for and observance of human rights and fundamental freedoms,

This phrase highlights a pledge by any member of the United Nations to promote human rights and basic freedoms everywhere. In this statement, the declaration adds the term "fundamental freedoms" to human rights without specifying those freedoms in later articles. Once again, freedom is a relative concept, and any definition of freedom must take into account numerous factors, including cultural, economic, political, and social traditions.

Whereas a common understanding of these rights and freedoms is of the greatest importance for the full realization of this pledge,

Not only is an understanding of human rights and freedoms important, but a "common" understanding also plays a key role in realizing universal human rights. In other words, opinions on what human rights and freedoms mean should correlate or at least bear some resemblance. This does not mean that any particular human right or freedom must be defined or interpreted the same by every country. However, some common ground for realizing human rights must exist among all nations. Otherwise, the Universal Declaration would remain nothing more than a theoretical proposition incapable of being put into practice.

Now, therefore,
The General Assembly
Proclaims this Universal Declaration of Human Rights as a common standard of achievement for all peoples and all nations, to the end that every individual and every organ of society, keeping this Declaration constantly in mind, shall

strive by teaching and education to promote respect for these rights and free-doms and by progressive measures, national and international, to secure their universal and effective recognition and observance, both among the peoples of Member States themselves and among the peoples of territories under their ju-risdiction.

This proclamation obligates signers of the declaration to promulgate human rights and explain them to peoples of the member States. Perhaps this provision is one of the most frequently violated by signatories. In the United States, only a few social work textbooks provide detailed discussions of human rights (Reichert 2001). However, textbooks that do address human rights generally classify them as an international concept. Little more than passing reference to human rights and their importance to the social work profession appears in those textbooks (Van Wormer 1996; Midg-ley 1997; Prigoff 2000; Healy 2001). This does not necessarily mean that au-thors of these textbooks are unaware of the importance of human rights to social work. However, by not addressing human rights in a more complete and direct manner, these textbooks simply do not sufficiently integrate human rights concepts into social work education.

The teaching of human rights in the United States appears to have a greater foothold in elementary and secondary schools than in higher edu-cation (Farah 2001). Clearly, if human rights are to mean anything, educa-tion about those rights must become more prevalent in all countries.

The provision of the preamble to the Universal Declaration of Human Rights concerning education concludes the introduction to the declaration. The next part of the declaration, separated into articles, defines specific rights and goals known as human rights.

Articles of the Universal Declaration The Universal Declaration of Human Rights contains thirty articles that list universal rights and goals applicable to everyone. These articles embody human rights that every government and individual should follow. The articles also include specific entitlements to rights that every government should strive to fulfill.

Article 1
All human beings are born free and equal in dignity and rights. They are en-dowed with reason and conscience and should act towards one another in a spirit of brotherhood.

This article derives from the concept of natural law and natural rights. Unjust acts create inequality. Everyone is born with the same human status and, because he or she has reason and a conscience, everyone should view other individuals as also having the same dignity and entitlement to human rights.

Article 2

Everyone is entitled to all the rights and freedoms set forth in this Declaration, without distinction of any kind, such as race, colour, sex, language, religion, political or other opinion, national or social origin, property, birth or other status.

Furthermore, no distinction shall be made on the basis of the political, jurisdictional or international status of the country or territory to which a person belongs, whether it be independent, trust, non-self-governing or under any other limitation of sovereignty.

This article specifies an entitlement to all human rights and freedoms without discrimination. At the time of the declaration, this language actually appeared quite radical in that many countries treated citizens differently on the basis of classification. For instance, in parts of the United States in 1948, segregation of whites and blacks existed in many respects, including use of bathrooms, drinking fountains, seats in buses, marriage, and an array of other segregated activities. In view of its segregation laws, how could the United States legitimately subscribe to human rights that contradicted those segregation laws? Of course, almost every country that has adopted the Universal Declaration encounters awkward questions about adherence to human rights listed there. Human rights often pose a dilemma for many nations bound by past traditions and laws that conflict with human rights.

The second part of this article emphasizes the universality of human rights. Regardless of an individual's origins, that individual is entitled to human rights and freedoms. The political system under which the individual resides must accommodate those rights. Obviously, many nations find the universality principle difficult to follow. For instance, governments frequently treat immigrant residents differently than citizens so that immigrants may not qualify for certain benefits viewed as human rights, while citizens do (Reichert and McCormick 1998). This favoring of citizens over immigrant residents violates the universality principle since everyone is entitled to human rights without limitation.

Article 3
Everyone has the right to life, liberty, and the security of person.

This human right highlights the sanctity of life and the right to be free in most pursuits and the right to be safe. However, precise definitions of liberty and security are difficult. Most likely, a common understanding among all nations would be difficult. In the United States, liberty and security of person take on a political and civil slant, meaning that government should not interfere with most individual activities nor arbitrarily threaten to detain someone. In China, this article could mean that government has a duty to prevent crime and ensure the safety of its residents, even if this involves restrictions on activities that would be allowed in the United States. Chinese officials may interpret this human right as the right to restrict individual activities when government believes that those activities negatively impact on society. Which country would be violating this human rights article? The United States or China? No clear-cut answers exist to this question, which requires detailed understanding of cultural, economic, and political circumstances. This example points out why accusations involving human rights violations should be clearly explained, with consideration given to whatever extenuating circumstances surround the so-called violation.

Article 4
No one shall be held in slavery or servitude; slavery and the slave trade shall be prohibited in all their forms.

As American citizens should know, no form of human domination can be more evil than slavery. Treating another human being as inferior or a piece of property can never be sanctioned. As a human right, the prohibition against slavery or servitude ranks as one of the most important.

Article 5
No one shall be subjected to torture or to cruel, inhuman, or degrading treatment or punishment.

This human right emphasizes the right of everyone to be free from torture and extreme methods of punishment or treatment. One instance where the United States possibly violates this human right involves the death penalty. Many countries around the world have prohibited the death penalty for crimes committed because they view the death penalty as inhumane (Human Rights Watch World Report 2001). The social work profession also advocates abolition of the death penalty: "As it is currently used, the death penalty violates the constitutional prohibition against cruel and unusual punishment. In addition, the unequal application of the death penalty deprives many people of color and low-income people" of equal protection under the law (NASW 2000:37).

Another instance of how this human right has influenced policies around the world involves domestic violence. Only recently have some countries viewed the battering of women as cruel and degrading behavior and, therefore, a violation of human rights. Acceptance of physical violence against women has been particularly prevalent in the private sphere: in general, it has been held, what goes on behind closed doors is nobody else's business. Now, however, this separation between the public and private physical abuse of women is dissolving, with special attention to the issue being raised through human rights documents subsequent to the Universal Declaration (e.g., CEDAW). The social work profession in the United States has also specifically addressed the issue of family violence in a human rights context: "The acceptance of family violence as a way of life, particularly violence against women and children, is pervasive in American culture. . . . Violence is presented as an acceptable form of behavior in literature, children's stories, theater, movies, athletic events, advertising, and radio and television programs" (NASW 2000:124). In some cases, bias in regard to sex, race, and class by social workers themselves help to perpetuate the problems of family violence:

> Many professionals blame the victims, believing that the wife, child, or elderly individual provokes or in some way is responsible for and contributes to the violence. All social workers should recognize the complex economic, emotional, cultural, and societal factors that keep the family member in the violent situation. The social work profession has a responsibility to address the problem of family violence through needed research, the development of prevention and intervention programs, and advocacy for adequate laws and funding for protective and treatment services. (NASW 2000:124–25)

The human right contained in this article touches upon important social work values. By addressing the issue of cruel and inhuman treatment and punishment in a human rights context, social workers can possibly be more effective in developing policies to prevent this human rights violation.

Article 6
Everyone has the right to recognition everywhere as a person before the law.

This human right is another example of the universality principle. No country should legally treat a foreign resident or immigrant differently than a citizen. It must treat them the same "before the law." A close reading of this human right limits the recognition as a person to those instances when a legal issue arises. Therefore, I or anyone else could say (as long as no law is involved) that I do not have to associate with or recognize a person whose religion differs from mine. From a human rights viewpoint, that interpretation could be justified provided that I or anyone else acts in a spirit of human dignity and brotherhood (art. 1). However, a more natural human rights position would be that an individual would always recognize a person as having inherent dignity. Therefore, in the spirit of sisterhood and brotherhood, an individual would not refuse to help people from all different walks of life.

Article 7
All are equal before the law and are entitled without any discrimination to equal protection of the law. All are entitled to equal protection against any discrimination in violation of this Declaration and against any incitement to such discrimination.

Generally, equal protection before the law prohibits discrimination against an individual because of a suspect classification, which includes gender, national origin, race, religion, and age. The purpose of this article is to promote a universal environment of nondiscrimination.

This equal protection provision resembles equal protection provisions in the U.S. Constitution (amend. 14). However, in the United States, discrimination may often be allowed if no underlying motive to discriminate exists. If a legitimate reason exists to justify an act, then generally the law overlooks any discriminatory effect of that act. For instance, suppose that an employer selects a non-African-American employee for a position requiring a highly specific background. African-Americans have applied for the job, but none has the background needed for the job. Because the job pool has not included African-Americans who have the required background, the employer is not viewed as unlawfully discriminating against African-Americans. Yet the *effect* of the selection process is discriminatory in that it has excluded African-Americans from the employment position at issue. The remedy would be to address this issue and ensure that African-Americans receive appropriate training to qualify for the employment position. To some extent, affirmative action programs adopt this type of remedial assistance to women and minorities. However, recent trends in the United States have been to move away from affirmative action in respect to issues of discrimination.

The U.S. view of equal protection could conflict with this human right provision since, under this provision, a zero tolerance level of discrimination appears to apply. In other words, even if a legitimate reason exists for an action that has a discriminatory effect, that action could violate this article of the declaration. To remedy the discriminatory effect, policies would be required to examine how to overcome the discriminatory effect and then actually address the issue.

Article 8

Everyone has the right to an effective remedy by the competent national tribunals for acts violating the fundamental rights granted him by the constitution or by law.

This legalistic article builds upon previous articles in ensuring that everyone has access to courts and other avenues of redress for constitutional and legal violations. The social work profession supports efforts to protect this human right. Social workers should oppose federal and state legislative initiatives and actions that discriminate against both legal residents and undocumented individuals (NASW 2000:173–74). "Social workers must take a forceful and assertive stand to ensure that policies, programs, and practices protect all individuals who reside in the United States" (173).

Article 9

No one shall be subjected to arbitrary arrest, detention, or exile.

This article further refines the limits of governments regarding criminal prosecution. After coming to power in 1933, the Nazis solidified their grip on the populace by eliminating procedural protections against arbitrary arrest and detention (Hansen 1991; Schnurr 1997). With horrific experiences suffered by victims of the Nazis being brought to light when the declaration was being written, this provision aimed to prevent a similar nightmare.

Article 10

Everyone is entitled in full equality to a fair and public hearing by an independent and impartial tribunal, in the determination of his rights and obligations and of any criminal charge against him.

This human right essentially guarantees to everyone the right to a fair and public hearing or trial, for not only criminal offenses but also any other proceeding that would affect the individual's rights and duties. (This latter part could refer to an administrative hearing to remove the license of a counselor, for instance.) Once again, the vagueness of the wording regarding this human right allows different interpretations. However, at a minimum, when an important right is at stake, an individual is entitled to an impartial public hearing.

Article 11

1. Everyone charged with a penal offence has the right to be presumed innocent until proved guilty according to law in a public trial at which he has had all the guarantees necessary for his defence.

2. No one shall be held guilty of any penal offence on account of any act or omission which did not constitute a penal offence, under national or international law, at the time when it was committed. Nor shall a heavier penalty be imposed than the one that was applicable at the time the penal offence was committed.

Paragraph 1 of this article essentially mimics the well-known phrase in the United States that everyone is innocent of a crime until proven guilty. The second part prohibits prosecution of acts not considered crimes at the time the acts were committed. For example, if five years ago no criminal penalty existed for driving 75 miles an hour, but now a penalty exists for that activity, no one who had driven 75 mph five years ago can be brought to trial at this time. Nor may a stricter penalty be imposed on a crime than the penalty that existed at the time of the crime. A primary purpose behind this human right is to prevent unfair tinkering with laws to prosecute unpopular opponents or individuals.

NASW states that, although "legitimate police activities are justified to protect human life and property, recent expansion of police and prosecutorial powers seriously infringes on the rights of the accused and violates the basic common law principle of presumed innocence" (NASW 2000:37). In contrast to a punitive view of those accused of crimes, NASW believes that "more can be done to fight crime by devoting greater resources to the elimination of its causes than by repressive measures that jeopardize the well-being of innocent people" (38).

Article 12

No one shall be subjected to arbitrary interference with his privacy, family, home or correspondence, nor to attacks upon his honor and reputation. Everyone has the right to the protection of the law against such interference or attacks.

This human right emphasizes the right to privacy and reputation, especially in the family setting. In the United States and other countries, laws exist to protect private e-mail correspondence, written letters, financial transactions, and other dealings. Courts in most countries also allow redress when an individual's reputation has been harmed. This type of action is known generally as defamation, or *libel* for written defamation and *slander* for verbal defamation.

The social work profession has incorporated elements of this human right into a policy statement that includes an "affirmative obligation to offer protection against excesses of authority that violate the rights of people whom social workers serve" (NASW 2000:39). The NASW condemns intrusions into the right of privacy, especially in its applications to health and human services settings.

Article 13

1. Everyone has the right to freedom of movement and residence within the borders of each State.

2. Everyone has the right to leave any country, including his own, and to return to his country.

This human right emphasizes the right of an individual to leave any country and to return to his or her country of citizenship. An individual also has the right to freely travel and reside within his or her country. This right does not specifically require a country to allow the entry of any individual. However, once an individual has been granted entry and permission to reside, restrictions on movement and place of residence may not exist. A gross violation of the second part of this right occurred when Germany existed as two parts, East and West Germany. East Germany would not allow its citizens to travel outside its jurisdiction and lined the border with machine gun nests and minefields for the express purpose of preventing its citizens from leaving. Hundreds of East Germans lost their lives trying to flee. While the East German government tried to justify its restrictions in regard to leaving the country on the basis that it was protecting its citizens from Western intrusion, such obstacles clearly violated the intent of this human right.

Article 14

1. Everyone has the right to seek and to enjoy in other countries asylum from persecution.

2. This right may not be invoked in the case of prosecutions genuinely arising from non-political crimes or from acts contrary to the purposes and principles of the United Nations.

The right of asylum relates to an individual who holds a well-founded fear of persecution on the basis of political, religious, or racial status. Every country must allow individuals the right to present their case for asylum. A need for this provision arose from the difficulty Jewish and other individuals experienced during World War II to escape persecution by the Nazi regime. However, asylum does not apply to cases where an individual is being prosecuted in his or her home country for nonpolitical crimes. Consequently, economic crimes or motives for seeking asylum fall short of satisfying the requirements of this human right.

Article 15

1. Everyone has the right to a nationality.

2. No one shall be arbitrarily deprived of his nationality nor denied the right to change his nationality.

Every individual has the right to belong to a nation. No country may take away this right without justification. However, if an individual wants to change citizenship, then he or she has that right.

Article 16

1. Men and women of full age, without any limitation due to race, nationality, or religion, have the right to marry and to found a family. They are entitled to equal rights as to marriage, during marriage and at its dissolution.

2. Marriage shall be entered into only with the free and full consent of the intending spouses.

3. The family is the natural and fundamental group unit of society and is entitled to protection by society and the State.

This right promotes marriage and elevates the family to a protected status. Of course, the wording of this right indicates why the declaration is a living and organic document, subject to future revision. This article reflects the time period in which it was drafted. Today, in some countries, the definition of family has broadened and includes same-sex families. However, under the Universal Declaration, drafters clearly intended the exclusion of same-sex relationships from the concept of family. The article appears to define family as one created by men and women. In countries or States that allow same-sex marriages, the spouses and their family, including offspring, would not necessarily be entitled to the rights specified in this article. However, other groups living together, such as a single mother and child, might also seem excluded from the term "family" under this article. In other words, the Universal Declaration does not appear to recognize families other than those composed of the traditional man, woman, and their offspring. Under the declaration, nontraditional families would not qualify for protection from society and the State. Yet today, human rights concepts do include same-sex and other living arrangements. For instance, NASW defines family as "two or more people who consider themselves 'family' and who assume obligations and responsibilities that are generally considered essential to family life" (NASW 2000:117). Family composition may cover a "range of constellations, including traditional married parents with biological children; divorced, separated, or unmarried parents who have individual, separate, or shared responsibility for the care of children; intergenerational arrangements for child or elder care; gay and lesbian couples with or without the care of children; and adoptive and foster families. Family social policy must recognize and respect this range of models and their respective specific needs" (117). This expansion of the traditional view of family is an example of how human rights concepts and documents are never static. In 1948, little recognition of family units outside the traditional existed. In the twenty-first century, the family has expanded to include all types of arrangements.

Article 16 further states that spouses must consent to the marriage, another provision that can run afoul of customs in some countries. In some societies, parents or the prospective husband chooses a spouse and arranges the marriage. This human right that spouses must consent to the marriage is an example of how culture comes into play. Why should a society be accused of a human rights violation for a tradition that has existed for centuries? The study of human rights frequently encounters this type of cultural issue (which chapter 7 addresses in more detail under "Cultural Relativism").

Article 17

1. Everyone has the right to own property alone as well as in association with others.

2. No one shall be arbitrarily deprived of his property.

This human right guarantees private ownership of assets. At the time of the declaration, many communist countries would have taken issue with this human right. According to communist doctrine, the people or State owns all the property, which does not allow individual ownership. In today's world, the pure doctrine of communism has given way to private ownership, even in countries that had communist governments. This article also prohibits the taking of property without justification. Protection of property rights plays a key role in human rights.

Article 18

Everyone has the right to freedom of thought, conscience, and religion; this right includes freedom to change his religion or belief, and freedom, either alone or in community with others and in public or private, to manifest his religion or belief in teaching, practice, worship, and observance.

This human right guarantees freedom of religion and thought. Western governments have accused China of violating this human right owing to

What happens when religion conflicts with government policies? Which controls? In the United States, constitutional and other legal principles require a separation of religion and state, and government must take a relatively neutral position toward religion. This does not mean government must ignore or shun religious perspectives. However, the favoring of any religion or the incorporation of religion into official policies generally would be taboo.

In contrast to the separation of religion and state in the United States, an intertwining of religion and government exists in some countries. In those countries, which would include some Middle Eastern lands, policies are frequently based on religious principles. Pressure unquestionably exists for everyone to join the dominant religion, allowing little room for other religious practices.

Certainly, the human right guaranteeing freedom of religion and thought does not contemplate an environment of fear when individuals wish to practice their beliefs. Failure to allow freedom of thought and religion can lead to repression of human dignity, a fundamental basis of human rights.

China's crackdown against a group known as Falun Gong, which considers itself a religious association. However, China does not view Falun Gong as a religion or its members as engaging in any spiritual practice. Because no precise definition for religion or religious belief exists within the declaration—this would be difficult to draft in any case—countries might view some practices as outside the realm of religion or belief. In that case, the right to freedom of thought should still prevail. Unfortunately, in many countries, suppression of religion and thought is commonplace.

Article 19
Everyone has the right to freedom of opinion and expression; this right includes freedom to hold opinions without interference and to seek, receive, and impart information and ideas through any media and regardless of frontiers.

This human right guarantees freedom of expression without interference by governments or others. While this right appears to mirror the First Amendment right in the U.S. Constitution, an important distinction is that the First Amendment prohibits government from interfering with free speech. The

First Amendment does not prohibit individuals from restricting opinions or information in a purely private setting. In that sense, this human right appears to be broader than the First Amendment because it does not provide for restrictions on the flow of information by private parties.

Article 20

1. Everyone has the right to freedom of peaceful assembly and association.

2. No one may be compelled to belong to an association.

This human right specifies the freedom to peacefully assemble and meet with others. No group may force an individual to join the group against the wishes of the individual. An interesting interpretation of this human right could actually prohibit an employee's union from requiring workers to join the union. However, the apparent intent of this article is to allow the individual a free choice of whether she or he wishes to join a political party or other association.

Article 21

1. Everyone has the right to take part in the government of his country, directly or through freely chosen representatives.

2. Everyone has the right of equal access to public service in his country.

3. The will of the people shall be the basis of the authority of government; this will shall be expressed in periodic and genuine elections which shall be by universal and equal suffrage and shall be held by secret vote or by equivalent free voting procedures.

This human right requires countries to hold free and democratic elections, which shall determine the desires of the people. An individual has the right to run for a government position or support candidates running for office. Governments may not discriminate against individuals in its provision of public services. Obviously, abuses of these human rights occur in many countries, including those with a strong democratic tradition, such as the United States. While everyone may have the right to take part in government, lack of financial resources can hinder this participation. Without adequate funding, an individual has little chance of being elected, particularly in state or federal elections. And while most U.S. citizens are eligible to vote, many do not, with the result that a minority of voters actually elects gov-

Efforts in the United States to restrict voting have included poll taxes, literacy tests, cumbersome registration, and holding elections during workdays. In other words, voting in the United States has rarely been considered inclusive of all citizens. An apparent result of placing obstacles in front of the voting booth is low electoral turnouts, with those eligible to vote knowing little about candidates and their positions on major issues.

In Australia, voting is compulsory, and turnout is usually close to 100 percent. However, do electors know more about their candidates or have more knowledge about issues? Unlikely.

Perhaps the key to obtaining a sincere and constructive participation in the voting process is a belief that a vote counts. If feelings of helplessness or cynicism prevail or if one feels that his or her vote is worthless, then the voting process will remain an academic exercise, even if compulsory as in Australia.

ernment officials. Does a minority of eligible voters truly represent the will of the people, especially where monetary interests have played a large role in determining electoral candidates? Probably not. Clearly, from a human rights viewpoint, governments should make sincere efforts to promote voting by its citizens.

Article 22

Everyone, as a member of society, has the right to social security and is entitled to realization, through national effort and international co-operation and in accordance with the organization and resources of each State, of the economic, social, and cultural rights indispensable for his dignity and the free development of his personality.

This human right introduces the concept of economic and social human rights. Everyone, by virtue of being human, is entitled to social security and the economic, social, and cultural rights necessary to obtain dignity and pursue individual development. These rights should be realized by national efforts and international cooperation, with consideration of the organization and resources of each State.

In a single sentence, this article addresses several key issues in human rights doctrine, although little research exists to explain these particular rights (Wronka 1998:13). A government must try to provide residents with social security and the means to realize important economic, social, and cultural rights, which would include the right to work, housing, health care, holidays, and allowable observance of cultural traditions. To realize these rights, governments should cooperate with each other through international organizations. Wealthier countries would be expected to assist less wealthy countries through transfers of assistance.

Social workers have significant involvement in these issues, with the NASW supporting a national health care policy that ensures the right to universal medical coverage (NASW 2000:152). NASW also advocates the goal of a "decent home" and "suitable living environment" for every American (158). All individuals and families have the right to housing that meets their basic needs for shelter at an affordable level and provides for a rewarding community life (166). In practicing their profession, social workers should also respect the cultural rights of others (61).

Article 23

1. Everyone has the right to work, to free choice of employment, to just and favourable conditions of work and to protection against unemployment.

2. Everyone, without any discrimination, has the right to equal pay for equal work.

3. Everyone who works has the right to just and favourable remuneration ensuring for himself and his family an existence worthy of human dignity, and supplemented, if necessary, by other means of social protection.

4. Everyone has the right to form and to join trade unions for the protection of his interests.

This human right creates a right to work, which elaborates on the generalized economic and social rights noted in the previous article. Certainly this human right appears grandiose in that unemployment is a fact of life the world over. Can governments really guarantee employment and a wage sufficient to provide an existence worthy of human dignity? Lesser developed countries would have an especially difficult time meeting the requirements of this article. Nonetheless, the goal of ensuring that everyone who wants to work has a job with sufficient income to provide for his or her family has merit. In other words, the right to work with a living wage makes sense as a human right even if the fulfillment of this right is not always possible.

In European countries, a paid four-week (or even greater) vacation from work is a sacred human right. Paid vacation is even cited as a human right in human rights documents adopted by countries all over the world. However, would the paid vacation have the same human rights status in less economically developed countries, where structured employment has much less relevance? Certainly, leisure time is indispensable to the human existence, regardless of culture. However, when Western concepts of paid vacation infiltrate human rights principles, resentment and impressions of arrogance might enter into the human rights equation of how non-Westerners view human rights.

This human right also raises the issue of equal pay for equal work. Women typically earn significantly less than men and encounter numerous obstacles in overcoming wage and salary differentials (NASW 2000:320). The social work profession advocates for remedies to gender inequity at all levels of traditional social work intervention: at the macro level through federal and state legislation and in the executive branches of government; at mezzo levels in communities and organizations; and at micro levels in direct practice with individuals, families, and groups (324).

Article 24
Everyone has the right to rest and leisure, including reasonable limitation of working hours and periodic holidays with pay.

As with the human right guaranteeing a right to work, this right also appears Western-oriented and lofty in its realization. However, the spirit of this human right is in the right place.

Article 25
1. Everyone has the right to a standard of living adequate for the health and well-being of himself and of his family, including food, clothing, housing and medical care, and necessary social services, and the right to security in the event of unemployment, sickness, disability, widowhood, old age, or other lack of livelihood in circumstances beyond his control.
2. Motherhood and childhood are entitled to special care and assistance. All

children, whether born in or out of wedlock, shall enjoy the same social protection.

This human right addresses other economic and social benefits, including health care, housing, and other social services. Here is where the United States, with its long tradition of political and civil protections, fails to devote equal attention in the area of human rights. While some countries may not have sufficient resources to provide these economic and social rights, the United States is certainly in a better position to provide those rights than most other countries. Those countries claiming they do not have the resources may also be challenged as to how they allocate resources. Who receives priority in determining social welfare policies?

Special care and assistance for motherhood and childhood also relate to cultural and social rights. A father might question the specific protection of motherhood and not fatherhood. However, this human right seems justified in that the mother carries the child for nine months before the actual birth of the child. Regardless of how much a father might like to duplicate that experience, this duplication remains an impossibility. For that reason, special protection to the mother is a legitimate human right.

Of course, a father who becomes the primary caregiver of a child after birth might argue that he should have special protection. Also, a father could claim that, in cases of adoption, where specific biological factors of motherhood do not enter into the situation, fathers are entitled to the same protection or recognition as the mother. This interpretation appears to go astray from the intent of the article. Motherhood, or the act of conceiving a child and bringing that child into the world, does hold unique attributes, and a human right recognizing the special needs of motherhood has merit.

Article 26

1. Everyone has the right to education. Education shall be free, at least in the elementary and fundamental stages. Elementary education shall be compulsory. Technical and professional education shall be made generally available and higher education shall be equally accessible to all on the basis of merit.

2. Education shall be directed to the full development of the human personality and to the strengthening of respect for human rights and fundamental freedoms. It shall promote understanding, tolerance, and friendship among all nations, racial or religious groups, and shall further the activities of the United Nations for the maintenance of peace.

3. Parents have a prior right to choose the kind of education that shall be given to their children.

This human right guarantees elementary or fundamental education, with parents having the right to choose either a religious or secular education. The second paragraph of this human right merits specific attention because that provision mandates education about human rights. Many countries are probably remiss in addressing this requirement. Some experts say that U.S. students lag behind Europeans in knowledge about human rights (Farah 2001). In a broader sense, education about human rights also relates to the educational environment, as well as specific learning exercises about the topic. Issues to consider include access to resources, discrimination, and overall treatment within the school environment. Simply learning about human rights from a book may have limited value if the educational environment does not promote what is being learned.

In reference to this human right, NASW states that public education is a "primary institution that shares with the family responsibility for raising and training children and youths. Furthermore, public education is a vital socializing force that, with the family, promotes the total development of the child—intellectually, socially, and physically" (NASW 2000:92).

Article 27
    1. Everyone has the right freely to participate in the cultural life of the community, to enjoy the arts, and to share in scientific advancement and its benefits.
    2. Everyone has the right to the protection of the moral and material interests resulting from any scientific, literary, or artistic production of which he is the author.

Participation in cultural life and benefits relating to technology is a human right. This article also guarantees ownership protection of inventions and productions.

Article 28
Everyone is entitled to a social and international order in which the rights and freedoms set forth in this Declaration can be fully realized.

This article addresses what are called third-generation human rights, which promote cooperation among different countries. To fully realize rights and freedoms specified in the Declaration, a spirit of working together must prevail. An example of this concept would be an environmental treaty that aims to reduce greenhouse emissions since global warming creates a worldwide problem and is not simply an isolated problem affecting just one country or region. For the treaty to be effective, many countries would have to obey its terms. In other words, international cooperation to realize human rights is the basis of third-generation human rights.

Article 29

1. Everyone has duties to the community in which alone the free and full development of his personality is possible.

2. In the exercise of his rights and freedoms, everyone shall be subject only to such limitations as are determined by law solely for the purpose of securing due recognition and respect for the rights and freedoms of others and of meeting the just requirements of morality, public order, and the general welfare in a democratic society.

3. These rights and freedoms may in no case be exercised contrary to the purposes and principles of the United Nations.

This article generally imposes duties on the individual to the community and other individuals. The duties would involve recognition and respect for rights and freedoms of others, and adherence to the purposes and principles of the United Nations. In other words, the realization of human rights is a two-way street. Governments must guarantee many of the rights stated in the Universal Declaration. However, in that process, individuals must recognize their duty to the community to respect the rights and freedoms of others.

Article 30

Nothing in this Declaration may be interpreted as implying for any State, group, or person any right to engage in any activity or to perform any act aimed at the destruction of any of the rights and freedoms set forth herein.

This final article acts as a safe harbor against violations of any human right or freedom specified in the declaration. The human rights and freedoms of the Universal Declaration are inviolate, and no State, group, or individual has the right to destroy those rights and freedoms.

ISSUES RAISED BY THE UNIVERSAL DECLARATION OF HUMAN RIGHTS

The Universal Declaration of Human Rights covers a wide range of fundamental do's and don'ts concerning individuals, groups, and governments. Yet drafting basic guidelines for human existence can only be viewed as the beginning of many challenges: Whose voices are being heard in the exercise of human rights? Who benefits from human rights and who does not? Who defines human rights? What interpretation does a nation place upon these rights? Who enforces human rights? Who pays for the provision of human rights? Clearly, many issues arise simply from the existence of a universal set of guidelines, especially in view of the vast number of nations that have been established since 1948. However, while challenges raised by the Universal Declaration appear daunting, familiarity with those challenges can help social workers better incorporate human rights into their practice.

Universality of Human Rights With a world comprised of almost two hundred different nations and countless cultural and social divisions, how can human rights ever be universal? To respond to this issue of universality, social workers must focus on the underlying reasons behind the Universal Declaration. The point of the Universal Declaration was to provide basic guidelines for all individuals and nations in how they act and interact with each other. The declaration establishes a code of conduct, much like a code of ethics for professional organizations. Social workers must subscribe to a code of ethics in how they act with clients, colleagues, and the public. While opinions of social workers may differ over the meaning of a particular statement of ethics, this disagreement does not prevent the existence of a code of ethics. Social workers also come from diverse backgrounds and do not always share a particular position on professional issues. A clinical social worker may have little familiarity with the difficulties of a community social worker, administrator, or academic. Does that mean universal themes or principles of social work have no relevance to the social work profession? The profession has many publications relating to social work practice, principles, and ethics that apply to all social workers.

The Universal Declaration of Human Rights resembles a code of conduct for a professional group, such as social workers. The obvious difference is that the declaration aims to include every individual and nation within its um-brella. This concept may initially appear grandiose but not when viewed in the context of a professional organization. If a code of conduct can exist for a professional organization that itself includes vast differences in cultural, economic, and political backgrounds, then a code of conduct can also exist for individuals and nations of the world. Differences in carrying out the code of conduct may always exist, but a general agreement on the necessity and principles within the code can be established. By viewing the Universal Dec-laration as a universal professional code of conduct, social workers can more readily grasp the significance and importance of the declaration. Social workers can also more readily understand that, as with any code of conduct, violations of the Universal Declaration do occur, with many alleged viola-tions falling within a gray area. However, by viewing alleged violations as a learning exercise and opportunity to better understand human rights, social workers can meet the challenge of universality. The seemingly impossible task of relating the Universal Declaration to all individuals and countries be-comes manageable.

Consider article 5 of the declaration: No one shall be subjected to torture or to cruel, inhuman, or degrading treatment or punishment. According to the organization Amnesty International, many countries violate this human right, including the United States. Yet few could argue with the intent behind this human right: nobody should undergo torture or cruel treatment. While countries may differ as to how they interpret torture or cruel treatment, cer-tain underlying principles concerning torture or cruel treatment apply on a universal basis. For example, should withholding food and water from a prisoner until he confesses to a crime constitute a human rights abuse? Clearly, withholding food and water is a life-threatening circumstance and a human rights violation. The justification for withholding food and water is to force a statement that most likely the prisoner does not want to make. Should he be made to confess in this manner? Perhaps the prisoner has not committed the crime. Does a culture or society have an interest in treating an accused individual in this manner? Is that interest outweighed by the harm done to the individual? From a human rights perspective, most cer-tainly. Yet where a human right has obtained a clear universal definition, cul-ture takes a backseat to that definition. When analyzing the universality aspect of human rights, social workers need to consider culture in deter-mining how to apply the human right in a particular social work context.

"Cultural competence" is nothing new to the profession and is even expected of social workers (NASW 2000:59–62).

While some human rights have clearly been accepted as universal, others are still evolving. For example, while article 5 of the Universal Declaration prohibits inhuman and degrading treatment or punishment, only recently have countries interpreted that provision to relate to violence in the domestic or private sphere. Many countries interpreted article 5 as relating mainly to torture of political dissidents and prisoners. Degrading treatment or physical violence in the domestic or private sphere escaped consideration as a human rights violation. However, through the efforts of women's organizations, many countries now view the human right prohibiting degrading inhuman and degrading treatment to include circumstances within the home. By connecting this human right to violence against women in a private setting, a universal norm is being established that domestic violence constitutes just as great a human rights abuse as torture against political dissidents. In other words, the issue of domestic violence becomes a societal and structural concern rather than simply an individual problem. Also, by highlighting the structural wrong of domestic violence, the human right to be free from domestic violence transcends any cultural norm that might tolerate domestic violence.

Understanding universality and culture is crucial to the study of human rights. In other words, appreciation of the universality concept requires an understanding of what lies behind the human right. By studying the purpose of a particular human right, social workers can better understand the concept of universality, even when encountering diverse backgrounds and work conditions.

Enforcement of Human Rights The understanding of universality when speaking of human rights leads naturally to the issue of enforcement. Granted, every individual and nation is subject to human rights and freedoms within the Universal Declaration. What mechanism exists with which to enforce violations of these rights and freedoms? And who determines when a violation occurs? Obviously, without enforcement of human rights, the declaration has no worth beyond the paper used to reproduce its many rights and freedoms.

Enforcement of human rights generally depends upon the goodwill or interest of individual countries. If an individual country has not enacted laws

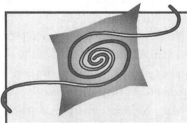

The Dynamics of Human Rights

▶ The universally acknowledged list of protected human rights (as found in the Universal Bill of Rights and subsequent human rights instruments) represents a powerful and important human consensus about the dignity that must be accorded all human beings and about the willingness of human society to respect basic rights for all. At the same time, human rights may exist that are not yet on any list of protected rights or acknowledged as part of the universal consensus. As a result, violations of human rights occur which are not seen as such and for which no one is held accountable.

▶ The history of human rights essentially traces two intertwining streams of human development: one stream represents the struggle to name previously unnamed rights and to gain their acceptance as human rights; the other stream represents the ongoing struggle to ensure the enforcement of established rights.

▶ This dynamic characteristic is what makes human rights a powerful tool for promoting social justice:

• If the right is not *recognized*, the struggle is to assure recognition.

• If the right is not *respected*, the struggle is to assure enforcement.

• The process of gaining recognition of a right leads to better enforcement and the process of enforcing leads to greater recognition of the rights.

FIGURE 2.1

that incorporate human rights contained in the declaration, then countries and individuals can circumvent the declaration. However, in recent years, countries have grown more sensitive to accusations of violating human rights and do take steps to recognize human rights. The "power of shame" does play a role today as an indirect enforcement tool (*Economist* 1998).

Aside from perhaps the desire of countries and individuals to avoid criticism for abusing human rights, the United Nations now has in force a monitoring body known as the Commission on Human Rights. The commission evaluates various complaints about human rights practices in different areas of the world. However, the commission itself has no direct enforcement powers, and politics often plays a role in positions taken by the commission (*Economist* 1998). Commission resolutions criticizing individual countries are often made for overtly political reasons. Governments with clout, such as China, are able to avoid criticism; those unable to marshal support, such as Cuba, fare less well (6). While this infiltration of politics into the commission may appear disheartening, one positive aspect is that countries do pay some attention to publicity about human rights violations.

In theory, the United Nations could take action against a member State for violating human rights, provided enough member countries voted to do so. The difficulty of enforcement through the UN lies in obtaining sufficient support to undertake action against human rights violations. For example, in 1994 the African country of Rwanda suffered a traumatic event that saw different ethnic groups perpetrating genocidal attacks on each other. The goal was to literally erase the other group. *Genocide,* or the deliberate and systematic destruction of a racial, political, or cultural group, violates several articles of the Universal Declaration (e.g., art. 1 and 2). Many countries, including the United States, knew about these genocidal acts through media and other outlets. Why did these countries not act to stop the atrocities? The answer is complex. A cynical response would be that those countries with the resources to intervene, such as the United States, do not value an African life as much as an American or European life. However, while that response has a superficial logic, many factors worked against intervention by the United States and Europe. Which African government wants to allow massive U.S. or European troops to occupy its country? Was there even a functioning Rwandan government at the time of the genocide? If the United Nations had approved an intervention against the genocide, what type of military action would have been necessary to halt it? Most likely, only well-trained and armed ground troops would have been effective. Could the

United Nations or any country or group of countries have effectively organized such a force within the short time frame necessary to take action? Any intervention by an outside force in human rights violations clearly presents profound challenges.

However, contrast the lack of intervention in Rwanda with interventions by the United States and allied countries against Iraq's takeover of Kuwait in 1991 and Yugoslavia's treatment of Kosovans in 1998. The United States took the lead in both those interventions, with possible justification because of human rights violations by Iraq and Yugoslavia. Did the United States and other countries intervene in Iraq and Yugoslavia because interests of the outside countries were greater than in Rwanda? Most likely, the relative interests of the outside countries did play a role in how they viewed the circumstances. These developments appeared to favor outside intervention when violations of human rights affected vast numbers of peoples in strategic areas.

Despite instances where outside forces have intervened to prevent violations of human rights within a country, the general view appears to be that countries will not directly intervene in the affairs of another country to correct alleged violations of human rights. For that reason, enforcement of human rights usually depends upon local policies and indirect pressure from outside a country.

Local views about human rights often influence attention paid to different rights. In China, government officials may view freedom of speech American-style as a threat to society and place little emphasis on allowing free expression. Instead, Chinese officials may consider human rights involving economic progress a greater priority—satisfying a hungry mouth has much greater importance than publicizing antigovernment sentiments. This juggling of priorities given to human rights occurs everywhere. The United States does not provide everyone with adequate education or health care, but certainly allows freedom of movement within its borders. This prioritizing of human rights conflicts with the indivisibility concept, meaning that no particular human right is more important than another. Unless governments and individuals acknowledge indivisibility among human rights, enforcement of those rights will always remain arbitrary and incomplete.

In addition to local policies that address human rights, another method of enforcing human rights lies in individuals and organizations that bring to light different violations. Amnesty International and other organizations focus on aspects of human rights and attempt to pressure governments to

MORAL RELATIVISM WON'T DEFEAT TERRORISTS

In the season finale this past spring [2002] of NBC's *The West Wing*, President Jed Bartlet struggles to decide whether to order the assassination of the foreign minister of Qumari (a fictitious Middle Eastern state), who is a known terrorist. The climactic scene shows the president arguing against the idea with his no-nonsense chief of staff, who, at one point, says something to the effect of: "The most horrifying aspect of your liberalism is that you think there are moral absolutes." The president felt that it wasn't worth sacrificing the basic principles of humanity to order an assassination. The chief of staff thought the assassination, while morally dubious, would ultimately save the lives of thousands who would suffer if the foreign minister stays in power. The plot thickens.

A similar back-and-forth has played out between a U.S. District Court judge in Washington and the State Department over the past few weeks in a federal case of corporate human rights abuse in Indonesia. International Labor Rights Fund, a human rights group in Washington, has filed a lawsuit alleging that the ExxonMobil Corporation looked the other way when its security guards, who are members of Indonesia's military, carried out torture, rape, and extrajudicial execution while guarding its plant in war-torn Aceh. The State Department recently answered a query by Exxon for its input on the possible foreign policy ramifications of allowing the lawsuit to proceed. The State Department's recommendation in a letter to the judge: the case should be dismissed because, if litigated, the matter could offend the Indonesian government, resulting in the possibility of even great human rights abuses, and a cold shoulder from America's most important ally in the war on terror.

So now the real-life judge (Judge Louis Oberdorfer), in considering the State Department's recommendations and deciding whether to dismiss the case, faces fictitious President Bartlet's quandary: Is calling Exxon to account for its complicity in human rights abuse a moral absolute? Or can diplomatic concerns outweigh that imperative, effectively putting justice on hold?

In the first place, the State Department's reasons for dismissal are not all terribly pressing—or even legitimate—foreign policy concerns. For instance, it states in its letters that the lawsuit might anger Indonesia to the point where it would drop its ties to American businesses and partner instead with countries less concerned about human rights, such as China. If American businesses don't behave better than those from less-enlightened

(continued)

countries, what's the point of State supporting them in the first place? The argument chases its tail.

A closer question is whether jeopardizing America's relationship with a major ally in the war on terror outweighs the importance of seeing a company answer to exploitative and harmful business practices. Moderate Muslim areas of southeast Asia are already a significant investment for the Bush administration: 1,200 American troops in the Philippines have just spent half a year training the military in counterterrorism fundamentals, and Indonesia, eager to impress its new Western friend, has deported scores of Middle Eastern Muslims on charges of collusion with Al Qaeda. Without Indonesia on our side, many say, terrorists fleeing central Asia will soon make the southeast their new headquarters.

Yet I argue that a moral absolute exists. There are certain basic rights, standards, and freedoms that must not be compromised, even to avoid future turmoil. Among them are freedoms from torture, rape, and murder, and the concomitant promise that when such freedoms are taken away, the law will find out why.

Sweeping under the rug ExxonMobil's role in unspeakable acts against the citizens of Aceh—like ordering the assassination of a despicable foreign leader—is tantamount to giving up the principles we fight for as we fight against terrorism: the means are poisoned and they sour the end.

Thus a triumph in the war on terror achieved by ignoring human rights abuse would be hollow because America's cherished principles—freedom, transparency in government, and above all, human dignity—would have been abandoned in the relentless drive for victory, making us no better than the terrorists we pursue.

Allowing Exxon to walk free is a moral failure, regardless of its perceived long-term benefits, not to mention a hypocritical betrayal of this country's new drive toward corporate responsibility.

President Bartlet, under pressure from his chief of staff, ultimately falters in his moral stand and orders the assassination. Here's hoping that Judge Oberdorfer won't do the same. (O'Donnell 2002:11) change their policies and better respect human rights. By bringing attention to human rights violations, these organizations have achieved some success in creating an environment where human rights are better respected.

Certainly enforcement of human rights remains a major issue in this field. Even where countries agree on an interpretation of a particular human right, enforcement can be troublesome. Perhaps the most effective means of enforcing human rights lies in education. If governments, groups, and individuals consciously strive to understand and practice human rights, enforcement would be much simpler.

SOCIAL WORK PERSPECTIVE ON THE UNIVERSAL DECLARATION

The Universal Declaration contains numerous rights and freedoms that aim to define what every individual, no matter where in the world he or she resides, should possess. The challenge of promoting those rights is enormous, but one that social workers can naturally embrace within their profession. For instance, the preamble to the *Code of Ethics* of the National Association of Social Workers could have been lifted right out of the declaration:

> The primary mission of the social work profession is to enhance human well-being and help meet the basic human needs of all people, with particular attention to the needs and empowerment of people who are vulnerable, oppressed, and living in poverty. (NASW 1996:1)

The code adds that social workers are "sensitive to cultural and ethnic diversity and strive to end discrimination, oppression, poverty, and other forms of social injustice" (9). Core values of the profession include service, integrity, competence, social justice, the dignity and worth of the person, and the importance of human relationships (9).

In a nutshell, the above language closely resembles what the Universal Declaration is all about. The human rights values of equality and the right to education, housing, food, and health care as well as freedom from discrimination and physical abuse are all social work values. Yet the NASW's *Code of Ethics* never mentions the term *human rights*. This omission of any reference to human rights may seem unimportant so long as social workers follow human rights values. However, by not devoting specific attention to human rights documents and provisions, social workers may not fully understand the significance of human rights. Because human rights are closely connected to social work, the study of human rights can only enhance competence within the social work profession.

Human rights incorporate a set of principles that provide the social worker with guidance in all types of circumstances. While many of these principles follow social work values, the concept of human rights goes beyond the issue of a client's needs. Human rights are based on what everyone should have to fulfill an inherent human dignity. Human rights recognize that gray areas exist within the application of human rights values to particular situations. However, in spite of conflicts that inevitably arise within the field of human rights, a basic foundation exists upon which to resolve that conflict. This basic foundation highlights the importance of human rights within the social work profession. To understand that foundation, social workers must learn about actual human rights instruments.

The legalistic nature of human rights instruments can present a significant obstacle to learning about human rights. However, social workers frequently have to know about other laws relating to the profession. The study of human rights should not be any different, especially since human rights are so closely connected to social work values and ethics.

QUESTIONS

1. What reasons can you cite for having the Universal Declaration of Human Rights?
2. Are governments legally required to respect the principles outlined in the Universal Declaration?
3. Discuss the concept of *universality* and how that might conflict with culture. Is it possible to have a common interpretation or understanding of human rights?
4. What is the importance of the concept of *indivisibility* as it relates to human rights?
5. The preamble of the Universal Declaration notes the inherit dignity of persons. What connection does human dignity have to human rights?
6. What human rights in the declaration are considered political and civil rights?

7. What human rights in the declaration are considered economic, social, and cultural rights?

8. What is meant by equal protection before the law?

9. Do equal protection laws in the United States adequately protect against racial, gender, or other discrimination? Explain.

10. How does article 5 of the Universal Declaration relate to domestic violence and rape?

11. A social worker makes an unannounced visit to a welfare recipient. Is this a human rights violation? Discuss.

12. Does the Universal Declaration balance the rights of the individual with the needs of the community?

13. What is meant by the phrase that the Universal Declaration of Human Rights is a living document? Give an example of how human rights in 1948 can be interpreted differently in 2002.

14. Does a minimum wage violate human rights? Discuss.

15. A person has a non-life-threatening condition but needs medical attention. The person has no health insurance and cannot afford medical treatment. Discuss any human rights issues raised by these circumstances.

REFERENCES

Economist, The. 1998. Human-rights law. (December 15): 4–16.

Farah, S. 2001. Taking note of human rights. Curriculum aims to bring an often-neglected topic into U.S. classrooms. *Christian Science Monitor* (February 13): 16.

Hansen, E. 1991. *Wohlfahrtspolitik im NS-Staat: Motivationen, Konflikte und Machstrukturen im "Sozialismus der Tat" des Dritten Reiches*. Augsburg: Maro.

Healy, L. 2001. *International Social Work: Professional Action in an Interdependent World*. New York: Oxford University Press.

Human Rights Watch World Report. 2001. *Events of 2000*. New York: Human Rights Watch.

Midgley, J. 1997. *Social Welfare in Global Context*. Thousand Oaks, Calif.: Sage.

Morsink, J. 1999. *The Universal Declaration of Human Rights: Origins, Drafting, and Intent*. Philadelphia: University of Pennsylvania Press.

National Association of Social Workers (NASW). 1996. *Code of Ethics*. Washington, D.C: NASW Press.

———. 2000. *Social Work Speaks: National Association of Social Workers Policy Statements, 2000–2003*. 5th ed. Washington, D.C.: NASW Press.

National Coordinating Committee for UDHR50. 1998. Franklin and Eleanor Roosevelt Institute home page (online). *See* www.udhr50.org/history/fribioer.htm.

O'Donnell, M. 2002. Moral relativism won't defeat terrorists. *Christian Science Monitor* (August 16): 11.

Otto, H. U. and H. Sunker. 1991. *Politische Formierung und soziale Erziehung im Nationalsozialismus.* Frankfurt: Suhrkamp.

Prigoff, A. 2000. *Economics for Social Workers: Social Outcomes of Economic Globalization with Strategies for Community Action.* Sacramento: Brooks/Cole.

Reichert, E. 2001. Placing human rights at the center of the social work profession. *Journal of Intergroup Relations* 28.1: 43–50.

Reichert, E. and R. McCormick. 1998. U.S. welfare law violates human rights of immigrants. *Migration World* 26: 15–18.

Schnurr, S. 1997. Why did social workers accept the New Order? In H. Sunker and H. U. Otto, eds., *Education and Facism*, 326–88. London: Falmer Press.

Witkin, S. 1998. Human rights and social work. *Social Work: Journal of the National Association of Social Workers* 43:197–201.

Wronka, J. 1998. *Human Rights and Social Policy in the 21st Century: A History of the Idea of Human Rights and Comparison of the United Nations Universal Declaration of Human Rights with United States Federal and State Constitutions.* Rev. ed. Lanham, Md.: University Press of America.

United Nations. 1948. *Universal Declaration of Human Rights.* Adopted December 10, 1948. GA. Res. 217 AIII. United Naitons Document a/810. New York: UN.

Van Wormer, K. 1997. *Social Welfare: A World View.* Chicago: Nelson-Hall.

3

Building on the Universal Declaration

The International Covenant on Civil and Political Rights

ROBERT J. MCCORMICK* AND ELISABETH REICHERT

As originally intended, the Universal Declaration of Human Rights embodied only the cornerstone of human rights protections. Drafters of the Universal Declaration viewed the declaration as a fundamental statement on human rights principles and concepts but also recognized that future action would be necessary to promote compliance with the declaration. Members of the United Nations also desired an initial, nonbinding statement on human rights—the Universal Declaration—with future documents providing the glue with which to bind countries to the declaration.

To better understand the intent of the declaration, an examination

*Robert J. McCormick, J.D. (1976), practices law in Illinois. He has served as a peace corps volunteer in Cameroon, Africa, and is the author of *The Other Side of Traveling Abroad*, a book on intercultural contacts.

of its language sheds useful light. For instance, the declaration usually avoids reference to any nation, state, or groups of nations and states, which highlights the general nature of the document. Rather, the point of view contained in the declaration generally mirrors that of the individual or group. The use of the word *everyone* throughout the declaration indicates an intent to include all persons within the area of human rights. However, the declaration rarely imposes any obligation upon a particular country or government. The declaration refers to various "rights" of individuals and groups but does not specify who must fulfill those rights or how those rights are to be fulfilled or enforced. The declaration resembles a code of conduct with which everyone should comply. However, without allocating responsibility onto government or individuals themselves as to the realization of human rights, the declaration can only remain a statement of intent with no power of enforcement.

Understanding that the declaration was only an initial step in promoting a uniform system of human rights, members of the United Nations contemplated the next steps that would lead to greater recognition of human rights. Steps to be taken after adoption of the Universal Declaration included the drafting of documents that would require States to recognize human rights contained in the declaration as legally binding within their jurisdiction.

The United Nations placed no specific time frame for completion of documents that would actually lead to the realization of human rights contained in the declaration. However, considering that the drafting of the declaration took only a few years, a similar time frame for the implementing documents might have appeared reasonable. In world politics, though, nothing seems to happen quickly. Struggles over drafting specific documents to implement the Universal Declaration encountered resistance. Countries balked at the thought of surrendering sovereignty to an instrument that could bind them to a worldly standard (*Economist* 1998). The Cold War, with the United States and its allies pitted against the former Soviet Union and its allies, also led to disagreements over the importance of various provisions that were to be part of the implementing documents. In the United States itself, debate raged over provisions within the declaration concerning racial equality and economic rights. Would the United States have to provide everyone with health care if the Universal Declaration became the law of the land? Would the United States have to provide equal educational opportunities if the Universal Declaration controlled? Other countries had their own agendas to consider. Under the declaration, the Soviet Union and other communist countries would have to recognize greater freedom of speech and allow freer movement of its peoples. South Africa would have to tear down its apartheid system.

Eventually, in 1966, after eighteen years of debate, members of the United Nations General Assembly adopted two key documents with which to implement the Universal Declaration: (1) the International Covenant on Civil and Political Rights and (2) the International Covenant on Economic, Social, and Cultural Rights. These documents derive from the declaration and contain standards for judging human rights violations. In contrast to the declaration, countries approving these covenants are required to enforce provisions contained within them.

AN INTERNATIONAL BILL OF RIGHTS

For social workers to understand what human rights involve, not only must they be familiar with the Universal Declaration of Human Rights, but they must also be familiar with the remaining components of what is called the International Bill of Human Rights. The two international covenants cited above aim to put force into provisions of the declaration. The purpose of the covenants is to ensure that countries take the Universal Declaration seriously and make efforts to legally bind their governments to protect human rights and freedoms outlined in the declaration. An adjoining document to the International Covenant on Civil and Political Rights, known as the Optional Protocol to the International Covenant on Civil and Political Rights, allows individuals, as opposed to countries, to raise human rights complaints based on that covenant. Only States that are party to the International Covenant on Civil and Political Rights may sign the Optional Protocol. Together, the Universal Declaration, the two international covenants, and the Optional Protocol constitute the International Bill of Human Rights.

As noted, the drafting of the two covenants took eighteen years, from 1948 until 1966, when the General Assembly voted to adopt the language of the covenants. However, it was not until 1976 that the covenants came into force: a covenant or convention comes into force only after a sufficient number of member countries of the United Nations have ratified the covenant. The number of countries required to ratify a covenant is specified in the text of the covenant. Countries ratifying a covenant are legally bound to enforce provisions contained in the covenant. The significance of ratification is that, at least in legal theory, a citizen or resident of the ratifying country has the right to rely on the ratified human right as legal principle. Consequently, if a country ratifies a covenant like the Covenant on Economic, Social, and Cultural Rights, citizens of that country should then be allowed to enforce provisions of the covenant in an applicable forum, including a court of law. If a country does not sign and formally approve a covenant, then that country has no obligation to follow terms of the covenant. Only by signing and approving a covenant does a country recognize provisions of the covenant.

When the U.S. government ratifies a treaty or covenant, the general idea is that terms of the treaty or covenant become the law of the land. However, this is not always the way things work out. If terms of a covenant are self-executing, then no further legislative action is necessary to enforce those terms or put the covenant into practice. Where a covenant is not self-executing, then further legislative action is required to incorporate terms of the covenant into existing legislation. In other words, even where the United States ratifies a United Nations covenant, unless the covenant specifies that its terms are self-executing, enforcement of the covenant does not occur until additional legislation more or less activates the covenant.

Neither the Covenant on Civil and Political Rights nor the Covenant on Economic, Social, and Cultural Rights contains self-executing provisions. Although the United States has ratified the Covenant on Civil and Political Rights, the government has not enacted specific legislation to put its provisions into effect. While many provisions in the covenant are similar to already existing laws in the United States, some of the provisions are unique. Yet because the covenant is not self-executing, its provisions are not legally binding in the United States and makes reliance on the document a tenuous proposition.

While addressing different aspects of the Universal Declaration, the two covenants nevertheless contain some duplication while promoting common themes: (1) the right to self-determination; (2) equality between men and women; and (3) indivisibility or interdependence of civil and political freedoms with economic, social, and cultural standards. The impact of these common themes should not be underestimated. The principle of self-determination has led to the formation of many new countries, based on the right of "peoples" to freely determine their political status and freely pursue their economic, social, and cultural development (part I, art. 1). The principle of gender equality has resulted in substantial legislation in many countries that promotes equality between women and men. Furthermore, many countries have sought to place the guarantees of health care, a minimum wage, and other social benefits on an equal footing with political benefits, such as the right to vote and free speech.

Social workers need to understand the two covenants and how those covenants interact with the Universal Declaration. Without these covenants, the declaration would remain nothing more than a nonbinding code of conduct. The two covenants aim to bring pressure to bear upon signatory countries by actually requiring those countries to recognize human rights contained within the Universal Declaration but further explained in the covenants. The rest of this chapter analyzes the International Covenant on Civil and Political Rights and the Optional Protocol to that covenant, while the next chapter will discuss the International Covenant on Economic, Social, and Cultural Rights.

THE INTERNATIONAL COVENANT ON CIVIL AND POLITICAL RIGHTS

Historically, the United States has paid much more attention to the human rights contained in this covenant than those in the covenant on economic rights. The U.S. Constitution clearly originates more from political than economic concerns. This focus on political and civil rights has often led the United States to take a one-sided view of human rights, without adequate recognition that human rights goes beyond the political sphere. For U.S. social workers, this focus on political human rights has undoubtedly led to a reluctance to study and integrate human rights into the social work profession. Yet, as will be evident upon analysis of the covenant, political and civil human rights have a close connection to interventions and principles of the profession.

Drafters of the covenant on civil and political rights divided the covenant into a preamble and six parts, which altogether contain fifty-three articles. The first three parts contain twenty-seven articles listing specific civil and political rights, while the last three parts address issues of procedure and interpretation as well as monitoring.

Preamble

The preamble to the International Covenant on Civil and Political Rights expressly lists civil and political rights that "derive from the inherent dignity of the human person" (see appendix B). The "ideal of free human beings enjoying civil and political freedom and freedom from fear and want can only be achieved if conditions are created whereby everyone may enjoy his civil and political rights, as well as his economic, social, and cultural rights" (preamble). This provision links political and civil rights with economic, social, and cultural rights, thereby creating the indivisible nature of these rights. To ensure enjoyment of economic, social, and cultural rights, individuals must also possess civil and political rights. The two sets of rights are inseparable.

The preamble makes it clear that political and civil rights are part of an inherent human dignity. For social workers, promoting human dignity is an important part of the profession. Consequently, the political and civil rights contained in the covenant have great importance to realizing the goal of human dignity.

Part I

Part I of the covenant guarantees the human right of self-determination to all "peoples" who may "freely determine their political status and freely pursue their economic, social, and cultural development" (Art. 1). The use of "peoples" and not States indicates that, within a State, various peoples may exist. A State or country may include numerous peoples within its borders. The purpose of self-determination in this context is to recognize that groups of the same ethnicity, religion, language, and other common traits have the human right to common association and development.

Self-determination has become a significant development in world politics since the Universal Declaration. Beginning in the late 1940s, European colonies in Africa and Asia began a dismantling process that resulted in dozens of newly formed nations, including India, Pakistan, Malaysia, Ghana, and Cameroon. Other nations formed on principles of self-determination include the Czech Republic, Macedonia, Croatia, and territories of the former Soviet Union. Native Americans and other Aboriginal peoples rely on the right to self-determination to establish their own self-governing nations within Australia, Canada, and the United States. Contemporary struggles involving the right of self-determination include Palestinians, Ti-

SOVEREIGNTY OF FIRST NATIONS PEOPLES

Unlike any other ethnic or racial group in the United States, First Nations Peoples are a political entity. The U.S. government recognizes Indigenous Peoples as having a special, legal government-to-government relationship with the United States (Pever 1992). By law, they are "distinct, independent, political communities possessing end exercising the power of self-govern-ment" (*Worcester v. Georgia* 1831). As a consequence of sovereignty, Indige-nous Peoples may participate in three levels of citizenship: indigenous, state, and United States. Indigenous families who belong to federally recognized tribes are eligible to receive federal services such as health care, education, and social services.

Sovereign Indigenous Nations have inherent powers of self-government. They have the right to make, pass, and enforce laws, implement taxation, create tribal constitutional codes, license social workers, declare war, and seek remedy in international courts of law. They also possess aboriginal ter-ritories (land) that are protected under trust agreement with the United States. Social workers who work with and on behalf of Indigenous Peoples must respect Indigenous sovereignty. They must agree to abide by all laws of the nations just as they would in any other country. . . . Any issues re-garding the welfare and protection of indigenous children fall under the province of Indigenous Nations. Sovereignty is essential to the preservation, the rights, and resources of Indigenous Nations and is a powerful protective factor. No other racial group in the United States has a similar sovereign po-litical and legal standing. (Waller and Yellow Bird 2002:51)

betans, and peoples within Indonesia. In connection with the right to deter-mine political status, self-determination allows peoples to freely pursue their economic, social, and cultural development. Individuals with common origins have the human right to form societies that promote historical tra-ditions and customs. Groups with common backgrounds might wish to form a union to discuss the difficulties of assimilating into a dominant cul-ture. The human right of self-determination protects all of these activities.

In exercising the human right of self-determination, individuals and groups have an obligation not to violate the rights and freedoms of others, including "just requirements of morality, public order, and the general wel-fare in a democratic society" (see appendix A: Universal Declaration, art. 29,

African-Americans at a public university wish to form their own clubs that do not allow other groups to join. Is this discrimination against whites and other non-African-Americans? Do the African-Americans have a human right to exclude others from their club? If a group of whites attempted to form their own club at a public institution, government laws generally would prohibit that type of exclusion. Does self-determination allow this exclusion?

The rationale for allowing groups other than mainstream Anglo-Americans to create their own niches relates to the promotion of culture and identity. Those of the majority culture might argue that allowing minority groups the right to exclude others inhibits assimilation and promotes exclusion. However, that is the point. In order to retain cultural identity, some degree of separation from the majority group is necessary. Unfortunately, the majority frequently views this type of self-determination as threatening to the social order. A clearer understanding of self-determination in a human rights context could help overcome anxieties about issues of cultural assimilation.

para. 2). The issue then becomes one of balancing the different human rights and coming to a resolution.

In addition to self-determination, part I of the covenant states that all peoples may "freely dispose of their natural wealth and resources without prejudice to any obligations arising out of international economic co-operation, based upon the principle of mutual benefit, and international law. In no case may a people be deprived of its own means of subsistence" (art. 1, para. 2). This provision allows "all peoples" to dispose of natural resources such as oil, coal, and water, as they please. Because all peoples have the right of self-determination, States party to the covenant should respect the right of its peoples to dispose of natural resources they may possess. However, the disposal of these resources should respect obligations of international economic cooperation. For example, assume that a tribe of Native Americans within the United States discovers oil upon their reservation. Under the covenant, the tribe would be allowed to dispose of that oil, as they want, subject to any international obligations. Assume that an international obligation between the United States and Mexico requires the tribe to sell part of

The creation of Israel in 1948 by the United Nations offended most of the Arab countries, who bitterly fought this decision from the beginning. While the UN also contemplated establishing a Palestinian state alongside that of Israel, this never occurred. Yet the push for a Palestinian state has never wavered.

Under self-determination principles of the Covenant on Civil and Political Rights, Palestinians would appear to be justified in wanting their own political entity. However, a claim for self-determination must not infringe upon the public order and welfare. Israelis could legitimately argue that, in seeking self-determination, the Palestinians have no right to use violence against Israelis. Palestinians might respond that, without violence, nobody—especially the Israelis—would pay attention to their plight. Palestinians might further argue that tactics used by Israelis also constitute violations of their human rights. The end result is a stalemate between Israelis and Palestinians, with both sides committing human rights violations against the other.

A human rights resolution to this conflict would require both parties to cease the violence against one another and recognize the inherent dignity of both sides. Palestinians have the right of self-determination and political status, with Israelis having the right to be free from violent attacks on their citizens. Of course, infusing human rights into this particular situation would require major commitments from both sides, which neither the Israelis nor the Palestinians currently appear ready to do.

its oil to a tribe in Mexico for the mutual benefit of both tribes. The tribe would be required to follow the terms of the international obligation and sell oil to the tribe in Mexico.

Self-determination ranks as a significant human right that States must respect. However, can every conceivable ethnic or religious group create its own political entity or State? At times, self-determination may seem to have gone too far, as in the Balkan regions of Bosnia, Kosovo, Macedonia, Yugoslavia, and other areas. Northern Ireland and Israel provide two examples of self-determination based on, in part, religion.

Perhaps more than any other human right, self-determination has most influenced today's world. Yet, as with many human rights, self-determination as a concept contains many subtleties and nuances. No clear-cut option exists in every set of circumstances involving issues of self-determination.

THE HUMAN RIGHT OF SELF-DETERMINATION
FROM A SOCIAL WORK PERSPECTIVE

Social workers are familiar with the concept of "self-determination" in the context of clients. The *Code of Ethics* of the National Association of Social Workers issues the following standard on self-determination:

> Social workers respect and promote the right of clients to self-determination and assist clients in their efforts to identify and clarify their goals. Social workers may limit clients' right to self-determination when, in the social workers' professional judgment, clients' actions or potential actions pose a serious, foreseeable, and imminent risk to themselves or others. (NASW 1996:1.02)

While the social work concept of self-determination relates to clients, this principle of self-determination is the same as that contained in the Covenant on Civil and Political Rights. Individuals and groups should be allowed to "identify and clarify" their own goals, with specified limitations. Social workers may intervene and limit a client's right to self-determination when a client is acting in a manner that could harm the client. This type of self-harm could occur in cases where a client wishes to end his or her life, although social workers may debate the ethics of euthanasia and physician-assisted suicide (Reamer 1998). Other, subtler issues arise in cases of self-harm: "How assertive should social workers be with battered women or men who decide to resume a relationship with an abusive partner? Should social workers interfere with hospital patients who want to return home while they are still in very frail condition and acting against medical advice? To what extent should social workers provide clients with access to information about themselves that is likely to be harmful to the clients?" (28).

Issues of self-harm within the standard of self-determination also relate well to the human rights notion of self-determination. For instance, should a social worker promote a group's right to isolate itself culturally from other groups if this isolation inhibits members of the group from receiving proper medical care? Should a social worker accept a cultural practice of touching a child's private areas if that touching would likely violate state laws on child abuse? These types of self-determination issues fall within the realm of human rights and indicate how difficult it can be to always have clear-cut answers to human rights issues.

(continued)

A second limitation on self-determination in a social work context involves potential harm by a client to others. The justification for social workers' placing limits on clients' right to self-determination is based on social workers' explicit concern for other people whose well-being is threatened by a client's actions (Reamer 1998). If a client credibly states that he intends to kill someone, then a social worker clearly has the duty to report this possible action to proper authorities. However, where circumstances indicate that a client's actions are ambiguous and may not cause any harm to others, then a social worker encounters one of those gray areas common within both ethical and human rights issues.

Suppose that the Native American parents of a child have been living in a suburb of Los Angeles where the child does superior work in an excellent school. The parents then decide to move to a reservation to take care of their own elderly parents. The child rebels against reservation life and runs away, back to friends in the suburb. Should the social worker accept the self-determination right of the parents to raise their child on the reservation or question that right because the child is being harmed by having to leave the better school? Or should the social worker be guided by what the child or adolescent wants? No clear answer exists, and the social worker would need to carefully evaluate the situation before proposing possible interventions.

Just as social workers encounter all types of dilemmas within the ethical standard relating to self-determination, similar dilemmas occur within the human rights concept of self-determination. As social workers become more familiar with human rights, the connection between social work ethics and human rights becomes more concrete.

Part II

The second part of the covenant requires that States not discriminate in the recognition of rights on the basis of "race, colour, sex, language, religion, political or other opinion, national or social origin, property, birth, or other status" (art. 2, para. 1). States are to ensure the "equal right of men and women to the enjoyment of all civil and political rights" contained in the covenant (art. 3). In times of true emergencies, States may take measures to

ON THE BORDER: LANGUAGE AFFECTS CITIZENSHIP

As greater numbers of people living in the United States do not speak English as their native language, a movement to promote English over other languages seems appropriate. Who could argue with the claim that all true-blue Americans should speak English? Compelling reasons exist for learning English in this country. Educational and professional opportunities will always be restricted if someone lacks fluency in English.

Conversations will be limited if English is deficient.

Yet, while English should be the primary language in the United States, deprecating other languages would be discriminatory to citizens and residents who, for whatever reasons, have not completely grasped the intricacies of English. I learned this lesson long ago.

My first year out of law school in 1976, I worked as a legal aid attorney in south Texas, near the Mexican border—occupied Mexico, as the locals called the area, with its mix of about 90 percent Hispanic and only 10 percent Anglo residents. English was the official language in court, but Spanish tended to be spoken everywhere else.

A few months after I started work, I was assigned to a case involving a young woman named Maria, who spoke no English. Every week or so, Maria, who lived in Texas, would cross the border to visit her Mexican parents. Upon reentering Texas, Maria would show U.S. immigration officials a baptismal certificate stating her birthplace as Texas. By having been born in Texas, Maria was a U.S. citizen, regardless of her parents' citizenship. One day, though, Maria lost her original certificate.

To obtain a replacement certificate, Maria went to the church in Texas where she had been baptized 21 years previously. At the church, she encountered the unexpected: records showed her birthplace as simply "Mexico." The current priest, not the one who had performed the baptism, could only issue a replacement certificate noting Maria's birthplace as Mexico. Our office advised Maria not to cross into Mexico again until we could clear up the issue of citizenship. However, Maria wanted to see her parents. She crossed the border and, as feared, on the return trip immigration officials refused her entry into the United States because the new baptismal certificate stated her birthplace as Mexico. Not speaking English and possessing little else that would convince border officials of her U.S. citizenship, Maria had to remain in Mexico.

At the request of our office, U.S. immigration scheduled a hearing before an immigration judge to determine whether Maria was a U.S. citizen. At that hearing, I called five witnesses, including Maria's parents, who all testified

(continued)

that Maria had been born in Texas. Although we had located the priest who performed Maria's baptism and had requested his testimony, he failed to appear that day.

As details of Maria's background emerged during the hearing, I realized that an entirely different America existed from that of the small, Midwest towns where I had grown up. Maria's parents had spent several years in Texas as migrant workers. On one occasion, the U.S. government had even welcomed them into a program known as *bracero*, Spanish for laborer, which officially allowed them to work here.

While circumstances surrounding Maria's birth presented me with a radically different version of an American, this revelation did little to support Maria's claim to U.S. citizenship.

The lawyer handling the case for the government spared no effort to discredit my witnesses. None of them spoke English, and they probably were biased, since they were related to Maria and wanted her to have the benefits of U.S. citizenship. Why should the judge accept their story as true? I needed the priest who had done the actual baptism.

Fortunately, the hearing dragged on for hours and the judge adjourned until a later date. The adjournment gave me an opportunity to contact the priest again in hopes that he would show up at the next hearing date. I pleaded with the priest to come and, on the appointed day, I found him waiting outside the hearing room. The priest became my star witness. He immediately put an end to all doubts about Maria's birthplace. Yes, he said, he did remember Maria's parents. He remembered baptizing Maria. His notation of Mexico instead of Texas in church records was a mistake.

After the priest had testified, the judge announced his decision: Maria was a U.S. citizen. Smiles broke out among everyone, including the government's lawyer.

Maria spoke not one word of English. Yet I knew that Maria was as much an American as anyone could ever be. (McCormick 1995:B2)

avoid their obligations under the covenant, provided those measures comply with international law and do not discriminate solely on the ground of race, colour, sex, language, religion, or social origin (art. 4, para. 1). However, discrimination in times of emergencies does not allow restrictions on political or other opinions, national origin, birth, or other status. Even in emergencies, States may not violate certain political and civil rights, including the right to be free from slavery, torture, and religious persecution.

Part III

Part III of the covenant contains the bulk of civil and political rights applicable to States party to the covenant. These rights include:

- *Article 6*—Every human being has the inherent right to life. Other provisions under this article clearly frown upon the death penalty. However, no outright ban on capital punishment exists except that no sentence of death may be imposed for crimes committed by persons under 18 years of age nor may the death penalty be carried out on pregnant women.
- *Article 7*—No one shall be subjected to torture or to cruel, inhuman, or degrading treatment or punishment.
- *Article 8*—This article abolishes slavery and forced labor except where punishment for a crime includes forced labor.
- *Article 9*—Provides safeguards against arbitrary arrest and detention by requiring information as to the reasons for the arrest allowing prompt challenges to the lawfulness of the detention.
- *Article 10*—This article specifies that accused persons shall be segregated from convicted persons and juveniles shall be separated from adults and brought as speedily as possible for adjudication. Rehabilitation shall be the "essential aim" of the penitentiary system, with humane and dignified treatment for all persons deprived of their liberty.
- *Article 11*—Nobody shall be imprisoned simply because he or she did not fulfill a contractual obligation.
- *Article 12*—Individuals lawfully within a country shall have the right to reside where they want within the country. Except in cases involving national security and public order, everyone shall be free to leave any country. No one shall be arbitrarily deprived of the right to enter his or her own county.
- *Article 13*—An "alien" lawfully in the territory of a State party to the covenant shall be entitled to legal safeguards, including representation, before being expelled. Only where compelling reasons of national security exist may a State expel an alien without legal due process.
- *Article 14*—This article lists a number of safeguards for any person charged with a criminal offense. These safeguards include the right to have legal assistance, to

The United States remains the only Western country to still allow the death penalty. European countries, Australia, and New Zealand have all abolished the use of capital punishment, no matter how egregious the crime.

A major issue surrounding the use of the death penalty in the United States involves the horrendous consequences if the wrong person is executed. The sad reality is that this could happen. Consider the following proposition: "A Columbia University study has found that judges are more likely to overturn death sentences in states and counties that use capital punishment most frequently, prompting the authors to suggest that narrowing the use of executions would cut down on mistakes" (Masters 2002:34). The express admission that mistakes occur in applying death sentences should send chills up anyone's spine. However, rather than simply abolishing the death penalty, the United States clings to the illusive goal that the system can be fixed. Yet consider these specific findings from the Columbia study:

- Jurisdictions that spent proportionally less per capita on their court systems had a larger share of cases overturned. This supports the commonly held view that poorly paid and incompetent court-appointed defense lawyers are a major source of error in capital cases.
- States with large black populations also had higher reversal rates on appeal of death sentences. This statistic indicates that jurisdictions where fear of crime might be driven by racial factors could have more trouble conducting fair trials.
- Reversals were more common in states where trial judges are popularly elected and, the authors of the study theorize, more subject to community pressure (Masters 2002:34).

Clearly, the use of capital punishment raises important human rights issues, including discrimination and due process. The difficulty of ever satisfying those issues creates a strong case against this type of punishment.

be informed in detail about the nature and cause of the charge, to examine witnesses against him or her, and to remain silent and not be compelled to testify. Nobody shall be tried twice for the same offense and everyone convicted of a crime shall have the right to appeal that conviction to a higher tribunal.

- *Article 15*—Nobody shall be guilty of any criminal offense on account of any act

Freedom of expression is a cherished right in constitutions of many countries. However, what that freedom does not include is the right to defame others. While the definition of defamation may differ from country to country, the underlying meaning is the same: that making malicious and untrue statements about an individual in the presence of others has consequences. Social workers should be vigilant in regard to defamatory statements directed at colleagues and clients. Defamation can easily lead to other human rights abuses, such as discrimination and even violence.

or omission, which did not constitute a criminal offense at the time the act or omission was committed. In other words, this guarantee prevents a State from prosecuting someone at a later date for an offense that was not criminal at the time of commission. This concept is known as an "ex post facto" law.

- *Article 16*—Everyone shall be recognized everywhere as a person before the law. This seemingly simple statement prohibits a State from barring certain individuals recourse through the State's courts. For example, a State may wish to exclude an individual unlawfully within the State from obtaining civil damages for personal injuries. The State may believe that an individual unlawfully within the country should not receive the same legal rights and privileges as a lawful resident. This article prevents a State from singling out individuals as less worthy of legal protection, either in civil or criminal courts.

- *Article 17*—This article prohibits arbitrary or unlawful interference with the privacy and reputation of individuals and families.

- *Article 18*—Everyone shall have the right to freedom of thought, conscience, and religion. Limits on the freedom to practice one's religion or beliefs may be restricted only when necessary to protect public safety, order, health or morals, or the fundamental rights and freedom of others. While this article appears to guarantee freedom of religion, States could broadly interpret the above limitation to essentially ban any religion.

- *Article 19*—Everyone shall have the right to freedom of expression. Restrictions on this freedom may be applied when necessary to protect the rights or reputations of others and to protect national security, public order, or public health and morals. As with the limitation on freedom of religion in article 18, a State

Following the September 11, 2001, terrorist attacks on the World Trade Center in New York City and on the Pentagon in Washington,D.C., the United States turned its attention to fighting terrorism. While most (but not all) Americans applauded the Bush administration's antiterrorism measures, voices outside the United States have been both more critical and more skeptical over the so-called "war on terrorism." Irene Khan, secretary-general of Amnesty International and a Muslim from Bangladesh, expressed concerns in an interview appearing in the *Far Eastern Economic Review* (Kahn 2002:26):

FEER: Does America's War Against Terrorism respect human rights?
Kahn: The first problem with terrorism is there is no objective, internationally recognized definition—everyone defines it as violence from a group they don't like. But if the violence is being committed by themselves, then that is not defined as terrorism. The other problem is that there are two broad international systems for protecting people. One is the system of international human rights that protects people in peacetime. The other is the international humanitarian law system which protects civilians in times of war. The war against terrorism appears to fall in neither category.
FEER: Is the U.S. in danger of losing its role as promoter of human rights, democracy, and the rule of law around the world?
Khan: The biggest danger to human rights always has been double standards. And when political and economic interest drives the human rights agenda—so that you pick and choose countries—you won't say anything about human rights abuses in Central Asia, or in Russia, or in Pakistan because these are your allies in the fight against terrorism. . . . You are damaging the whole notion that human rights are global universal standards.

While fighting terrorism should occupy a central role in government policies, ignoring human rights principles in that fight can only work against the ultimate goal of eliminating terrorist activities. Playing favorites, racial profiling, circumventing due process, all in the name of fighting terror, chips away at established human rights principles.

could broadly interpret the allowable restrictions to essentially bar any type of expression. The extent of this type of human right generally reflects culture or society, with a Western-type culture generally having fewer restrictions on expression than an Asian-type culture. The term *cultural relativism* addresses this issue and will be covered in more detail in later chapters.

- *Article 20*—War propaganda and any advocacy of national, racial, or religious hatred that constitutes incitement to discrimination, hostility, or violence shall be prohibited. Certainly, under this article, the practice of racial profiling, or adversely singling out individuals because of physical and other characteristics, is prohibited.

- *Article 21*—The right of peaceful assembly shall be recognized with customary limitations based on national security, public safety, public order, protection of public health or morals, and protection of rights and freedoms of others. Taking the limitations literally, a State could apply the above limitations to ban most assemblies.

- *Article 22*—Everyone shall have the right to freely associate with others and to form and join trade unions, with the usual limitations (e.g., national security) applying. However, this article shall not prevent a State from placing "lawful restrictions" on members of the armed forces and police. For example, a lawful restriction on police could consist of a "no strike" clause in their labor contract.

- *Article 23*—This article entitles the family as the "natural and fundamental group unit of society" to protection by society and the State. A State shall recognize the right of "men and women" of marriageable age to found a family— same-sex marriages do not appear to fall under this human right.

- *Article 24*—Children shall have the right to protection, immediate registration after birth, a name, and a nationality.

- *Article 25*—This article generally guarantees citizens the right to participate in public affairs and to vote without discrimination based on race, color, sex, language, religion, political or other opinion, national or social origin, property, birth, or other status. A citizen shall have equal access to public services in his or her country. Note that this article specifies "citizen" and not lawful resident. In other words, this provision does not prevent States from barring noncitizens from voting.

- *Article 26*—All persons shall be equal before the law and entitled to equal protection without discrimination. Equal protection refers to the legal concept of not being singled out for different treatment on the basis of some status. This human right resembles the ethical responsibilities of social workers. For example, the NASW's *Code of Ethics* states that social workers "should not practice, condone, facilitate, or collaborate with any form of discrimination on the basis of race, ethnicity, national origin, color, sex, sexual orientation, age, marital status, political belief, religion, or mental or physical disability" (NASW 1996:4.02). This ethical responsibility essentially provides that social workers are not to discriminate on any of the listed classifications. The U.S. Constitution also has an equal protection clause, although the classes of discrimination are not as extensive as the human rights article, which bars discrimination on the basis of "property." In the United States, the imposition of a law that favors property owners would not necessarily violate equal protection principles. The failure to own property does not create circumstances that trigger equal protection.

- *Article 27*—This article addresses the cultural rights of ethnic, religious, or linguistic minorities within a State. Those minorities shall have the right to enjoy their "own culture, to profess and practise their own religion, or to use their own language." This human right appears to conflict with proponents who favor English-only usage in the United States. Under this article, the Hispanic minority within the United States would be allowed to use Spanish as its own language. Social workers have an ethical responsibility to understand the culture of clients and be sensitive to differences among people and cultural groups (NASW 1996:1.05).

The third part of the covenant contains many civil and political rights that in some countries already exist, at least on paper. Because one State may interpret a particular article differently than another State, distinctions in what any given article means can arise. These distinctions often occur in the areas of freedom of speech and religion. Yet to say that any single State knows and follows the *definitive* interpretation of a human right is both arrogant and incorrect. Room for differences must exist, particularly considering the vast number of States and cultures involved. However, general themes permeate articles 6 through 27, which create principles that social workers everywhere can apply to their practice. Social workers in the United States have already incorporated many of these human rights principles into their association's *Code of Ethics*. This connection between human rights and social work ethics and practice exists throughout the area of human rights.

Part IV

The fourth part of the covenant establishes a Human Rights Committee with the apparent purpose of monitoring steps that States party to the covenant have taken in implementing rights guaranteed by the covenant. The committee consists of eighteen members who are nationals of the States Parties to the covenant (art. 28, para. 1). Those members shall be persons of "high moral character and recognized competence in the field of human rights" (art. 28, para. 2). Each State party to the covenant may nominate two persons to serve on the committee (art. 29, para. 2). However, only one national from the same State may serve on the committee at the same time (art. 31, para. 1). Members are elected by secret ballot by States party to the covenant (art. 30, para. 4). Members serve for a term of four years but may be reelected for subsequent terms (art. 32, para. 1). When electing committee members, States shall consider an "equitable geographical distribution of membership" and "representation of the different forms of civilization and of the principal legal systems" (art. 31, para. 2).

Within one year from the date the covenant enters into force for a State, that State must submit an initial report for consideration by the committee on "measures they have adopted which give effect to the rights" within the covenant and the "progress made in the enjoyment of those rights" (art. 40, para. 1[a]). After the initial report, States must submit periodic reports for consideration by the committee (art. 40, para. 1[b]). The committee may make comments on the reports to a State, with a State having the right to respond to those comments (art. 40, para. 4–5). The current policy of the committee requires that States submit reports every five years from the date of their initial report.

In some instances, the committee may also receive written complaints from one State about the failure of another State to fulfill its obligations under the covenant (art. 41, para. 1). However, before the committee may consider or handle this type of complaint, both States must declare that they recognize the competence of the committee to consider communications involving the failure of a State to fulfill its obligations under the covenant. Procedures for considering and resolving these complaints are specified in detail (art. 41 and 42). Generally, a complaining State must first raise the matter by written communication to the other State (art. 41, para. 1[a]). Within three months after the receipt of the communication, the receiving

State must give the complaining State a written explanation or statement of the matter at issue. The written explanation should include any relevant references to domestic procedures and remedies taken or available in the matter. If the States cannot resolve the issue within six months after the receipt of the initial written communication, either State may refer the matter to the Human Rights Committee (art. 41, paragraph 1[b]).

The committee shall deal with a matter only after it has determined that all the States have exhausted all available domestic remedies to resolve the issue (art. 41, para. 1[c]). An exception to this jurisdictional bar exists where an unreasonable length of time has passed in the application of a remedy. In that case, the committee would not restrict itself from entertaining the matter. In all cases that the committee accepts under these provisions, it shall hold closed meetings when examining communications (art. 41, para. 1[d]). The committee's role in these cases is to offer its services to the States "with a view to a friendly solution of the matter on the basis of respect for human rights and fundamental freedoms as recognized" in the covenant (art. 41, para. 1[e]). States involved in a matter before the committee may make oral and written submissions to the committee (art. 41, para. 1[g]). Within twelve months from the date the committee first received notice of a matter, the committee shall submit a report that specifies any solution reached by the committee (art. 41, para. 1(h)(i)). If the committee has not reached a solution, then the committee confines its report to a brief statement of the facts to which submissions by the concerned States are attached (art. 41, para.1(h)(ii)).

In cases where the committee has not resolved the matter to the satisfaction of the concerned States, with prior consent of those States the committee may appoint an *ad hoc* Conciliation Commission (art. 42, para. 1[a]). In other words, no permanent Conciliation Commission exists for this purpose, and the committee would only create this commission when the concerned States have previously consented to the appointment of this commission. The purpose of the Conciliation Commission is to assist the concerned States in reaching an "amicable solution" to the matter at hand. As with the procedure for the Human Rights Committee, the Conciliation Commission has twelve months in which to submit a report briefly specifying a solution or, if it has not reached a solution, presenting its views on the possibility of an amicable solution to the matter (art. 42, para. 7[b] and [c]). In cases where the commission has not reached a solution, the concerned

States shall notify the chair of the committee whether or not they accept the contents of the report within three months of having received it (art. 42. para. 7[d]).

In 1997, forty-four countries, including the United States, had officially recognized the competence of the Human Rights Committee to hear complaints involving their countries under the above procedure (Women, Law, and Development International/Human Rights Watch Women's Rights Project 1997:30). However, at that time, no State had submitted a complaint about another State. The lack of participation in the procedure to hear interstate complaints by the committee indicates reluctance by States to open themselves to examination by other States. Undoubtedly, if one State files a complaint against another State, the receiving State would also find a human rights issue to raise with the other State. Charging a country with a human rights abuse can be ticklish business, as no State wishes to hear that it violates human rights. Perhaps, though, the positive aspect of this development is that human rights do matter. No State can afford to simply brush off complaints about violations of human rights. The lack of participation in the procedures for hearing interstate complaints could also indicate that countries do take charges of human rights abuses seriously but do not want to be judged by other States concerning those charges.

Aside from procedures involving the Human Rights Committee, States may use any other mechanism or procedure in settling a dispute in accordance with general or special international agreement in force between them (art. 44). Each year, the committee must submit to the General Assembly of the United Nations, through the Economic and Social Council, an annual report on its activities (art. 45).

Some States might find the Human Rights Committee cumbersome or indecisive, since no authority exists for the committee to issue a binding decision. Unless a State has previously accepted the competence of the committee, the State does not have the right to submit a complaint. However, by subjecting itself to the competence of the committee, the complaining State might also find itself on the receiving end of a human rights complaint.

On the other hand, the committee clearly offers States a mechanism with which to air human rights concerns involving other States. The purpose of the committee is not to punish States for alleged violations of human rights but to assist States in meeting their obligations under the covenant. With that purpose in mind, States have much to gain by utilizing the committee and its expertise in sorting out human rights issues.

Part V

Part V of the covenant states that nothing in the covenant may impair provisions of the United Nations Charter or constitutions of specialized agencies involved with matters contained in the covenant (art. 46). For instance, the Commission on Human Rights of the United Nations is a specialized agency dealing with matters contained in the covenant. Therefore, nothing in the covenant may be interpreted in a manner that conflicts with the constitution of that agency. On a broader level, nothing in the present covenant shall be interpreted as impairing the inherent right of all peoples to enjoy and utilize fully and freely their natural wealth and resources (art. 47). This provision ensures that nothing contained in the covenant may prevent "peoples" from enjoying and using their natural wealth and resources. Therefore, a State party to the covenant may not take natural wealth and resources from peoples residing within the boundaries of that State. People are entitled to enjoy natural wealth and resources without interference from a State. Unfortunately, the broad sweep of this provision raises issues of interpretation not easily resolved. However, the intent appears to be an interpretation limiting the power of a State.

Part VI

The final part of the covenant contains procedural points, including who may sign the covenant and when the covenant becomes effective. Generally, any member of the United Nations or any State invited by the General Assembly of the United Nations to become a member can become a party to the covenant (article 48, para. 1). By its terms, the covenant enters into force three months after the date of deposit with the Secretary-General of the United Nations instruments of ratification or accession from thirty-five States (art. 49, para. 1). In 1976, ten years after the General Assembly adopted the language of the covenant, thirty-five States had either acceded to or ratified the covenant and, therefore, the covenant entered into force at that time. For those thirty-five States, the effective date of the covenant was three months after the covenant entered into force. For a State that acceded to or ratified the covenant after the covenant entered into force, the effective date of the covenant was three months after the accession or ratification (art. 49, para. 2). The terms *accede* and *ratify* relate to the means by which a State expresses consent to be bound by a treaty.

Under the U.S. Constitution, the president has the power, with the advice and consent of the Senate, to make treaties, provided two-thirds of the Senate present concur with the treaty (U.S. Constitution, art. 2). Often, a president may sign a human rights treaty, with the Senate delaying its approval or ratification for many years. With respect to the ratification by the United States of the International Covenant on Civil and Political Rights, the U.S. placed five reservations on that treaty. Those reservations modified the covenant in the following manner (Newman and Weisbrodt 1996):

- Preserved the higher protection of free speech and association guaranteed by the U.S. Constitution;
- Ensured that the United States could continue to impose the death penalty as punishment for persons under the age of 18 convicted of appropriate crimes;
- Limited the proscription against "cruel, inhuman, or degrading treatment or punishment" to definitions under the U.S. Constitution;
- Preserved the U.S. rule allowing imposition of any higher penalty in force at the time an offense was committed; and
- Preserved the right to treat juveniles as adults in exceptional circumstances.

The above reservations involving juveniles could certainly be viewed as incompatible with the object and intent of the covenant, which prohibits the death penalty for individuals less than 18 years of age. However, without these reservations, the United States would not have ratified the covenant.

Clearly, the process of drafting and obtaining acceptance of a treaty on human rights involves numerous factors. The initial wording of the treaty contains its own set of challenges, with some countries or groups wanting a particular wording to satisfy their own political or social agenda. After the inevitable tug-of-war over language of a treaty comes the vote on the treaty. Will enough countries in the General Assembly of the United Nations vote to adopt the treaty? If so, then comes the subsequent process of putting the treaty into effect, which requires a specific number of countries accepting the treaty as the law of their lands. Even acceptance of the treaty as law does not prevent a country from placing reservations on the treaty. If a country wants to accept the treaty generally but does not like a particular provision, then that country may reserve enforcement of that provision. Finally, after ratification of the treaty, a country has to decide whether the treaty is self-implementing or requires specific legislation to implement its terms. The

United States has usually viewed UN treaties as requiring specific legislation to implement the treaty. In other words, an individual who might be affected by the treaty could not simply refer to the treaty in a court of law but would need to refer to specific implementing legislation. If such legislation does not exist, the individual cannot rely on the treaty for legal support.

The International Covenant on Civil and Political Rights addresses human rights and freedoms as they relate to States or the governments of States. Without additional provisions, the Human Rights Committee would have no authority to receive complaints about human rights violations from individuals. Yet political and civil human rights impact in particular on individuals. For that reason, the United Nations adopted an Optional Protocol to the International Covenant on Civil and Political Rights (see appendix C).

OPTIONAL PROTOCOL TO THE INTERNATIONAL COVENANT ON CIVIL AND POLITICAL RIGHTS

To create a forum for individuals alleging violations of human rights contained in the International Covenant on Civil and Political Rights, the United Nations drafted an additional instrument to give voice to individuals. That instrument is known as the Optional Protocol to the International Covenant on Civil and Political Rights.

The Optional Protocol consists of fourteen articles which generally address procedures under which an individual may submit a written communication to the Human Rights Committee. Any State that has signed the International Covenant on Civil and Political Rights may also sign the protocol (appendix C: art. 8, para. 1). States that have acceded to or ratified the covenant may then ratify the protocol (art. 8, para. 2). This language clearly indicates that not only must a State sign the protocol but its government must also accept the protocol as binding. Without ratification of the protocol, a State is not subject to the terms of the protocol.

A State party to the Optional Protocol must recognize the competence of the Human Rights Committee to receive and consider communications involving alleged human rights violations from individuals subject to the State's jurisdiction (art. 1). The committee may not receive any communication if that communication concerns a State party to the Covenant but not a party to the Optional Protocol (art. 1). In the communication, individuals must allege that the State has violated one or more of their rights listed in the International Covenant on Civil and Political Rights (art. 1). The committee will not accept any communication that is anonymous, nor will the committee accept communications that it considers incompatible with the provisions of the covenant (art. 3). The Optional Protocol does not specify any particular format for a communication other than the communication must be in writing.

After receiving an acceptable communication, the Human Rights Committee shall bring the communication to the attention of the State alleged to be violating the covenant (art. 4, para. 1). Within six months, the receiving State shall provide the committee with written explanations or statements clarifying the matter and the remedy, if any, that may have been taken by that State (art. 4, para. 2).

The committee shall consider communications received in light of all written information made available to it by the individual and the State concerned (art. 5, para. 1). However, the committee shall not consider any communication from an individual unless the committee has determined that the individual has exhausted all available domestic remedies (art. 5, para. 2[b]) and that the same matter is not being examined under another procedure of international investigation or settlement (art. 5, para. 2[c]). If a State has unreasonably prolonged the application of domestic remedies to the alleged human rights violation, the committee may then consider the matter without regard to the exhaustion of domestic remedies (art. 5, para. 2). The committee shall hold closed meetings when examining communications and shall forward its views to the State and individual concerned (art. 5, para. 3–4).

The intent of the Optional Protocol is to provide individuals with an avenue through which to address possible human rights violations against their government when domestic procedures have failed to resolve the alleged violation. For many countries, provisions of the Optional Protocol may appear intrusive in that a United Nations committee may examine an alleged human rights violation after the relevant government has already dealt with the matter. Not surprisingly, the United States has not signed the Optional Protocol, although almost one hundred other States are now party to the protocol.

A second and more specific document—the Second Optional Protocol to the International Covenant on Civil and Political Rights—addresses the

death penalty. As with the First Optional Protocol, the United States has neither signed nor ratified the protocol.

SOCIAL WORK PERSPECTIVE ON THE INTERNATIONAL COVENANT ON CIVIL AND POLITICAL RIGHTS

The title of the International Covenant on Civil and Political Rights may
seem far removed from social work practice. However, nothing could be
more wrong. Many provisions within the Covenant on Civil and Political
Rights directly relate to the ethical standards of social workers. At times, language in the covenant mirrors language in the NASW's *Code of Ethics* and
policy statements.

The purpose of the Covenant on Civil and Political Rights is to guarantee
that everyone can voice opinions, preserve cultural backgrounds, carry out
religious practices, and organize employment unions. The covenant also
prohibits torture, slavery, cruel and degrading treatment, discrimination,
and other violations of the person. Social workers can easily find common
cause with these human rights. In fact, social workers have an obligation to
take social and political action to promote the bulk of human rights contained in the covenant (NASW 1996:6.04).

The importance of recognizing that the social work profession is closely
tied to human rights lies in the additional strength that this connection provides the profession. By tying particular injustices or circumstances to
human rights, social workers can better advocate for clients and fulfill the
primary mission of the profession. Promoting human rights attracts more
attention than simply saying that social workers are fulfilling their ethical
obligations.

By now, the link between human rights and the social work profession
should be coming into focus. Unquestionably, the social work profession is
a human rights profession.

QUESTIONS

1. What does the International Bill of Human Rights mean? What documents are included in the International Bill of Human Rights?
2. What is a major distinction between a covenant and a declaration in
   terms of human rights documents?

3. Both the Covenant on Civil and Political Rights and the Covenant on Economic, Social, and Cultural Rights mentions the term *self-determination*. What does that term mean in the context of those two covenants? Does the use of this term in human rights documents have any connection to the use of that term in the social work profession?

4. What types of human rights are contained in the Covenant on Civil and Political Rights?

5. Do you believe that the human rights contained in the above covenant should be guaranteed to everyone? Why or why not?

6. List at least one human right contained in the Covenant on Civil and Political Rights that could be subject to different interpretations.

7. What is meant by the term *equal protection*? How is this term important to the social work profession?

8. Should the right to practice one's religion or participate in cultural traditions be allowed without restriction?

9. What provisions does the Covenant on Civil and Political Rights contain for monitoring compliance with human rights contained in the covenant?

10. Has the United States ratified the Covenant on Civil and Political Rights? Did the United States place any reservations upon its ratification? If so, what are those reservations?

11. What relevance does the Covenant on Civil and Political Rights have to the social work profession?

REFERENCES

Economist, The. 1998. Human-rights law. (December 15): 4–16.

Kahn, I. 2002. Cost of countering terror. *Far Eastern Economic Review* (February 21): 26.

Masters, B. 2002. Saved for "the Worst of the Worst." The death penalty is reversed often in states that use it frequently, a review shows. *Washington Post National Weekly Edition* (February 18–24): 34.

McCormick, R. 1995. On the border: Language affects citizenship. *Southern Illinoisan* (October 13): B2.

National Association of Social Workers (NASW). 1996. *Code of Ethics*. Washington, D.C: NASW Press.

Newman, F. and D. Weisbrodt, eds. 1996. *International Human Rights: Law, Policy, and Process*. 2d ed. Cincinnati, Ohio: Anderson Publishing.

Pever, S. 1992. *The Rights of Indians and Tribes: The Basic ACLU Guide to Indian and Tribal Rights.* 2d ed. Carbondale, Ill.: Southern Illinois University Press.

Reamer, F. 1998. *Ethical Standards in Social Work: A Critical Review of the NASW Code of Ethics.* Washington, D.C.: NASW Press.

United Nations. 1948. *Universal Declaration of Human Rights.* Adopted December 10, 1948. GA. Res. 217 AIII. United Nations Document a/810. New York: UN.

Waller, M. and M. Yellow Bird. 2002. Strengths of First Nations Peoples. In Dennis Saleebey, ed., *The Strengths Perspective in Social Work Practice,* 51. 3d ed. Boston: Allyn and Bacon.

Worcester v. Georgia, 31 US (6 Pet) 515 (1813).

Women, Law, and Development International and Human Rights Watch Women's Rights Project. 1997. *Women's Human Rights Step by Step.* Washington, D.C.: Women, Law, and Development International.

4

The International Covenant on Economic, Social, and Cultural Rights

ROBERT J. MCCORMICK AND ELISABETH REICHERT

The second major covenant derived from the Universal Declaration of Human Rights is the International Covenant on Economic, Social, and Cultural Rights. This covenant aims to make States responsible for providing human rights falling under what might be termed "quality of life" categories.

Some countries, like the United States, emphasize civil and political rights over economic, social, and cultural rights. After all, without civil and political rights, how can any country promote economic rights? Should not the human rights focus be on civil and political guarantees, with other rights then naturally following, with no requirement to "guarantee" those rights? Some countries struggle to guarantee freedom of speech, free elections, and other political rights. Yet the economic status of these countries may be barely above the subsistence level. How can these countries provide economic rights to their residents? Should they be labeled as violators of human rights if they cannot provide adequate food for all their residents? These are some of the questions and issues that arise when comparing the two covenants derived from the Universal Declaration.

PREAMBLE

The International Covenant on Economic, Social, and Cultural Rights consists of five parts and thirty-one articles. As with the International Covenant on Civil and Political Rights, a preamble provides the broad purpose of the covenant. States party to the covenant recognize that the "ideal of free human beings enjoying freedom from fear and want can only be achieved if conditions are created whereby everyone may enjoy his economic, social, and cultural rights, as well as his civil and political rights" (preamble). States party to the covenant recognize that rights under the covenant derive from the inherent dignity of the human person. States party to the covenant realize that the individual, having duties to other individuals and to the community to which he belongs, is under a responsibility to strive for the promotion and observance of the rights recognized in the covenant.

The language in the preamble to this covenant closely follows language in the International Covenant on Political and Civil Rights. Indivisibility of the two covenants is clearly intended by language that freedom from fear and want can only occur if conditions are created whereby everyone may enjoy economic, social, and cultural rights. The covenant on political and civil rights contains similar language except the reference to freedom from fear and want focused on enjoyment of civil and political rights. While drafters may have intended that economic, social, and cultural rights occupy the same status as civil and political rights, as noted above, that has not always been the case, especially in the United States.

Language in the covenant may appear sexist. However, as explained in chapter 2 (on the Universal Declaration), drafters of these documents addressed the issue of gender in the drafting process. No favoring of one gender over another is intended, a point made clear in provisions addressing nondiscrimination. The preamble also makes it clear that the covenant is applicable to States and not a general declaration of intent or aspiration. Countries that accept the document have an obligation to carry out provisions within the document.

PART I

This section of the covenant is identical to part I of the International Covenant on Civil and Political Rights. All peoples have the right of self-determination (art. 1, para. 1). As part of this right to self-determination, peoples can freely pursue their economic, social, and cultural development (para. 1). Reading between the lines of this language indicates that States should not interfere in economic, social, or cultural affairs of other countries. Under self-determination, other States should accept a State having an economic and social system based on substantial government control, provided that State does not violate other human rights. The position of Cuba and the United States provides an example of how countries can become enmeshed in human rights struggles without fully examining principles of human rights. The United States has enacted economic sanctions against Cuba on the basis that Cuba violates political and civil human rights, including freedom of speech and assembly. These sanctions prohibit citizens of the United States from doing business with Cuba and traveling to Cuba. However, under the right of self-determination, Cuba could argue that it has the right to freely determine its own political status, which allows varying interpretations of political rights. Cuba might also claim that the United States itself violates human rights in respect to racial discrimination. Consequently, policies of the United States or any other country based on human rights violations in other countries risk charges of hypocrisy.

States shall promote the realization of the right of self-determination and respect that right in conformity with the Charter of the United Nations (art. 3, para. 3). This recognition of self-determination does not prevent monitoring of human rights violations within States' jurisdiction. States should evaluate the status of human rights in other countries. However, as previously noted, a State criticizing other States for violations of human rights can easily run afoul of human rights charges itself. Evaluation of human rights violations requires thought and knowledge about human rights documents and sensitivity to differing ways of life.

PART II

The purpose of part II to the covenant is that of explaining limitations and interaction with other human rights recognized by States party to the covenant. Generally, States must respect all rights guaranteed in the covenant. However, in certain instances, a State may limit those rights.

Each State party to the covenant must take steps to progressively realize the rights contained in the covenant by all appropriate means, including particularly the adoption of legislative measures (art. 2, para. 1). This provision indicates that the covenant is not self-executing, or requires additional legislation to implement its provisions. Each State shall undertake these steps individually and through international assistance and cooperation, especially economic and technical, to the maximum of its available resources (art. 2, para. 1). These provisions require States party to the covenant to work toward fulfilling the economic and other human rights specified in the covenant. In the exercise of human rights specified in the covenant, States shall not discriminate on the basis of race, color, sex, language, religion, political or other opinion, national or social origin, property, birth, or other status (art. 2. para. 2). Developing countries, with due regard to human rights and their national economy, may determine to what extent they would guarantee the economic rights recognized in the covenant to non-nationals (art. 2, para. 3). In other words, less economically developed countries may favor citizens over residents in the guarantee of economic rights, provided those countries respect other human rights. This provision applies only to developing countries and to economic—not social and cultural—rights. In 1996, when the United States enacted reforms of its welfare laws, many immigrant residents in the United States found themselves excluded from economic rights granted to U.S. citizens (Reichert and McCormick 1998). Legal challenges to this exclusion have generally failed based on U.S. laws (Kim 2001). Had the United States ratified and implemented the covenant on economic, social, and cultural rights, exclusion of welfare benefits to immigrants would most likely have been an illegal violation of human rights.

States party to the covenant undertake to ensure the equal right of women and men to the enjoyment of all economic, social, and cultural rights in the covenant (art. 3). States may limit rights in the covenant only to the extent that those limitations promote the general welfare in a democratic society (art. 4). This language appears to allow a State to impose limits to economic, social, and cultural rights but only if those limits are compatible with the nature of the rights and promote the general welfare. For example, a country might decide to limit economic rights specified in the covenant when those limitations are necessary to overcome an economic crisis. However, that country could not discriminate on the basis of gender in the measures taken to overcome the crisis. No State, group, or person may engage in any activity aimed at the destruction of any rights in the covenant, or their limitation to a greater extent than is provided in the covenant (art. 5, para. 1). A State may not use the covenant as a pretext for violating human rights that the State recognizes in other legal instruments (art. 5, para. 2). Rights contained in the covenant do not act to limit or exclude other human rights.

While States party to the covenant generally must ensure specified human rights, provisions exist to consider the circumstances of a particular State. Where economic resources are insufficient to satisfy all economic rights listed in the covenant, a State may limit its guarantee of those rights. A State may restrict rights provided in the covenant if the restriction would promote the general welfare in a democratic society. Instances of this restriction appear limited to crisis situations.

PART III

This part lists the substantive economic, social, and cultural rights contained in the covenant.

- *Article 6, para. 1*—This provision recognizes the right to work. Everyone shall have the opportunity to gain his living by work that he freely chooses or accepts. States party to the covenant "will" take appropriate steps to safeguard this right. (An interesting point is the use of the word *will* and not *shall* regarding the duty of a State to take steps to safeguard the right to work. *Will* does not have the same mandatory tone as *shall*.) Consequently, the guarantee of this right to work appears less stringent than if the drafters had used the word *shall*. Possibly recognizing that a State cannot always guarantee employment freely chosen or accepted by an individual, the drafters toned down the mandatory nature of this human right.
- *Article 6, para. 2*—Steps to be taken by a State to effect the right to work "shall" include technical and vocational guidance and training programs and policies and techniques to achieve steady economic, social, and cultural development and full and productive employment. A State may take these steps only under conditions which safeguard individual political and economic freedoms. Assuming a State does take steps to guarantee employment, those steps would in-

The human right to productive work raises all types of issues, with perhaps the most obvious one being how to pay a wage sufficient to actually live within an individual's means. For instance, in 1996 the U.S. government enacted new welfare laws that focused on work as a requirement to receive governmental assistance (Reichert and McCormick 1997). In addition, those new laws limited many individuals to only five years of public assistance during their lifetime. The overall effect of the new U.S. welfare laws has been a significant reduction in welfare recipients. Politicians from all philosophical corners have touted the new laws as an unqualified success story.

But while U.S. welfare laws have certainly decreased the number of welfare recipients, an inescapable irony in this "success" story emerges: By working, even at minimum wage jobs, individuals and family members often become ineligible for public assistance because their income exceeds the caps for that assistance. Yet without health insurance and greater benefits, insufficient income exists with which to adequately provide for the household. Has the move to get people off welfare actually resulted in individuals' obtaining productive work that provides sufficient income to exist? Some groups would say no.

The Poor People's Economic Human Rights Campaign and other groups have charged the U.S. government with human rights violations caused by the 1996 Welfare "Reform" Act (Poor People's Economic Human Rights Campaign 2001; Zucchino 2001). The Poor People's Economic Human Rights Campaign is a national effort led by poor and homeless women, men, and children of all races to raise the issue of poverty in the United States as a human rights violation. The campaign fights for "basic human rights" as provided in the Universal Declaration of Human Rights: the right to a decent job at a living wage, the right to a suitable home, the right to food, the guarantee of quality education and quality health care, and a future for individuals and families. The crux of this movement is to provide sufficient resources to the poor in order to fulfill basic human rights. Perhaps the most important part of this movement lies in providing what is known as a "living wage"—in other words, an income that is sufficiently substantial to adequately support those in the family or household.

Calls for a "living wage" would seem to belie the purported success of the U.S. welfare law. Merely being able to obtain work does not mean that an individual can thereby make ends meet (which seems to be the underlying premise of the welfare law):

> Three years ago, Juana Zatarin couldn't make ends meet. The mother of three, a baggage handler at Los Angeles International Airport, was subsisting on an income about half that of the federal poverty rate of $17,028 for a family of four. Today, thanks to a "living wage" law requiring city

(continued)

contractors to pay employees a minimum of $8.97 per hour, Ms. Zatarin earns more than $24,000 a year. Now life is good. "I can make my payments on time now and even have a chance to take some time off," she says. (Wood 2002:1)

But doesn't paying individuals higher wages reduce the availability of jobs? Fears about the benefits of substantial pay increases for workers being overshadowed by a huge reduction in available jobs do not seem to have materialized (Wood 2002:4). A study by the Public Policy Institute of California examined thirty-six cities within the United States that have imposed a living wage on contractors doing business with those cities. That study found that slight job losses caused by living wage laws are more than compensated by the decrease in family poverty (4).

Welfare laws that require work should aim to satisfy the human right to productive work and other related human rights. That requires more than simply viewing the obtaining of *any* type of work as a success: indeed, work that does not provide a living wage falls far short of the mark.

clude both micro- and macro-level policies. Unfortunately, the language describing these steps appears sufficiently broad to include just about anything. At the micro level, a State is to establish technical and vocational programs as part of an overall plan to ensure full and productive employment. Obviously, resources must be available to establish and staff these programs. Many countries may not have sufficient economic or social resources to do this. At the macro level, a State must devise policies and techniques to achieve full employment. The difficulty here is that world economic conditions may not be conducive to achieving full employment. A global recession may inhibit employment possibilities in any country.

- *Article 7*—This article requires States party to the covenant to "recognize the right of everyone to the enjoyment of just and favourable conditions" of work. In particular, these conditions require fair and equal remuneration for work of equal value without distinction. In particular, women are guaranteed conditions of work equal to those enjoyed by men, with "equal pay for equal work." The ar-

MOBBING—A WORKPLACE PHENOMENON

While "just and favorable conditions" of work is a human right within the International Covenant on Economic, Social, and Cultural Rights, the focus of that human right has typically been on equal pay issues relating to gender. However looming behind the harm of unequal pay lies another significant evil: mobbing.

Before 1982, reference to mobbing as a workplace phenomenon did not exist. In that year, however, Dr. Heinz Leymann, a German industrial psychologist, began research into emotional abuse at the workplace. Dr. Leymann referred to a particular type of this abuse as mobbing (Davenport, Schwartz, and Elliott 1999:14). Dr. Leymann defined mobbing as psychological terror involving hostile and unethical communication directed in a systematic way by one or a few individuals mainly toward one individual (22). Further research into mobbing has given us the "mobbing syndrome" (40):

- The mobbing syndrome is a malicious attempt to force a person out of the workplace through unjustified accusations, humiliation, general harassment, emotional abuse, and/or terror.
- It is a "ganging up" by the leader(s)—organization, superior, coworker, or subordinate—who rallies others into systematic and frequent "mob-like" behavior.
- Because the organization ignores, condones, or even instigates the behavior, it can be said that the victim, seemingly helpless against the powerful and many, is indeed "mobbed." The result is always injury—physical or mental distress or illness and social misery and, most often, expulsion from the workplace.

Workplace mobbing can take many forms. For instance, a petition by employees to remove a coworker from their midst on false pretenses without allowing the coworker any opportunity to respond to the petition would be mobbing. Another instance of mobbing would be the hiring of an outside consultant by the employer on the pretext of helping employees work better together. The employer and other employees then target an unpopular employee as a troublemaker and tell the consultant, who simply rubber-stamps this label in a report to the employer.

In trying to reduce workplace mobbing, some European countries have enacted legislation against this human rights violation (26). Curiously, the United States lags behind Europe in recognizing mobbing as a workplace hazard. While mobbing is a household word in Germany, many Americans

(continued)

would have no idea as to a literary connection of mobbing to the workplace. While mobbing may occasionally run afoul of laws against discrimination or sexual harassment, mobbing frequently constitutes an entirely different evil.

By not directing sufficient attention to mobbing at the workplace, the United States runs the risk of allowing enormous emotional harm to continue there (Keashly 1998). This can only increase harm to not only the victims of mobbing but also employers that must ultimately pay in lost productivity and poor morale.

---

ticle also guarantees a "decent living" for workers and their families. Additional rights guaranteed to workers include "safe and healthy working conditions"; "equal opportunity for everyone to be promoted in his employment to an appropriate higher level, subject to no considerations other than those of seniority and competence"; and "rest, leisure, and reasonable limitation of working hours and periodic holidays with pay, as well as remuneration for public holidays."

Many of these stated rights of workers can only exist on paper in many countries. States with insufficient resources can hardly guarantee these rights. Even in the United States, to require an employer to pay a "living wage" meets resistance from employers, many of which would probably shut down rather than increase wages. In less economically developed countries, many of these rights might also be unknown in the culture. In a society where leaders are chosen based on family lineage, cultural norms would obviously clash with the requirement to promote workers only on the basis of "seniority and competence." The dichotomy between political and civil human rights and economic and social rights becomes evident when actually analyzing the different rights.

- *Article 8*—States party to the covenant "undertake to ensure" that everyone has the right to form and join a trade union of his choice, subject to restrictions necessary in a democratic society to preserve national security, public order, and rights of others. States also ensure that trade unions have the right to form federations and that union members have the right to strike, with allowable restrictions on members of the armed forces, police, and administration of the State.

While many countries have laws that satisfy the right to form trade unions, the reality is that membership in trade unions continues to decline. The underlying purpose of this human right is to allow employees a voice in their employment conditions. Unfortunately, management and employees simply do not always view the needs of a business or entity through the same lens. Employees who have organized into trade unions become nuisances to management. In some cases, trade unions may indeed become nothing more than a thorn in management's side. Why should management have to listen to employees who know little about running a business or government agency? Yet how could any operation exist without laborers? Don't they have a right to assist in determining their working conditions? Human rights principles say that they do.

- *Article 9*—States recognize the right of everyone to social security, including social insurance. No explanation of "social security" or "social insurance" appears in the article. Obviously, the article refers to a level of support sufficient to enable an individual to maintain an existence. That level would be relative to the standard of living in a particular country, with higher levels of support customary in more economically developed countries such as Germany and the United States.
- *Article 10*—This article provides protection for the "family, which is the natural and fundamental group unit of society." The article also states that, "Marriage must be entered into with the free consent of the intending spouses." This provision appears aimed against arranged marriages common in some cultures. Other protections concerning the family include "special protection" for "mothers during a reasonable period before and after childbirth." During this period, working mothers "should be accorded paid leave or leave with adequate social security benefits." Children should be protected from "economic and social exploitation." States should prohibit paid employment of children below a set age.

  Many countries, whether parties to the convention or not, support these human rights principles. However, in the United States, an employer generally makes the decision on whether to provide paid maternity leave. In less economically developed countries, paid maternity leave may not even be possible.
- *Article 11*—Under this article, States party to the covenant recognize the "right of

everyone to an adequate standard of living for himself and his family, including adequate food, clothing, and housing, and to the continuous improvement of living conditions." In undertaking the satisfaction of this right, States "will" recognize the "essential importance of international co-operation." In recognizing the fundamental right of everyone to be free from hunger, States shall establish programs to improve methods of food production and attempt to ensure an equitable distribution of world food supplies in relation to need.

This human right addresses the important issue of food and housing, basic needs in any society. Clearly, governments must cooperate with one another in order to achieve the aims of this human right.

- *Article 12*—States party to the convention recognize the right of "everyone to the enjoyment of the highest attainable standard of physical and mental health." States are to take steps to reduce infant mortality; improve environmental and industrial hygiene; prevent, treat, and control diseases; and create conditions that would assure medical services to everyone in the event of sickness.

   These goals are laudable and should not be objectionable to any country. However, guaranteeing health care to all citizens and residents remains a difficult issue in the United States.

- *Article 13*—This article details the human right to education, which has the primary goals of fully developing "the human personality and the sense of its dignity" and enabling everyone to participate effectively in a free society. Primary education shall be compulsory and free, with secondary and higher education being accessible to all subject to available means. While not requiring free secondary and higher education, States are to progressively introduce free education on these levels. States are to allow parents freedom to place their children in private schools that meet minimum educational standards.

   Education occupies a central position in human rights principles. Without education, the full development of an individual is not possible.

- *Article 14*—This article allows a State that, at the time of becoming a party to the covenant, has not been able to provide free and compulsory primary education within its "metropolitan territory," to present a plan to accomplish free and compulsory primary education. Rural areas appear exempt from this requirement.

- *Article 15*—States recognize the right of everyone to "take part in cultural life" and to "enjoy the benefits of scientific progress and its applications." This article also imposes the recognition that everyone has the right to benefit from the

Health care in the United States is never a given. Individuals and families must either receive health benefits from an employer or hope to qualify for a governmental program, like Medicare. An interesting point here is that, while the government pretty much guarantees health coverage to elderly citizens through Medicare, it does not provide any guarantee of health coverage to children and families. While government programs have recently expanded to include many children, gaps still exist, especially for the parents of those children.

> For a single mother of twin boys living on income from two part-time minimum wage jobs, the issue of health care often takes precedence. "My main concern is for Jack and Jeremy, when they get sick," said the mother, who does not make enough income at her fast-food restaurant job to purchase insurance. "I have [government medical] cards for the boys, which I can't do without, but I don't have anything for myself at all. It just leaves us with a regular round-robin of colds and flu, especially in the winter. They get sick, I get sick, I give it back to them. It's just a vicious cycle. . . . I'd love to have insurance. It would be a good safeguard to have. I worry about what will happen to me if I should get really sick or something." (Krutsinger 2001:1)

The lack of adequate health insurance for all Americans continually falls upon deaf ears with politicians, who of course could not imagine *themselves* being without medical coverage. Unfortunately, while politicians always give lip service to the importance of universal health coverage, significant action to reach that goal never seems to occur.

"protection" of the moral and material interests resulting from any scientific, literary, or artistic production of which a person is the author.

This article raises important issues concerning the provision of benefits from scientific progress. The protection of material benefits from scientific inventions can conflict with other human rights that guarantee medical care and food. Under this article, States must respect patents on medicines to prevent or treat HIV/AIDS. However, States also have an obligation to prevent and control diseases. If a country cannot afford to purchase patented drugs to treat a high incidence of AIDS within that country, should that country then try to duplicate the patented drugs without respecting the patent? This issue pits countries whose corporate citizens have produced and patented drugs to treat AIDS against countries that must purchase those drugs, often at great cost. Generally, this results in a conflict between corporations from wealthy countries and governments of less economically developed countries where AIDS affects many individuals.

Interaction and cooperation among countries is needed to promote the human rights cited within this article. The article contemplates international discussion by recognizing the "benefits to be derived from the encouragement and development of international contacts and co-operation in the scientific and cultural fields." The difficulty arises when the dominant country or group pressures other countries or groups to accept conditions that become counterproductive.

No further provisions appear in part III of the covenant. In summary, economic, social, and cultural benefits focus on five main areas: employment; protection of the family; social security, including adequate food, housing, and medical care; education; and participation in cultural and scientific endeavors. Many of the benefits unquestionably present challenges in their fulfillment. Current debate questions whether economic benefits should even be part of the human rights umbrella (*Economist* 2001a, 2001b).

PART IV

This part of the covenant addresses reports and methods of informing others about steps taken to achieve observance of economic, social, and cultural rights listed in the covenant.

- *Article 16*—States party to the covenant submit reports on the measure they have adopted and the progress made in achieving the observance of rights in the covenant. States submit the reports to the Secretary-General of the United Nations, who then forwards copies of the reports to the Economic and Social Council. The Secretary-General also forwards copies or relevant parts of the reports to specialized agencies of the United Nations responsible for matters discussed in the reports.
- *Article 17*—States submit their reports in stages in accordance with a program

established by the Economic and Social Council. Reports may indicate factors and difficulties affecting fulfillment of obligations under the covenant.

- *Article 18*—The Economic and Social Council may arrange with specialized agencies that report on progress made in observing rights in the covenant the type of reports it desires. Those reports may include particulars of decisions and recommendations on such implementation adopted by the agencies.
- *Article 19*—The Economic and Social Council may transmit reports it receives under articles 16, 17, and 18 to the Commission on Human Rights for study, general recommendation, or information.
- *Article 20*—States party to the covenant and any specialized agency may submit comments to the council on any general recommendation or reference to this recommendation in any report by the Commission on Human Rights.
- *Article 21*—The council may submit reports on progress made in achieving general observance of the rights contained in the covenant to the General Assembly.
- *Article 22*—The council may bring to the attention of other agencies within the United Nations any matters that would assist those agencies in meeting their own goals.
- *Article 23*—States party to the covenant agree that international action to achieve rights contained in the covenant include the conclusion of conventions or treaties, adoption of recommendations, furnishing of technical assistance, and holding of regional meetings for consultation.
- *Article 24*—Nothing in the covenant may be interpreted as infringing upon the Charter of the United Nations and other UN agencies.
- *Article 25*—Nothing in the covenant may be interpreted as impairing the inherent right of all peoples to enjoy and utilize fully and freely their natural wealth and resources.

In comparison to the Covenant on Civil and Political Rights, monitoring provisions within the Covenant on Economic, Social, and Cultural Rights are less stringent. In the latter covenant, no country has the right to complain about another country for possible violations of the covenant. Reading between the lines of both covenants, States party to the economic covenant appear to have more leeway or acceptance in whether they fulfill provisions of the covenant. Perhaps this reflects an implicit acknowledgment that many countries, including wealthy countries, may have difficulties fulfilling provisions of the covenant.

PART V

This part concludes the provisions of the covenant. Generally, articles under part V are similar to those in part VI of the Covenant on Civil and Political Rights. States wishing to adopt provisions of the covenant may either ratify or accede to the provisions. As discussed under part VI of the covenant on political rights, ratification and accession refer to the method by which a State agrees to make legally binding provisions of the covenant.

THE SOCIAL WORK PERSPECTIVE ON THE INTERNATIONAL COVENANT ON ECONOMIC, SOCIAL, AND CULTURAL RIGHTS

Social workers can unquestionably find common cause with the International Covenant on Economic, Social, and Cultural Rights. Many of the human rights listed in that covenant mirror goals and ethical principles of social workers. Yet the status of economic, social, and cultural rights as human rights has never quite matched that of civil and political rights (*Economist* 2001b:18–20). Some Western countries, especially the United States, have never subscribed to the theory that universal rights should include a job, housing, and generous welfare benefits. While many Western countries attempt to provide economic and social rights to every citizen, no guarantee of those rights exists. For instance, the U.S. Welfare Reform Act specifically states that, in most cases, nobody may receive welfare benefits after a five-year period. This provision clearly conflicts with articles 9, 11, and 12 of the covenant. Also, while the 1996 welfare act promotes work over government handouts, it does not provide any guarantee of work at a living wage, a possible violation of article 7 of the covenant.

Studies now clearly indicate that the number of individuals on welfare in the United States has dramatically decreased since the 1996 welfare act became law (Figlio and Ziliak 1999; Henly 2000; Cancian 2001). Of course, this should be no surprise. By imposing fixed time-periods for receiving welfare benefits, governments can easily reduce the number on welfare. The crucial issue remains, however, whether those who leave the welfare rolls actually receive sufficient income and benefits to adequately provide for themselves and their families.

WELFARE REFORM—SELF-SUFFICIENCY IS ELUSIVE GOAL

The underlying theme of the new welfare reform law [in the United States] is that of self-sufficiency: Every individual adult residing in the United States should be able to support his or her family without significant or prolonged government assistance. Unlike the guarantee of assistance to everyone meeting guidelines under the former Aid to Families with Dependent Children [AFDC] program, the new welfare law aims to prevent any entitlement to government support.

Although experiencing similar social problems as the United States such as out-of-wedlock births and high rates of divorce, Germany has enacted a Child and Youth Welfare Act that entitles all families to numerous benefits, including kindergarten and child care. A primary goal of the German law is that of developing a family-oriented environment and proactive child welfare system.

Based on international comparison, about 22 percent of all children in the United States live in poverty, while in Germany the corresponding rate is only 8 percent. Because of cultural and other intangible differences between the two countries, it would be simplistic to conclude that a German-style welfare system could help reduce child poverty in the U.S. Yet it would be equally simplistic to totally ignore the effect of providing a minimum safety net for children.

The new U.S. welfare law highlights work and marriage as the remedy to government assistance for children. In theory, this makes sense. Studies show that parents who work generally feel better about themselves than those who do not. Married parents also fare better financially than the single parent, and children are less prone to delinquency in two-parent families.

In reality, though, the twin pillars of work and marriage can be difficult to construct. Marriage may not always be an option for some mothers who, for whatever reason, become pregnant. The frequency of divorce is disturbing, but ways to prevent divorce remain elusive.

While favorable employment figures in the United States suggest that anyone who wants a job can get one, significant huffing and puffing accompanies the level of employment. Somebody who works even one hour a week is considered employed, and those who have given up looking for work are no longer counted as unemployed.

Many jobs in this country do not offer health coverage, which is required by the government for most workers in Germany. Finding affordable child

(continued)

care is another concern of many parents. Taking a job can be a losing proposition when medical or child care costs outweigh income from employment.

Compared to U.S. welfare reform, the German Child and Youth Welfare Act promotes a much more active stance by government in administering child welfare. The Germans do not rely as heavily on the private sector to bring about improvements in social conditions. In Germany, children are legally entitled to support and guidance that enables them to become responsible adults, with additional goals of self-determination and ties to the social community. The government encourages a broad partnership among those needing assistance, private institutions, the community, and government.

Of course, not all is perfect with the German welfare system. While the Child and Youth Welfare Act provides many benefits, the bureaucracy resulting from its expansive social net may be its biggest deficiency. The law resembles a panacea, with entitlements to cover every conceivable need that might arise among today's families. Funding mandated services imposes a huge burden on government, and proposals exist to reduce welfare spending.

Americans can criticize the German welfare system for creating a dependency on government handouts. However, a major fallacy contained in U.S. welfare reform is the myth of the self-sufficient American. Since World War II, governments in the U.S. have presided over an unprecedented distribution of benefits to corporations and individuals. In addition to direct government subsidies, the federal tax code has become a continuous source of goodies. Major perks include nontaxable health benefits, tax-deferred retirement funds, and deductible home mortgage interest.

In Germany, government assistance to all families undoubtedly plays a major role in preventing children there from falling into the well of poverty. Government here also provides assistance to many citizens but frequently views those living in poverty as less deserving than others.

Our bias against low-income residents may help explain why this country experiences greater poverty levels than any other industrialized country. (Reichert and McCormick 1996:A6)

In 1978, President Carter signed the Covenant on Economic, Social, and Cultural Rights. However, the Senate has never ratified the treaty, as required under the U.S. Constitution for the covenant to become effective. Why has the United States not ratified the Covenant on Economic, Social, and Cultural Rights? The difficulty in accepting the covenant arises in the guarantee of economic benefits that the United States has traditionally not accepted as a right. For example, the United States does not guarantee health care to every U.S. national and resident. By not providing medical care to every resident, the United States could immediately find itself accused of violating human rights principles. From a philosophical position, should this be the case? The *Economist* magazine had this response to a movement by Amnesty International to incorporate economic rights into its existing mission of ensuring political rights:

> Even if economic and social rights appear to have the same status on paper as civil and political rights, their philosophical grounding is often questioned. Designating a good as a universal human rights means that reasonable people believe that under no jurisdiction, and under no circumstances, may that good be justly denied to anybody. Although freedom from torture certainly now falls into this category—arguably due to the efforts of groups like Amnesty—goods such as food and a decent home do not. Governments may intentionally torture their citizens; they do not usually intentionally inflict on them poverty and ill health. The moral imperative to stop poverty or disease is therefore not as convincing as the moral imperative to stop torture. (*Economist* 2001b:19)

Perhaps the moral imperative to stop poverty or disease is not as convincing as the moral imperative to stop torture. However, that position is itself a question of values. If government policies inflict unnecessary physical suffering upon its citizens by not providing adequate food, shelter, or health care, then why should those policies not be condemned as strongly as those permitting torture? Certainly in the United States sufficient resources exist to provide every child and adult with adequate health care. Germany and other Western countries certainly make health care a right, and their government policy is to provide every child and adult with adequate medical treatment (Reichert and McCormick 1997). If, in the United States, few instances of torture occur but many children fail to receive basic health care, is the "moral imperative" less convincing than if it were the other way around? If U.S. policies *intentionally* deprive children of basic medical care, what is the moral difference between those children being free from torture but not being provided with adequate medical care?

Elevating the status of economic, social, and cultural rights to those of civil and political rights unquestionably presents challenges, especially in countries less economically developed than the United States:

> To guarantee civil and political rights is relatively cheap, whereas to guarantee economic and social rights is potentially enormously costly. The cost of ensuring the right to vote, for example, is well-defined: the nature of universal franchise is set out in a century of case law and statute, and the costs of staffing and equipping the ballot are easy to assess. Even when an election turns out to require independent observers, extended court sessions, and a lot of recounting, as in Florida last November and December [2000], it is still relatively easy for a democratic government to protect its citizens' right to vote. Endorsing a universal right to health care, by contrast, seems a sure start to an expensive ride down a slippery slope. Who is to say when a person has had enough money spent on keeping him fit? (*Economist* 2001b:20)

While the above position sounds reasonable, what about the costs of *not* providing sufficient economic and social rights? By far, the United States has one of the highest imprisonment rates in the world. The cost of operating those prisons runs into billions of dollars each year. Additional expenses arise just from running the courts and law enforcement agencies, as well as providing restitution to victims of crime. If a link exists between failing to provide economic benefits (such as education and health care) and a life of crime, then can it really be said that it is cheaper to guarantee mainly political and civil rights? Would it not be less expensive (not to mention more worthwhile) to provide better educational facilities and social assistance programs during the formative years of a person who, owing to poverty, might grow up to engage in criminal activities than to fork over the huge infusion of government funds necessary to run the legal and prison systems that now house the (often nonviolent) criminal?

By studying both of the major international covenants, social workers can better understand the connection that exists between political and economic human rights. In many instances, the failure to provide one type of human right can lead to the deprivation of another type. This symbiotic relationship between different sets of human rights raises valid questions as to whether one set of rights should be favored over another.

QUESTIONS

1. What types of human rights are contained in the Covenant on Economic, Social, and Cultural Rights (CESCR)?
2. Are the rights contained in the CESCR as important to an individual or community as the rights contained in the Covenant on Civil and Political Rights? Give reasons for your response.
3. What concession is made to "developing countries" in the CESCR concerning the guarantee of economic rights? Is this concession justified?
4. Does the United States violate principles contained in the CESCR when it excludes lawful immigrants from the receipt of welfare benefits available to citizens?
5. What is meant by the "right to work" as a human right? Does this mean that everyone is entitled to a job if he or she wants a job?
6. Why is education considered a human right?
7. Should wealthy countries be required to contribute to the progress of developing countries under human rights principles contained in the CESCR?
8. Why are human rights contained in the CESCR different from human rights contained in the Covenant on Civil and Political Rights?
9. Has the United States signed the CESCR? Has it ratified the CESCR? If not, why not? Give reasons.
10. Of what relevance is the CESCR to the social work profession?

REFERENCES

Cancian, M. 2001. Rhetoric and reality of work-based welfare reform. *Social Work: Journal of the National Association of Social Workers* 46.4: 309–14.

Davenport, N., R. Distler Schwartz, and G. Parsell Elliot. 1999. *Mobbing: Emotional Abuse in the Workplace.* Ames, Iowa: Civil Society Publishing.

Economist, The. 2001a. The politics of human rights. (August 18): 9.

———. 2001b. Special report on human rights: Righting wrongs. (August 18–24): 18–20.

Figlio, D. N. and J. P. Ziliak. 1999. Welfare reform, the business cycle, and the decline in AFDC caseloads. In S. Danziger, ed., *Economic Conditions and Welfare Reform*, 17–48. Kalamazoo, Mich.: W. E. Upjohn Institute for Employment Research.

Henly, J. R. 2000. Mismatch in the low-wage labor market: Job search perspective. In K. Kaye and D. Smith Nightingale, eds., *The Low-wage Labor Market: Challenges and Opportunities for Self-sufficiency*, 145–67. Washington, D.C: Urban Institute Press.

Keashly, L. 1998. Emotional abuse in the workplace: Conceptual and empirical issues. *Journal of Emotional Abuse* 1.1: 85–117.

Krutsinger, L. 2001. Lack of health care a costly problem. *Southern Illinoisan* (July 19): A3.

Kim, R. 2001. Welfare reform and "ineligibles": Issues of constitutionality and recent court rulings. *Social Work: Journal of the National Association of Social Workers* 46.4: 315–23.

Newman, F. and D. Weisbrodt, eds. 1996. *International Human Rights: Law, Policy, and Process*. 2d ed. Cincinnati, Ohio: Anderson.

Poor People's Economic Human Rights Campaign. 2001. *See* www.kwru.org/updates/12–11–00.

Reichert, E. and R. McCormick. 1996. Welfare reform—Self-sufficiency is elusive goal. *Southern Illinosan* (December 3): A6.

——. 1997. Different approaches to child welfare: United States and Germany. *Journal of Law and Social Work* 7.1: 17–33.

——. 1998. U.S. welfare law violates human rights of immigrants. *Migration World* 26.3: 15–18.

Wood, D. 2002. "Living wage" laws gain momentum across U.S. *Christian Science Monitor* (March 15): 1 and 4.

Zucchino, D. 2001. Streetfighting woman: The activist issue. *Ms. Magazine* 11.3 (April–May): 62–67.

5

Vulnerable Groups

Women

Look at the World Through Women's Eyes
—NGO Forum on Women (4th UN World Conference on Women,
Beijing, China, 1995)

The Universal Declaration on Human Rights, the International Covenant on Civil and Political Rights and the Optional Protocol to that covenant, and the International Covenant on Economic, Social, and Cultural Rights each address many fundamental aspects of the human existence. Together, these documents constitute the International Bill of Human Rights. However, human rights never remain static and continually require new interpretations, more detailed explanations, better enforcement, and greater promotion. For those reasons, numerous other declarations, resolutions, covenants, treaties, and other documents emanate from the United Nations and other groups devoted to human rights. In particular, human rights groups have focused on so-called vulnerable populations—that is, segments of society that require extra attention in the area of human rights.

WHAT IS A VULNERABLE GROUP?

Before analyzing human rights documents dedicated to particular segments of the population, we should consider the key question as to why a
need even exists for these documents? The general response is that certain
population groups have traditionally encountered discrimination on the
basis of gender, national origin, ethnicity, age, or other classification. In addition, some of these population groups (such as children) require special
attention to avoid potential exploitation.

In virtually all societies, women encounter an array of obstacles in obtaining many of the same rights and benefits as those held by men. For instance, those who hold political and economic power are more likely to be
male than female. The male domination of power thus tends to omit a
woman's perspective on particular issues, which can often lead to discriminatory results.

Alongside women as a vulnerable group, children also receive special attention in the area of human rights (although not for the same reasons). The
maturity level of children cannot match that of their elders, who must then
be vigilant to protect their rights. Less fragile than children, adults generally
have no need for special protection against parental or other mistreatment,
as children do.

Other vulnerable groups include cultural, ethnic, and religious minorities
that reside within the mainstream of their societies. The Walloons in Belgium, the Catholics in Northern Ireland, the Gypsies in Europe, Native
Americans and African-Americans in the United States, the Kosovars in Ser-
bia, and the Palestinians in Israel (and other countries) are all examples of
vulnerable groups.

The realities of age and disabilities also create vulnerable groups. The older
an individual is, the more likely discrimination and exploitation may occur
because of frailties associated with advanced age. An individual with a physical or mental disability also needs special protection where the disability inhibits activities readily available to those without the particular disability.

Certainly governments are aware of this increased likelihood of oppression or exploitation and enact laws that focus on vulnerable groups. In the
United States, federal and state laws prohibit discrimination in connection
with employment, real estate transactions, access to financial credit, and
availability of public accommodations on the basis of gender, national ori-

GENDER DISEMPOWERMENT

Although women and children comprise 75 percent of the world's population, they bear the brunt of human rights violation and endure some of the worst atrocities committed by men. In their most horrifying form, the litany of injustice includes various forms of physical, psycho-social, and sexual abuse, exploitation, and homelessness as a result of wars precipitated by ill-informed decisions and the practices of patriarchy. (Kawewe 2001:471)

The above passage should sound the alarm for any social worker advocating social justice and human rights. The disproportionate number of human rights violations with regard to women and children in comparison to men raises serious issues about global society. Human rights documents, supposedly aimed at all segments of society, irrespective of gender, appear ineffective in the face of such stark circumstances.

Part of the difficulty in overcoming human rights violations against women and children lies in the "historical practice of emphasizing individual civil and political rights of men" (471). The "systemic diminution of opportunities for women to exercise power is translated into socioeconomic and political disenfranchisement at the micro-, mezzo-, and macro-levels of society" (472).

Of course, simply installing women into positions of power does not guarantee women's rights either. "The social work profession has to become aware of that fact, so as not just to promote women as political tokens" (481). The process required to overcome gender or any other type of discrimination must address structural, as well as individual, obstacles.

Because women tend to encounter a particular set of discriminatory structures, human rights groups have specifically focused on women. Several international documents and treaties now exist on eliminating discrimination against women. However, these documents are only a start in recognizing women's rights as human rights. The real key to progress is the empowerment of women in all areas of society: political, economic, social, and cultural.

gin, age, disability, and other classifications (e.g., Illinois Human Rights Act 1992). These laws aim to protect vulnerable groups in situations most likely to impact on significant events encountered by individuals who are part of the vulnerable group. Children receive special protection in laws prohibiting abuse and neglect.

However, while many countries have, like the United States, enacted laws addressing human rights issues affecting vulnerable groups, many of those laws address only certain situations and do not provide a sufficiently broad and coherent approach to human rights of vulnerable groups. For example, laws prohibiting discrimination against gender and other vulnerable classifications often do not apply to small employers or private clubs (Illinois Human Rights Act 1992). This exclusion allows many acts of discrimination to continue without consequence. Even when laws prohibiting discrimination apply, filing complaints can be time-consuming and cumbersome, and are often beyond the complainant's expertise. Further, large companies typically have the resources to hire legal professionals and will often go to considerable expense in contriving responses to allegations of discrimination. In other words, charges of discrimination not only frequently do *not* prompt action to change unlawful practices but can instead *promote* action to defend and uphold current practices. Occasionally, a law firm might undertake a class action case against a mighty icon of corporate enterprise on behalf of a large group of plaintiffs, but few individuals have the necessary resources with which to battle large corporations. As Richard Grossman, a historian on corporations, law, and democracy has stated: "There's a corporate class that has enormous wealth, and the power of law behind it, and it dominates the way issues are framed. I mean, is it really true that the majority of the American people over the last twenty-five years didn't want a major transition in energy to move to efficiency and solar, didn't want universal health care, but wanted pig genes in fish?" (Conniff 2002:34).

To counter existing power structures, particularly those relevant to vulnerable populations, a different way of approaching discrimination and other violations of the human existence must be established. Human rights principles provide a means with which to alter the overall structures that allow discrimination and other violations. Unfortunately, laws can sometimes harden attitudes if compliance with those laws requires significant economic and political change. Instead of always relying on laws to assist vulnerable populations, attention should also be directed toward the mind-

Many states have formed agencies that investigate violations of "human rights." For instance, in Illinois a state agency exists that calls itself the Illinois Department of Human Rights. That agency investigates certain complaints relating to alleged discrimination on the basis of age, gender, national origin, disability, and religion. Discrimination on the basis of sexual orientation is not included within the type of complaints the department investigates.

To claim discrimination, a "complainant" must allege facts indicating that some action, usually by an employer, resulted in the loss of a benefit. The complainant must also present facts that show the action taken was based on the complainant's age, gender, national origin, disability, or religion.

The authority of the Illinois Department of Human Rights to investigate complaints of discrimination is limited to employers that have at least ten employees, thus exempting small employers from "human rights" complaints. In addition to complaints of discrimination involving employers, the department may investigate complaints against public facilities and landlords. Private clubs are also exempt from investigation.

The effectiveness of the Illinois Department of Human Rights in preventing discrimination may be minimal. Large companies often make it extremely difficult to pursue these complaints unless the complainant has a lawyer (which costs money). Investigators may also demand hard facts as to the alleged discrimination, which generally is subtle in nature and not obvious.

An unintended result of the department's activities may actually be to entrench discriminatory practices, especially where complaints are dismissed or settled out of court with no real consequence to the (alleged) offender. Unless employers and other entities find it costly to discriminate, most likely discriminatory practices will continue. Unfortunately, government agencies assigned to investigate discriminatory practices may not have sufficient resources to actually do the job they are required to do. In addition, complainants may also find it easier to abandon their cause once they discover how difficult (and expensive) it can be to prove discrimination and to persevere against their employer. Of course, anyone who files a complaint of discrimination must be prepared to face the wrath of their employer (and perhaps even of coworkers), although retaliation by an employer is prohibited.

The bottom line for those who wish to file complaints of discrimination is to be prepared for quite a struggle. Discrimination in the eyes of the complainant is simply not the same as discrimination in the eyes of the alleged offender.

set of those who control societal institutions. Regardless of circumstances, every individual is entitled to an existence that encompasses human rights. The starting point for any government, corporation, school, religious group, and other entity should be to focus on satisfying human rights, without feeling coerced into doing this. This initial step becomes particularly relevant when involvement with vulnerable populations occurs.

While the International Bill of Human Rights frequently addresses these vulnerable groups, additional human rights documents provide greater context and detail concerning these groups. This chapter focuses on women as a vulnerable group and on those human rights documents that specifically address women. The next chapter will consider additional vulnerable groups and the specific human rights documents relating to those groups.

WOMEN AS A VULNERABLE GROUP

A primary goal of the social work profession is to work with vulnerable populations. Perhaps the largest of the vulnerable populations encompasses women and the girl child. Historically, this population has encountered all types of discriminatory abuse.

Women perform two-thirds of the world's work but earn only one-tenth of all income and own less than one-tenth of the world's property (Human Rights Watch World Report 2001:456). Two-thirds of the 110 million children in the world who are not receiving an education are girls (456). Women and children in female-headed households comprise almost all the population in poverty (Sidel 1996). Women constitute the majority of the world's poor as defined by income level (Human Rights Watch World Report 2001). Seventy percent of the world's 1.3 billion people living in poverty are women (456). The number of rural women living in absolute poverty (i.e., life-threatening poverty) has risen by 50 percent over the last two decades as opposed to 30 percent for men (456). Because of their greater incidence of poverty, women do not always receive adequate health care. Socioeconomic factors, as well as chance genetic inheritance and geographical availability of nutritional resources, determine an individual's health status. Relatively affluent people and those content with their lives enjoy better health status than impoverished—and oppressed—people who suffer a poor self-image in addition to the disrespect they may encounter in their own communities.

Cheri Honkala is a woman with a mission. On the first day of the Republican National Convention in July 2000, Honkala was determined to rally hundreds of people to march for "economic human rights" (Zucchino 2001:62). The police wanted to stop Honkala and the marchers from coming close to the location of the convention, in the heart of Philadelphia. However, Honkala and her group prevailed, with the police forced to lead the marchers to a point only two blocks from the convention hall. "If they can make accommodations for all the Republicans coming into town, they can take a few hours and make accommodations for poor people," said Honkala (62).

Honkala is founder of the Kensington Welfare Rights Union, which insists that the poor and dispossessed be treated with respect and dignity. Honkala's tactics are much more aggressive than what some might like—housing takeovers, office sit-ins, picketing of bureaucrats' homes—all fit into the methods used by Honkala to get her point across: poverty and homelessness in the United States are simply unacceptable (64).

Today, women remain economically disadvantaged in most countries, which makes them both vulnerable to violence and unable to escape violence (Human Rights Watch World Report 2001). The correlation between gender and poverty is a problem for developed countries as well as developing countries.

WOMEN'S SUBORDINATION AND EXCLUSION

In societies around the world, female-gendered status is viewed as inferior and subordinate to male-gendered status (Bunch 1991). Societies have modeled their gender-role expectations on these assumptions of the "natural order" of humankind. Historic social structures reflect this gender difference of male dominance and female subordination, including

- the organization and conduct of warfare;
- the hierarchical ordering of influential religious institutions;

- attribution of political power;
- authority of the judiciary;
- influences that shape the content of the law (Bunch 1991).

In most, if not all, societies, women assume inferior, servile social roles. The historic subordination, silencing, and imposed inferiority of women is not simply a feature of society but a condition of society (Cook 1995). Legal precepts traditionally exclude women from centers of male-gendered power, including legislatures, military institutions, religious orders, universities, medicine, and law. In social work, although women constitute the majority of social workers, men hold the vast majority of leadership positions in teaching social work (Bricker-Jenkins, Hooyman, and Gottlieb 1991).

However, while women can readily understand their lack of power in relation to men, women also encounter diversity of power within their own gender. For instance, a white, heterosexual, and married upper-class woman possesses greater privileges in society than a lesbian African-American woman with limited income. The white woman obviously has many more doors open to her in terms of housing, education, esteem within the community, and other opportunities. Such imbalance of power does not occur simply at the individual level; society, government, religious institutions, and other forces maintain this imbalance, which is frequently directed against particular groups.

A woman's access to resources, work, housing, education, government benefits, and many other advantages often determines the level of power she possesses. For that reason, when considering the application of human rights, social workers must always acknowledge how differences in power among and between groups can result in discrimination and inequality.

Women throughout the world share many common experiences of violations of their rights. A human rights perspective helps to illuminate the complicated relationship between gender and other aspects of identity such as race, class, religion, age, sexual orientation, disability, culture, or immigrant status. The types of discrimination and violence against women and girls are usually shaped by how gender interfaces with those aspects of identity (Bunch and Frost 1997). The absence of women in public office and decision-making positions may indicate cultural discrimination. The norms of a society may dictate that women do not belong in those positions. Class distinctions may also determine whether a girl child has access to health care

LIFTING THE VEIL ON WOMEN'S SUBJUGATION

Imagine spending five years without ever feeling the warm glow of the sun on your face. Five years in which your only view of the outside world is filtered through a mesh rectangle over your eyes. Five years cocooned, head to toe, in yards of hot, scratchy fabric that makes you look like a whaling tent—a faceless, shapeless being robbed of your individuality and public identity.

Then imagine the unexpected pleasure two weeks ago, of suddenly being able to take off that imprisoning garment and experience the world as you once did, unencumbered. Your oppressors have fallen from power and you are free.

No wonder new photos coming out of Kabul in the past two weeks will rank among the most joyous journalistic images of 2001. They show the strong, proud faces of elated Afghan women, no longer under the cruel thumb of the Taliban, emancipated from the often-hated burqas. Last week the women walked freely, savoring their right to leave the house without a male relative, to shop, attend school, even work outside the home again. Before the Taliban rule, women accounted for 70 percent of teachers in Afghanistan and half of all government workers.

The burqua and the laws imposed by Taliban rule represent the most extreme forms of repression against women in modern memory. They also serve as reminders of other ways, large and small, obvious and subtle, in which clothing and other practices have shackled the female form and imprisoned women's spirits.

Burqas can take many symbolic forms depending on the area and culture.

Think of the ancient custom of foot-binding in China. Beginning in the 10th century, parents compressed the feet of daughters in thigh bandages so their feet would not exceed four inches. Tiny feet suggested that the woman's family was so wealthy that she did not need to work. The painful practice hobbled women. It severely restricted their mobility and insured their dependence on men. The government made foot-binding illegal in 1911.

Today, women can hobble their own feet by choice, in milder ways. Stiletto heels, first popular in the 1950s, fell from favor with the rise of feminism. This year stilettos are back, thinner and higher than ever. So are narrow, pointed toes.

Another form of fashion-imposed bondage involves the corset. For centuries women's desire for an hourglass figure kept many tightly bound. As a 19th-century publication called *The Englishwoman's Domestic Magazine*

(continued)

wrote, "If you want a girl to grow up gently and womanly in her ways and feelings, lace her tight."

Letter writers to the magazine used words as "suffering," "torture," "pain," "agony," and "discipline" to describe this type of armor.

Today most women no longer rely on whalebone stays and laces to create a willowy figure. Instead, they count calories and work out at the gym. Taken to an obsessive extreme, the latter solution, encouraged by media images of slimness, can be more punishing and dangerous to woman's well-being then the former.

One of the most extreme methods of subjugating women is surgical—female genital mutilation. This cultural practice, still common in parts of Africa, is usually performed on girls before puberty—as many as 6,000 a day worldwide, by one estimate. It can cause a host of reproductive problems and even lead to death.

There are many ways to keep women "in their place."

As Afghan women begin rebuilding their lives and educating their daughters, the world will be watching and cheering their transformation. Burqas may disappear. But they remain an important symbol of the ways in which those who care about women must continue to speak out on behalf of their rights and freedoms. The burqa and everything it represents must not happen again somewhere else. (Gardner 2001:14)

or education. While the particular issue concerning women's rights might vary from country to country, the theme remains the same: women and the girl child have less value than men.

The notion that human rights are universal and belong to all people is centrally connected to principles of equality. Everyone, everywhere, is born with the same human rights, although she should have the same opportunities to enjoy those rights. In a human rights context, equality does not necessarily mean treating everyone in the same manner. When people are in unequal situations, treating them in the same manner invariably perpetuates, rather than eradicates, injustices (van Wormer 2001). Women often require different treatment than men in order to enjoy the same rights. For example, to enjoy the human right to work, women may require child care and recognition of the work they typically do in the home. A woman's right to work would then require measures to balance the unequal situations between men and women. Emphasis on the role of a man in raising children and doing work at home could help women achieve this human right. Merely enacting a law stating that women have the same right to a job as a man does little in helping women to exercise their human right to work. Consequently, human rights are not gender neutral. In addressing violations of human rights against women, social workers must acknowledge the unequal positions of women and men in society and how this situation has become the cultural norm.

WOMEN'S RIGHTS ARE HUMAN RIGHTS

The Universal Declaration of Human Rights does not contain any provisions specific to women. The language of the declaration refers to "man" and uses the pronoun "he" when referring to individuals. However, during the three years in which representatives of countries drafted the Universal Declaration, drafters actively exchanged thoughts about women and the rights of women (Morsink 1999). Although the declaration introduced innovative and progressive rights for everyone, the articulation of those rights reflects a male-dominated world by incorporating generally male perceptions and priorities. After adoption of the Universal Declaration in 1948, central concerns about the male focus persisted. The concept of human rights had not been expanded sufficiently to account for the social, economic, cultural, and political circumstances in which a woman's identity is shaped and experienced (Human Rights Watch World Report 2001:455). Essentially, the failure of human rights documents and principles to sufficiently highlight the equal status of women to men led to a need to specifically recognize that "women's rights are human rights."

> Creating an awareness of women's rights as human rights within mainstream human rights organizations, as well as within the international human rights system has not been easy. Existing human rights concepts, language, and practice are fundamentally flawed by male-bias.
>
> There are disproportionate numbers of men involved in human rights work at international, inter-governmental, governmental, and nongovernmental lev-

els. Much innovative work needs to be done in order to make human rights texts and mandates truly sensitive to the specificity of violations of women's human rights, and to create space inside and outside the systems for women to actively participate in shaping the human rights agenda for the future. (Whrnet 2001)

The movement to promote women's rights as human rights began in the years following the Universal Declaration. In 1966 the United Nations adopted two international covenants that gave more force to human rights as specified in the declaration: the International Covenant on Civil and Political Rights and the International Covenant on Economic, Social, and Cultural Rights. However, these documents did not highlight the pressing need to address women's rights as human rights. Countries ratifying those treaties signified a greater commitment to human rights, at least on paper. However, the specific recognition of a woman's entitlement to human rights did not yet appear.

For the first time, in 1975, the United Nations held a World Conference on Women in Mexico City (United Nations 1976). At this conference, those attending linked the oppression of women to their inequality. Leaders at the conference also urged governments to eliminate violence against women (Reichert 1998). To improve the status of women, leaders acknowledged that much needed to be accomplished. Therefore, the UN proclaimed the next ten years as the Decade of Women (Reichert 1998).

Five years after its first world conference on women, the UN in 1980 held its 2nd United Nations World Conference on Women in Copenhagen, Denmark (Reichert 1998). At this conference, delegates from the UN endorsed the Convention on the Elimination of All Forms of Discrimination Against Women (CEDAW) (United Nations 1980). This convention aimed to place women on an equal footing with men within any field, including political, economic, social, and cultural arenas. Social workers have called this convention a Magna Carta for the human rights of women (Wetzel 1993). The convention establishes a bill of rights for women with internationally accepted standards for achieving equal rights (Wetzel 1993) Under provisions within CEDAW, thirty days after the twentieth country deposited its instrument of ratification or accession to the treaty, CEDAW would come into force. On September 3, 1981, CEDAW entered into force. At least 170 States have either ratified or acceded to the treaty.

CONVENTION ON THE ELIMINATION OF ALL FORMS OF DISCRIMINATION AGAINST WOMEN

This convention, or CEDAW, contains six parts and thirty articles, with a clear focus on elevating the status of women to that of men in the area of human rights. In CEDAW's opening statements, States ratifying or acceding to this convention acknowledge that the Universal Declaration of Human Rights and subsequent international covenants all aim to eliminate discrimination on the basis of gender. However, concerns exist that "despite these various instruments extensive discrimination against women continues to exist" and "in situations of poverty women have the least access to food, health, education, training, and opportunities for employment and other needs." States party to CEDAW are convinced that the "full and complete development of a country, the welfare of the world, and the cause of peace require the maximum participation of women on equal terms with men in all fields." States bear in mind "the great contribution of women to the welfare of the family and to the development of society, so far not fully recognized." States also bear in mind the "social significance of maternity and the role of both parents in the family and in the upbringing of children." States are "aware that the role of women in procreation should not be a basis for discrimination but that the upbringing of children requires a sharing of responsibility between men and women and society as a whole." States are aware that "a change in the traditional role of men as well as the role of women in society and in the family is needed to achieve full equality between men and women." States party to CEDAW then agree to adopt measures required for the elimination of gender discrimination in all its "forms and manifestations."

Part I

Part I of CEDAW provides the following definition for "discrimination against women":

> Any distinction, exclusion, or restriction made on the basis of sex which has the effect or purpose of impairing or nullifying the recognition, enjoyment, or exercise by women irrespective of their marital status, on a basis of equality of men and women, of human rights and fundamental freedoms in the political, economic, social, cultural, civil, or any other field. (art. 1, para. xx)

By stating that any distinction, exclusion, or restriction having the "effect" as well as "purpose" of discriminating, this definition includes unintentional as well as intentional discrimination.

Other articles in part I require States party to CEDAW to take steps to eliminate discrimination against women in a broad range of areas. For instance, article 3 requires States to take appropriate measures in all fields, particularly the "political, social, economic, and cultural fields, to ensure the full development and advancement of women, for the purpose of guaranteeing them the exercise and enjoyment of human rights and fundamental freedoms on a basis of equality with men." One provision even requires States to take all appropriate measures to "modify the social and cultural patterns of conduct of men and women, with a view to achieving the elimination of prejudices and customary and all other practices which are based on the idea of the inferiority or the superiority of either of the sexes or on stereotyped roles for men and women" (art. 5[a]). CEDAW also requires States to suppress all "forms of traffic in women and exploitation of prostitution of women" (art. 6).

Other Provisions of CEDAW

Part II of CEDAW focuses on equality within political and public life of the country, including equality in voting and participation in formulating government policies. Part III addresses equality of men and women in the fields of education, employment, health care, and economic benefits. A special provision requires States to take into account particular difficulties experienced by rural women in areas of health, education, and other aspects of rural life (art. 14). Part IV establishes equality between men and women in civil matters, including the right to conclude contracts and administer property. Women shall also enjoy the same rights with regard to freedom of movement and choice of residence as men. States shall also eliminate discrimination in marital and other family matters, allowing women equal rights with respect to choosing a spouse, choosing a family name or profession, and owning and disposing of property.

Part V of CEDAW establishes a Committee on the Elimination of Discrimination Against Women for the purpose of considering the progress made in implementing the treaty (art. 17). States party to CEDAW must submit periodic reports on measures taken to effect provisions of CEDAW to the Secretary-General of the United Nations, for consideration by the committee (art. 18). Part VI contains procedural provisions, including a settlement procedure for resolving disputes between two or more States concerning the interpretation or application of CEDAW. However, States party to CEDAW may opt out of the settlement procedure. An Optional Protocol to CEDAW would allow individuals to submit complaints of alleged violations of rights to the committee and also allow the committee to initiate an inquiry into alleged serious violations of rights protected by CEDAW by a State party to the convention (CEDAW 1979). The UN adopted the optional protocol in 1999, with ratification or accession of only ten countries needed for the protocol to become effective.

The United States' Position on CEDAW

Most countries of the world have now ratified CEDAW, thereby obligating their governments to enforce provisions within the convention except for any reservations cited by said governments. As noted previously, a country can ratify a treaty but may single out particular provisions that it will not enforce. Generally, this expression by a government not to enforce particular provisions of a treaty consists of reservations specifically stated at the time of ratification. One notable holdout in ratifying CEDAW is the United States. While the United States has signed the treaty, the U.S. Senate must approve the document. However, Senate approval of CEDAW does not appear imminent. On International Women's Day in 2000, influential Sen. Jesse Helms (R-NC) publicly vowed never to allow the Senate to vote on CEDAW. Instead, he promised to leave the treaty in the "dustbin" for several more "decades" (Human Rights Watch World Report 2001:457). Not satisfied with simply leaving it at that, in May 2000 Senator Helms introduced a resolution calling for the Senate to actually reject CEDAW (457).

What objections do members of the U.S. Senate have against CEDAW? A ratification of the treaty (assuming the enactment of implementing legislation) would require significant changes in present laws concerning discrimination against women. For instance, present U.S. laws simply do not go so far as CEDAW in prohibiting discrimination against women. CEDAW contains many provisions that cover all types of instances where discrimination may occur. Existing laws tend to focus on discrimination in the workplace or at public facilities. Private entities oftentimes enjoy loopholes in discrim-

As of June 2002, 170 countries had ratified the Convention on the Elimination of All Forms of Discrimination Against Women. The United States does not belong to this group, even though the U.S. considers itself a world leader in human rights (*see* www.feminist.org 2001).

The United States took an active role in drafting CEDAW, with President Carter signing it on July 17, 1980, and referring it to the Senate Foreign Relations Committee in November 1980. In the summer of 1990, ten years later, the Senate Foreign Relations Committee finally held hearings on the convention. At that time, the U.S. State Department testified that it had not prepared a legal analysis of the convention to determine how it comports with U.S. law.

While several senators expressed a desire to ratify the convention, the Senate effectively stalled the convention for years. On March 8, 1999, International Women's Day, Sen. Jesse Helms, chair of the Foreign Relations Committee, stated his "deep concerns" over the increased efforts to bring CEDAW to a hearing and eventual ratification" (www.feminist.org 2001).

Even if the Senate were to ratify CEDAW, that body has placed four reservations on the convention, which state that the United States is not obligated to (1) assign women to all units of the military; (2) mandate paid maternity leave; (3) legislate equality in the private sector; and (4) ensure comparable worth, or equal pay for work of equal value. In addition, an understanding attached to the convention is that any free health services to benefit women would be determined by the states and automatically mandated by U.S. ratification of the convention. And, of course, the convention would not be "self-executing," which means that the U.S. government would have to enact specific legislation to place CEDAW into force even after ratification.

As of September 2002, the United States still had not ratified CEDAW. However, with all the qualifications placed upon the convention by the Senate, the question arises as to whether ratification would have much importance.

ination laws. CEDAW would provide no loopholes and would actually require positive efforts by government to eliminate discrimination. Existing laws generally require the victim of discrimination to take the initiative by filing a complaint, a process that can be costly and intimidating.

Unquestionably, the broad-based legal approach of CEDAW to ending discrimination against women does not always find favor among lawmakers and others. What would be the cost to businesses and agencies if they had to comply with every relevant provision of CEDAW? What would be the cost to government? What would be the cost to individuals? How could such costs be met? Of course, these are all relevant questions. Complying with several layers of government regulations against discrimination would require substantial resources. However, this cost analysis also overlooks certain key points in regard to any type of discrimination: What are the economic, political, social, and cultural costs if a society *allows* discrimination to exist, particularly against a group so numerous as women? Is the cost any less than that required to take positive steps against discrimination? If one-half of the world's citizens are unable to utilize fully their intellectual and social potential because of obstacles imposed by social or cultural norms, tremendous damage to world societies is incurred. Recognition of that fact is the basis upon which drafters of the CEDAW treaty have approached the issue of discrimination against women.

DEVELOPMENTS AFTER CEDAW

Events after CEDAW continued to highlight its goals. At the end of the "women's decade," UN leaders in 1985 held the 3rd World Conference on Women in Nairobi, Kenya. The purpose of this gathering was to appraise achievements and the current status of women. Conference delegates concluded that much still needed to be done in this area and developed strategies for improving conditions for women. The final document of the Nairobi conference, known as the Nairobi Forward-Looking Strategies for the Advancement of Women, identified areas of concern to women and children, including violence, poverty, health, and education (Reichert 1996, 1998). Some of the key points of this document state that

- Women's universal oppression and inequality are grounded in a patriarchal system that ensures the continuance of female subservience and secondary status everywhere;
- Women do two-thirds of the world's work, yet two-thirds of the world's women live in poverty. This work is usually unpaid, underpaid, and invisible. Perpetuation of women's fiscal dependency occurs despite the fact that women do almost all of the world's domestic work, plus working outside the home and growing half of the world's food;

- Women are the peacemakers, yet they have no voice in arbitration. War takes a heavy toll on them and their families as they struggle to hold them intact, in the face of physical and mental cruelty that leaves more women and children tortured, maimed, and killed than men in combat;
- Sexual exploitation of girls and women is universal, often resulting in sexual domination and abuse throughout women's lives;
- Women provide more health care (both physical and emotional) than all the world's health services combined. Women are the chief proponents of preventing illness and promoting health. Yet women enjoy fewer health care services, are likely to experience chronic exhaustion due to overwork, and are likely to be deprived emotionally and physically by their men, their families, their communities, and their governments (Wetzel 1993).
- Women are the chief educators of the family; yet women outnumber men among the world's illiterates at a ratio of three to two. Even when educated, women generally are not allowed to lead.

The Forward-Looking Strategies document also viewed domestic violence as a learned behavior that would harm future generations. Delegates urged governments to increase antiviolence services for women and to hold perpetrators of violence legally accountable.

After the third women's conference, the next major event concerning women occurred in 1992 at the UN Conference on Environment and Development held in Rio de Janeiro, Brazil. This conference recognized the role of women in sustainable development and environmental protection.

In 1993 a second World Conference on Human Rights was held in Vienna, Austria. By the time this conference convened, the notion that "women's rights are human rights" had become a central tenet of thousands of advocates all over the world. At the conference, women presented UN delegates with a petition that demanded the recognition of violence as an abuse of women's rights. Almost 500,000 individuals from 128 countries signed that petition. The participants also held an international tribune of violence, where women presented documented and moving cases of gender-based abuse. The final declaration at the Vienna conference affirmed that women's rights are human rights (Heise 1995). For the first time, many governments officially recognized women's rights as human rights (Bunch 1995). Gender-based violence and all forms of sexual harassment and exploitation, including those resulting from cultural prejudice and international trafficking, are incompatible with the dignity and worth of the human person, and must be eliminated (*Vienna Declaration* 1993). While many statements flowed from the Vienna conference, clearly the overriding significance of the conference lay in the recognition that "the human rights of women and the girl child are an inalienable, integral, and indivisible part of universal human rights," a development that took more than fifty years!

Two years later, in 1995, at the World Summit for Social Development, governments acknowledged that, to combat poverty and social disintegration, women would have to attain equality. Governments also acknowledged that poverty was a form of violence against women (United Nations 1995).

Finally, in September 1995 the much-publicized UN 4th World Conference on Women took place in Beijing. At that conference, delegates realized that many of the strategies developed ten years earlier at Nairobi to promote the status of women and children had not been effective. Violence, poverty, illiteracy, and poor health continued to affect women disproportionably. Women still occupied only a small minority of leadership positions. In the hope of accelerating progress in advancement of women's rights, delegates adopted a final document referred to as a Platform for Action (PFA), which expressly stated that women's rights are human rights. The platform addressed twelve areas of critical concern affecting the well-being of women and the girl child. In addition to violence, the platform addresses poverty, health, armed and other conflicts, human rights, education, economic participation, power-sharing and decision-making, national and international mechanisms, mass media, environment and development, and the social role and treatment of the girl child. The platform recommends measures to promote the status of the girl child, noting that the "girl child of today is the woman of tomorrow" (United Nations 1996). The platform is the most supportive official statement on women ever issued by the United Nations and reflects the sentiment that all issues are women's issues.

The platform inspires many positive developments regarding women. It reflects an extensive grassroots effort by nongovernmental organizations (NGOs) and women from all areas of the world, not simply economically developed countries. It addresses oppression of women at all societal levels and provides a comprehensive strategy for advancement of women. A major position of the platform elevates women's rights over cultural norms. However, even though the platform represents a unique and extremely important step forward for women, drawbacks to the platform exist. A primary difficulty in transforming the platform from mere words to action lies in its nonbinding legal status. No government is obligated to follow directives or strategies outlined in the platform. At times, the wording of the platform also becomes cumbersome, thereby losing clarity.

Despite its shortcomings, the platform still embodies an admirable effort to present an agenda for advancement of women in society. Along with the CEDAW, the platform holds great potential for improving the overall status of women in society.

After the Beijing conference, efforts began to realize the areas of critical concern listed in the Platform for Action. In countries where United Nations treaties and agreements carry the weight of law, women have been able to use the Platform for Action to prod their governments to repeal legislation that worked against women (Meillon and Bunch 2001:2). However, as part of the ongoing process of promoting women's rights, government representatives at the Beijing conference decided to meet again in five years to evaluate their progress toward implementing the Platform for Action. This evaluation process was known as the Beijing + 5 Review, which would end in a special session of the UN General Assembly in June 2000. A formal document to evaluate achievements and obstacles experienced by governments in trying to fulfill goals of the Platform for Action was called the "Outcomes Document" (Meillon 2001).

The Beijing + 5 Review involved a multitude of voices and perspectives. Certainly in evaluating progress made in fulfilling areas of concern listed in the PFA, the importance of action versus words became paramount. In this respect, governments were aware that they had made little progress toward fulfilling the Beijing promises and were reluctant to make more commitments (Bunch 2001:134). The assessment of women's status also became more complex with significant improvements in some areas for some women offset by economic decline and growing violence in others (Bunch 2001:134). Backlash may have entered into the reluctance of governments to pay greater attention to the Platform for Action. Political leaders may have tired of hearing how difficult women have it and acted accordingly. The aspect of "globalization" played a more significant role in the Beijing + 5 Review, with women living in less economically developed countries encountering more conflict with women living in wealthy countries. Where insufficient resources exist to even implement basic human rights, how can

While pleased that the United Nations Beijing Plus Five Conference in New York ended with 180 nations reaching consensus on a document that reaffirmed the platform approved at the 1995 4th World Conference on Women, some groups expressed disappointment with the failure to implement a stronger statement (*see* www.feminist.org, 11/06/2001:1). Nongovernmental organizations lamented the lack of "more concrete benchmarks, numerical goals, time-bound targets, indicators, and resources aimed at implementing the Beijing Platform" (1). Disagreements on progress centered on issues of abortion and sexual orientation. Some groups opposed greater access to abortion and birth control, and greater protection for gays and lesbians.

However, not all was contentious, with delegates agreeing on a statement to eradicate harmful customary or traditional practices against women, including marital rape and forced marriages. Other gains included attention to the gender aspects of various infectious diseases, women's access to health services, inheritance rights, and gender-related asylum. Delegates also directed attention toward negative impacts on women and gender differences in globalization, privatization, and economic restructuring.

the focus be on equality in the workplace or other concerns typically found in wealthy societies?

Overall, the Beijing + 5 Review reaffirmed the Platform for Action, and governments pledged to implement areas of concern in the PFA. Of course, as with any area of human rights, women's rights can be enshrined in gold-plated ink but have little meaning if the will to recognize those rights fails. Without understanding human rights and their importance, laws simply are not enough to ensure the actual recognition of human rights, especially for a vulnerable population like women.

SOCIAL WORK SYMPOSIUM ON HUMAN RIGHTS AND VIOLENCE AGAINST WOMEN

From their inception, the UN's world conferences on women were structured to include both governmental and nongovernmental groups. Parallel to each of those conferences, nongovernmental organizations have held their own forums from which to present recommendations to conference

BRACKETING OF TEXT

Drafting a document for a human rights conference requires all types of give-and-take on specific language to be used within the document. Because so many different countries and groups have an interest in the language of the document, delegates assigned the role of drafting the document generally have to walk a fine line.

During the preparatory stage of the conference, drafters of the proposed document insert square brackets around those parts of the text upon which delegates are unable to agree. Delegates to the conference pay special attention to the bracketed text in hopes that they can reach some resolution on that particular language, either before the conference or at the conference itself. Participants at the conference view bracketed parts of text as controversial statements and proposals that need particular attention. Deliberations by interested parties focus primarily on reaching consensus on the bracketed text.

An example of the extent to which bracketed text can infiltrate a human rights document concerns the Platform for Action at the 1995 World Conference on Women in Beijing. When the PFA document arrived in Beijing, approximately 40 percent of the document contained bracketed text. Brackets had been placed around all references to gender, apparently because some delegates suddenly discovered that they did not even understand what the term *gender* meant. The phrase *right to live* also created confusion or dissent. The Holy See (Vatican) instigated much of this bracketing exercise, along with several Islamic States and NGOs.

The process of linking human rights to rights and freedoms without regard to sex was nothing short of a revolution in the thinking of many participants in the Beijing conference.

delegates. The NGO Forum on Women held in conjunction with the 4th UN World Conference on Women in 1995 met in Huairou, a small city about one hour's traveling time from Beijing. The forum conveyed an atmosphere of diversity, with over 30,000 participants, mainly women, from every corner of the world.

During past UN conferences on women, no organized meeting of social workers had occurred (Reichert 1998). Yet underlying themes of the conferences addressed issues of great importance to social workers. To emphasize the importance of the social work profession in issues presented at the conference, Dr. Janice Wetzel of Adelphi University organized a Social Work Symposium on human rights and violence against women at the 1995 NGO forum. Joining Dr. Wetzel in sponsoring the symposium was the Women's Caucus of the International Association of Schools of Social Work, a nongovernmental organization having consultative status with the United Nations. This symposium represented the first organized gathering of international social workers in conjunction with a UN world conference on women (Reichert 1998). A primary goal of this symposium was to bring social workers together from all parts of the world to exchange ideas and information. The women's caucus provided social workers with information about attending the symposium.

Two hundred women and men from twenty-seven countries attended the four-hour symposium (Reichert 1998), which highlighted a human rights approach in order to counter the view that violence against women is a cultural norm. By emphasizing women's rights and human rights, participants at the symposium hoped to create a common thread among social workers in response to violence. The symposium also encouraged governments to consider cultural background when taking measures against violence. Participants divided themselves into groups based on the following themes:

- treatment of groups and individual affected by violence
- poverty as violence against women
- violence affecting female refugees and displaced women
- social action against violence
- teaching about violence and research of violence
- women who kill their batterers

Following the symposium, volunteers drafted a resolution to schools of social work and delegates attending the UN women's conference. That resolution consisted of ten elements derived from a model called the "Global Zeitgeist," a synthesis of programs initiated by women for personal, social, and economic development which have proved successful worldwide (Wetzel 1993, 1996). The ten elements originating from the symposium are as follows:

1. *Look to the women: listen to the women*: Always begin with the personal experiences of indigenous and local women, generalizing then to state,

national, and international policies so that the connections between all forms of violence become clear.

2. *Require economic self-determination*: Women must lead and define economic and development policies and programs that impact communities. Current policies leave women with a heritage of destruction in health, environment, education, livelihood, culture, and autonomy. Investment priorities must be in the human community.

3. *Free women from fear and domination*: War, dislocation, and state-sponsored violence as well as violence in the street and in the home feed the epidemic. It is a fundamental human right of all women and children to live with respect and without fear.

4. *Value all women's work*: The invisibility and undervaluing of women's work within and outside the home lead to women's status as the poorest, least educated, and most vulnerable to health problems, both physical and mental. Overwork and lack of pay impedes human progress.

5. *Place women in decision-making positions*: With women's personal development, relevant social development and action is not only possible but most appropriate and successful.

6. *Promote shared responsibilities in all forms of family and social partnerships*: Human rights include equal sharing of home care and family care. Respect for all forms of human families is basic to promoting human rights and building healthy communities.

7. *Invest in health care and education*: The prevention of women's physical and mental illness requires access to appropriate and affordable health services. Literacy, numeracy, and other forms of basic education improve women's economic status, delay pregnancies, and better educate future generations.

8. *Educate all women regarding their legal rights and other laws pertinent to them*: Include in legal education the execution of critical analyses and the development of corrective laws and policies.

9. *Promote positive perceptions of and by women*: Within the context of human rights, provide opportunities for women to share experiences, acknowledge differences, and recognize the value of diversity.

10. *Press for relevant gender-specific data collection and research*: Consider new models, such as participative action research, whereby women themselves select the issues and guide the design, analyses, and implementation of results.

> ## Examples of Women's Human Rights Advocacy
>
> **International-level advocacy strategies:**
> The worldwide initiative by women to add women's human rights to the agenda of the World Conference on Human Rights held in Vienna, Austria, in 1993.
> The effort of human rights advocates to make human rights the framework for the entire Platform for Action adopted at the Fourth World Conference on Women in Beijing, China, in 1995.
> Regional efforts to establish the Inter-American Convention on Violence Against Women.
> Campaigns to expose rape as a war crime in Bosnia and Rwanda.
> The campaign to compensate the "comfort women" who suffered systematic sexual abuse by the Japanese military during World War Two.
> Elaboration of additional Protocols on Women to the African Charter.
> **National-level advocacy strategies:**
> Efforts in Ecuador, Peru and other Latin American countries to bring national laws into conformity with the new Inter-American Convention to eliminate violence against women.

FIGURE 5.1

These ten elements provide social workers all over the world with guidance in addressing women's issues and human rights. In conjunction with CEDAW, the Platform for Action (United Nations 1996), and other human rights documents, the resolution can provide schools of social work a valuable tool in promoting the human rights of women.

THE IMPORTANCE OF WOMEN'S HUMAN RIGHTS TO THE SOCIAL WORK PROFESSION

In bringing a gender perspective to the understanding of rights, women have struggled to ensure that *all* human rights—civil, political, economic, social, and cultural—are equally guaranteed to women. The promotion of gender perspective has resulted in increased recognition of interdependence among all human rights (Human Rights Watch World Report 2001:456). By examining human rights through women's eyes, critical questions emerge: Who in society is a citizen? What are the criteria for consideration as a citizen? Are issues and themes accepted as "legitimate" political debate truly representative of the concerns of the majority of its citizens? These questions all relate to the recognition that women's rights are human rights.

How does the movement to recognize women's rights as human rights have relevance to the social work profession? A primary mission of the social work profession is to advocate and work on behalf of vulnerable populations. In regard to women, a human rights perspective helps to illuminate the complicated relationship between gender and other aspects of identity such as race, class, religion, age, sexual orientation, disability, culture, and refugee or migrant status.

Viewing women's and girls' lives within a human rights framework provides a new perspective. For example, the movement to draw attention to violence against women and girls emanates from article 5 of the Universal Declaration of Human Rights. The concept of human rights has helped to define and articulate women's and girls' experiences of violations, such as rape, female genital mutilation, and domestic violence. Understanding such violence in terms of human rights establishes that States and individuals are responsible for such abuse whether committed in the public or private sphere. A human rights perspective also addresses the issue of how to hold governments and individuals accountable when they are indifferent to such abuses.

A human rights framework creates a space in which the possibility for a different account of women's lives can be developed. The human rights concept gives each person the entitlement to human dignity. Human rights provide women all over the world with a common vocabulary by which they can define and articulate their specific experiences. This common vocabulary enables women to share those experiences with other women.

Of course, for human rights to have relevance to women or any vulnerable group, official acknowledgment of those rights is crucial. Knowing about human rights is only the first step to recognizing those rights. Legal processes must also integrate human rights into laws and policies and actively enforce those rights.

Despite a growing body of human rights documents acknowledging women's rights as human rights, resistance to recognizing women's rights as human rights still exists, based, in part, on the following reasons:

- Sex discrimination is too trivial or not as important as larger issues of survival that require more serious attention;
- Abuse of women, while regrettable, is a cultural, private, or individual issue and not a political matter requiring State action; and,
- While women's rights exist, those rights are not human rights per se.

As discussed in this chapter, none of these reasons is persuasive. Unless women's rights are fundamentally established as human rights, the role of women will always be secondary in overall societal structures. By promoting human rights for women, the social work profession will be working toward the fulfillment of its primary mission to assist vulnerable populations.

QUESTIONS

1. Why are women considered a vulnerable group?
2. What is meant by the phrase "women's rights are human rights?"
3. Discuss the term *gender disempowerment*.
4. Give an example of how difference of power can lead to discrimination.
5. Respond to the following statement: The Universal Declaration of Human Rights is outdated and does not reflect women's rights.
6. Discuss why human rights are not gender neutral.
7. Why has CEDAW been called the Magna Carta for women?
8. What is the significance of the 1993 World Conference on Human Rights in Vienna?
9. How does CEDAW relate to social work values?
10. What is the significance to social work of the Social Work Symposium held in Huairou during the 4th UN World Conference on Women in Beijing in 1995?
11. What does the "bracketing of a text" mean?
12. The Platform for Action is not a legally binding document. Does this lessen its importance?
13. Although the United States has not ratified CEDAW, it has signed CEDAW. Does the United States have an obligation to follow provisions of CEDAW?
14. What would it mean legally if the United States ratified CEDAW? What would it mean for the social work profession if the United States ratified CEDAW?

REFERENCES

Bricker-Jenkins, M., N. Hooyman, and N. Gottlieb, eds. 1991. *Feminist Social Work Practice in Clinical Settings*. Newbury Park, Calif.: Sage.

Bunch, C. 1991. Women's rights as human rights: Toward a re-vision of human rights. In C. Bunch and R. Carrillo, eds., *Gender Violence: A Development and*

Human Rights Issue, 3–18. New Brunswick, N.J.: Center for Women's Global Leadership.

——. 1995. Beijing backlash and the future of women's human rights. *Health and Human Rights: An International Quarterly Journal* 1.4: 449–53.

——. 2001. Taking stock: Women's human rights five years after Beijing. In Meillon and Bunch, eds., *Holding on to the Promise.*

Bunch, C. and S. Frost. 1997. Women's human rights: An introduction. *See* www.cwgl.rutgers.edu/whr.html.

Charlesworth, H. 1994. What are "women's international human rights"? In R. J. Cook, ed., *Human Rights of Women: National and International Perspectives.* Philadelphia: University of Pennsylvania Press.

Conniff, R. 2002. The *Progressive* interview: Richard Grossman. *The Progressive* (March): 32–36.

CEDAW. 1979 (1981). Convention on the Elimination of All Forms of Discrimination Against Women. G. A. Res. 34/180, U.N. GAOR, 34th Sess., Supp. No. 46 at 193, U.N. Doc. A/34/46, adopted September 3, 1981. New York: United Nations.

Convention of the Rights of the Child. 1991. New York: United Nations.

Cook, R. 1995. Gender, health, and human rights. *Health and Human Rights: An International Quarterly Journal* 1.4: 350–66.

Dominelli, L. 1997. International social development and social work. In M. C. Hokenstad and James Midgley, eds., *Issues in International Social Work: Global Challenges for a New Century.* Washington, D.C.: NASW Press.

Gardner, M. 2001. Lifting the veil on women's subjugation. *Christian Science Monitor* (November 28): 14.

Health Division of Children's Defense Fund. 2000. *See* www.npnd.org.mortality. htm.

Heise, L. 1995. Violence against women: Translating international advocacy into concrete change. *American University Law Review* 44: 1207–11.

Human Rights Watch World Report. 2001. *Events of 2000.* New York: Human Rights Watch.

Illinois Department of Children and Family Services. 2001. Fostering Illinois: Linking families together for children's futures. *Our Kids* (September) 5: 3.

Illinois Human Rights Act, 775 ILCS 5/1–101 et. seq. (1992).

Kawewe, S. 2001. The impact of gender disempowerment on the welfare of Zimbabwean women. *International Social Work* 44.4: 471–85.

Meillon, C. 2001. Beginning and ending with women's human rights. In Meillon and Bunch, eds., *Holding on to the Promise.*

Meillon, C. and C. Bunch, eds. 2001. *Holding on to the Promise: Women's Human Rights and the Beijing + 5 Review.* Rutgers, N.J.: Center for Women's Global Leadership.

Morsink, J. 1999. *The Universal Declaration of Human Rights: Origins, Drafting, and Intent.* Philadelphia: University of Pennsylvania Press.

Reichert, E. 1996. Keep on moving forward: NGO Forum on Women [4th UN World

Conference on Women], Beijing, China [1995]. *Social Development Issues* 18.1: 61–71.

——. 1998. Women's rights are human rights: A platform for action. *International Social Work* 15.3: 177–85.

Reichert E. and R. McCormick. 1997. Different approaches to child welfare: United States and Germany. *Journal of Law and Social Work* 7.1 17–33.

——. 1998. U.S. welfare law violates human rights of immigrants. *Migration World* 26: 15–18.

Sidel, R. 1996. *Keeping Women and Children Last: America's War on the Poor*. New York: Penguin Books.

United Nations. 1948. *Universal Declaration of Human Rights*. Adopted December 10, 1948. GA. Res. 217 AIII. United Nations Document a/810. New York: UN.

——. 1976. *Report of the World Conference of the International Women's Year*. Mexico City, June 19–July 1975. United Nations Publication no. E.76.IV.I (E/Conf.66/34). New York: UN.

——. 1980. *Report of the World Conference of the United Nations Decade for Women: Equality, Development, and Peace*. Copenhagen, July 14–30, 1980. United Nations Publications no. E.80.IV-3 (A/CONF. 94/35). New York: UN.

——. 1995. *World Summit for Social Development*. U.S.State Department.

——. 1996. *The Beijing Declaration and the Platform for Action*. 4th World Conference on Women, Beijing, China, September 4–15, 1995. New York: UN Department of Public information.

U.S. Department of Health and Human Services, Centers for Disease Control. 2000. Fact Sheet. *See* www.cdc.gov.nchs/releases/00facts/infantmo.htm.

Van Wormer, K. 2001. *Counseling Female Offenders and Victims: A Strengths-Restorative Approach*. New York: Springer.

Wetzel, J. 1993. *The World of Women: In Pursuit of Human Rights*. London: Macmillan.

——. 1996. On the road to Beijing: The evolution of the international women's movement. *Affilia: Journal of Women and Social Work* 11.22 (Summer): 221–36.

Whrnet (Women's human rights net). 2001. *See* www.whrnet.org.

www.feminist.org. 2001 (June 14).

Vienna Declaration and Programme of Action. 1993. 2nd World Conference on Human Rights. New York: UN Department of Public information.

Zucchino, D. 2001. Streetfighting woman: The activist issue. *Ms. Magazine* 11.3 (April–May): 62–67.

6

Vulnerable Groups

Children, Persons with Disabilities and/or HIV-AIDS, Gays and Lesbians, Older Persons, and Victims of Racism

Prejudice is a burden which confuses the past, threatens the future, and renders the present inaccessible.

—*Maya Angelou (1986:155)*

In addition to women, human rights documents address other vulnerable groups. Human rights declarations, conventions, and resolutions focus on children, persons with disabilities (including HIV-AIDS), gays and lesbians, older persons, and victims of racism. These documents parallel the primary mission of the social work profession, which aims to assist vulnerable populations.

While the above list of vulnerable groups is not complete, discussion of documents relating to those specific groups provides the social worker with a basic understanding of how human rights relate to the broader range of all vulnerable groups. In contrast to the previous chapter on women, the linking of human rights to these groups lacks a similar depth and experience. Yet the human rights of *any* vulnerable group should hold equal importance, and no group is less deserving of human rights than another.

CHILDREN AS A VULNERABLE POPULATION

Unfortunately, in today's world a vulnerable population group needing recognition beyond generic documents and principles is that of children. Perhaps more than most other groups, children need special protection because of their fragile state of development. Children are readily susceptible to abuse and neglect. Certainly in the United States and many other countries, children have occupied a special status in need of protection because of their maturing stage of development.

In the United States, individual states have created agencies with specific goals of protecting children from abuse and neglect. The Department of Children and Family Services in Illinois oversees the safety of children and views the following as a child's basic rights:

- the right to be protected against neglect, cruelty, abuse, and exploitation;
- the right to safe housing, health care, and education that prepares them for the future;
- the right to be a unique person whose individuality is protected from violation;
- the right to prepare for the responsibilities of parenthood, family life, and citizenship;
- the right to maintain relationships with people who are important to them;
- the right to a stable family;
- the right to safe, nurturing relationships intended to last a lifetime (all the above from Illinois Department of Children and Family Services 2001)

The Universal Declaration of Human Rights and other UN documents echo a similar need to protect the child. As indicated in the Declaration on the Rights of the Child, "The child, by reason of his physical and mental immaturity, needs special safeguards and care, including appropriate legal protection, before as well as after birth" (United Nations 1989). In view of this need for special protection regarding children, the United Nations drafted a Convention on the Rights of the Child.

CONVENTION ON THE RIGHTS OF THE CHILD

On November 20, 1989, the General Assembly of the United Nations adopted the Convention on the Rights of the Child (United Nations 1989).

Comprised of three parts divided into fifty-four articles, the convention specifies a number of basic rights that every child should enjoy. As with other conventions, this convention also establishes a committee to oversee progress made in fulfilling provisions of the convention. Before the convention could become effective, twenty countries had to ratify or accede to the convention. Response to the convention by the world community was overwhelmingly positive. Within less than a year after its adoption, on September 2, 1990, the required number of countries had either ratified or acceded to the convention. To date, almost every member country of the UN has ratified or acceded to the convention, with the United States being one of only a few countries that has not acceded to or ratified the convention.

Preamble

In the preamble to the Convention on the Rights of the Child, States party to the convention recognize that "in all countries in the world, there are children living in exceptionally difficult conditions, and that such children need special consideration." States duly account for the "importance of the traditions and cultural values of each people for the protection and harmonious development of the child" and further recognize the "importance of international co-operation for improving the living conditions of children in every country, in particular in the developing countries." Goals stated in the preamble indicate that governments of countries adopting the convention truly recognize the need to protect children.

Of course, as with other human rights documents, merely signing and ratifying a convention does not necessarily mean that a country will actually fulfill duties specified in the document. The hope is that a country will take human rights obligations seriously, especially when it legally commits itself to do so.

Part I

Following a common pattern of conventions or treaties dealing with human rights, the first part of the Convention on the Child specifies actual rights that apply to children. These rights cover many areas crucial to the development of a child. Some rights appear to be Western-oriented, but in general, few countries could legitimately quibble about the universality of these rights.

Under part I of the convention, a child "means every human being below the age of eighteen years unless, under the law applicable to the child, majority is attained earlier" (art. 1). This definition of "child" leaves open the possibility that a particular State may define a child as having reached adulthood before the age of 18 years. In the United States, one example of a child being treated as an adult before the age of 18 would be the prosecuting of a child under that age as an adult in serious felony cases.

States shall not discriminate against a child regardless of the child's—or his or her parents' or legal guardians'—"race, color, sex, language, religion, political or other opinion, national, ethnic, or social origin, property, disability, birth, or other status" (art. 2, para. 1). States shall take appropriate measures to ensure that the child is protected against all forms of discrimination or punishment on the basis of the status, activities, expressed opinions or beliefs of the child's parents, legal guardians, or family members" (art. 2, para. 2).

In all actions concerning children, whether undertaken by public or private social welfare institutions, courts of law, administrative authorities, or legislative bodies, the best interests of the child shall be a primary consideration (art. 3, para. 1). The convention does not define the "best interests" of a child, which leaves open all types of interpretations among States party to the convention. Generally, the term *best interests* requires the interests of the child to take priority over interests of a parent or other guardian. Also, at a minimum, States are obligated to comply with provisions specified in the convention (art. 4). In other words, the best interests of a child must be based on terms contained in the convention, as well as on local policies. With regard to economic, social, and cultural rights, States shall undertake measures to the maximum extent of their available resources and, where needed, within the framework of international cooperation (art. 4).

States shall respect the responsibilities, rights, and duties of parents, legal guardians, and, where applicable, members of the extended family or community, in the provision of rights recognized by the convention (art. 5). This provision clearly requires States not to interfere with parents or legal guardians in the raising of their children. However, this provision also requires parents and other responsible parties to carry out their responsibilities "in a manner consistent with the evolving capacities of the child." This qualification allows States to intervene when parents are not able, for whatever reason, to take care of the child.

Does abortion conflict with ensuring the survival and development of the child? This would depend on whether the life of a human being begins at conception or birth or some point in between. The convention does not address this issue, thereby leaving open the question of whether an unborn child, through a legal or other representative, could prohibit abortion as a violation of the unborn child's human rights.

States recognize that "every child has the inherent right to life" and "shall ensure to the maximum extent possible the survival and development of the child" (art. 6).

A child shall be registered immediately after birth and have the right to a name, acquire a nationality, and as far as possible, to know and be cared for by his or her parents (art. 7, para. 1). This provision imposes a duty upon parents to care for their children. Under the convention, States must also respect the right of a child to preserve his or her identity, including nationality, name, and family relations without unlawful interference (art. 8). Past examples of stripping a child of his or her identity include the forced relocation of Native American or Aboriginal children to adoptive families outside the child's birthright culture. In Australia, this practice—with its obvious purpose of ridding the country of future Aboriginal generations—existed until the 1970s.

States may separate a child from his or her parents against the will of the child only when competent authorities subject to judicial review determine that separation is necessary for the best interests of the child (art. 9, para. 1). Separation may be necessary in cases of abuse or neglect and in cases where parents live separately and a decision must be made as to the child's residence. A child separated from one or both parents has the right to maintain personal relations and direct contact with both parents on a regular basis, unless that contact is contrary to the child's best interests (art. 9, para. 3). This right to maintain contact with both parents also applies when the parents reside in different countries (art. 10, para. 2). To prevent any improper or illegal nonreturn of a child, the convention requires States to "take measures to combat the illicit transfer and non-return of children abroad" (art.

The cultural aspect of child kidnapping became prevalent with the case of U.S. citizen Betty Mahmoody, who found herself trapped in Iran with her Iranian husband, who would not allow Ms. Mahmoody to leave Iran with their daughter. The Mahmoodys had lived several years in the United States and went to Iran only to visit relatives, or so Ms. Mahmoody believed. Shortly after the couple and their daughter arrived in Iran, the husband made it clear that neither he nor the daughter would return to the United States. Eventually, Ms. Mahmoody found a way out of Iran, with her daughter (Mahmoody and Hoffer 1987). (Many readers will be familiar with this story from the 1991 film, *Not Without My Daughter*.)

The problem of children getting caught between two parents of different nationalities is not uncommon. While many of these tugs-of-war involve conflicting cultures, not all do. Germany has been notorious for dragging out child custody cases involving American and German parents, often making it next to impossible for the American parent to have access to the child.

Unfortunately, even when a court recognizes the need for a child to have contact with both parents, one of whom is not a citizen of the local court, enforcement of visitation and custody orders can become prohibitively expensive. What good is a court order that grants visitation to the foreign parent, when enforcement of that order requires all types of legal proceedings that are beyond the resources of the ordinary person? The best interests of the child do not always seem to matter when it comes to custody and visitation issues.

11, para. 1). However, what one country considers to be "illicit" may not coincide with another country's view of that term.

A child "capable of forming his or her own views" shall have the right to express those views with due weight given in accordance with the age and maturity of the child (art. 12, para. 1). This rule particularly applies with respect to any judicial or administrative proceeding affecting the child (art. 12, para. 2).

A child shall have the right to "freedom of expression," which includes the freedom to "seek, receive, and impart information and ideas of all kinds, regardless of frontiers, either orally, in writing, or in print, in the form of art,

The idea that children would turn into unmitigated monsters if the United States ratified and put into place provisions of the Convention on the Rights of the Child seems to be a prevalent objection to the treaty. Family psychologist and syndicated newspaper columnist John Rosemond presented this view of the convention in one of his columns:

> In February 1993, President Clinton signed an international treaty known as the United Nations Convention on the Rights of the Child. It extended to children a host of privileges, including freedom of association, freedom of access to information (of all sorts, without restriction), and in essence, freedom from punishment.
>
> Needless to say, the document sent me into apoplexy. Thankfully, it was immediately assigned to legislative limbo by Sen. Jesse Helms. (Rosemond 2002:D5)

Comparing actual provisions of the convention to comments by Rosemond makes it clear why negative publicity can be instrumental in determining the outcome of human rights treaties in the United States. Rosemond has a broad audience but unfortunately does not portray the child convention accurately. Yet his language is lively and easy to grasp. He is persuasive, if not correct in his judgment about the convention.

or through any other media of the child's choice" (art. 13, para. 1). A state may restrict this broad grant of freedom of expression in regard to respect of the rights or reputations of others and in regard to the protection of national security, public order, public health, or morals (art. 13, para. 2).

Under the convention, a child has the right to freedom of thought, conscience, and religion (art. 14). A child also has the right to freedom of association and peaceful assembly (art. 15). While these rights appear sufficiently broad to allow all types of mischievous activity, they are not open-ended. Reference to these rights should always include the consideration that states may protect the public order, health, and morals. Therefore, a child cannot simply do whatever he or she wants in terms of expression and association where states have reasonable policies against these actions.

A child also has the right to be free from arbitrary or unlawful interference with his or her privacy, family home, or correspondence (art. 16). The use of the qualifying terms "arbitrary" and "unlawful" restrict this provision to what is reasonable and lawful. In other words, a child does not have unrestricted privacy in the family home, which would allow the child to essentially dictate living conditions to his or her parents.

States are to encourage mass media to make available to the child all types of information, especially those aimed at the promotion of the child's social, spiritual, and moral well-being and physical and mental health (art. 17). Clearly, interpretation of these freedoms assured to the child will vary from country to country. Should a 15-year-old child be free to view violent material? Under the convention, a state could restrict this freedom by claiming the restriction necessary to protect public morals. Some states may choose to do this, while others may not.

While provisions of the convention appear to favor a child having free reign in his or development, both parents have common responsibilities for the upbringing and development of the child (art. 18, para. 1). Parents (or legal guardians) have the primary responsibility for the upbringing and development of the child, with the basic concern of parents being the best interests of the child. To assist parents with their responsibilities, states shall provide appropriate assistance to parents and shall ensure development of "institutions, facilities, and services for the care of the children," including child care (art. 18, para. 2 and 3).

States shall take all appropriate measures to protect the child from all forms of physical or mental violence, neglect, maltreatment, or exploitation, including sexual abuse, while in the care of parents, legal guardians, or caretakers (art. 19). A child temporarily or permanently deprived of his or her family environment is entitled to special protection and assistance from the State (art. 20). Many countries already have provisions relating to abuse and neglect that are similar to those within the convention. However, the level of state assistance can vary among countries (Reichert and McCormick 1997). For instance, Germany offers strong assistance in these matters through all types of laws regarding children and youths.

Within States that recognize or permit adoption of children, the convention provides guidelines to ensure that adoption proceedings take into account the best interests of the child (art. 21). With respect to intercountry adoption, the convention requires countries to ensure that the placement of a child does not result in "improper financial gain" for those involved (art. 21[d]). The convention also requires countries to take appropriate measures to protect children who are seeking refugee status (art. 22).

Children with mental or physical disabilities "should enjoy a full and decent life, in conditions, which ensure dignity, promote self-reliance, and facilitate the child's active participation in the community" (art. 23). States must provide education, training, health care services, rehabilitation services, preparation for employment, and recreation opportunities in a manner conducive to the child's achieving the fullest possible social integration and individual development (art. 23, para. 3). States shall exchange appropriate information relating to treatment of children with disabilities, with the aim of assisting countries, particularly developing countries, to improve their capabilities and skills within this area (para. 4). While the convention lists admirable goals of assisting children with disabilities, the difficulty of accomplishing these goals obviously depends upon sufficient resources, which often will be lacking. Yet countries ratifying the convention legally obligate themselves to fulfilling these goals.

Under the convention, children are entitled to adequate health care (art. 24), treatment for mental health (art. 25), social security (art. 26), adequate standard of living, including nutrition, clothing, and housing (art. 27), and primary education (art. 28).

States agree that the education of the child shall include development of the child's personality, talents, and mental and physical abilities to their fullest potential (art. 29, para. 1[a]); respect for human rights and fundamental freedoms (1[b]); development of respect for the child's parents, his or her own cultural identity, language, and values, and his or her own country and other civilizations (1[c]); preparation of the child for responsible life in a free society (1[d]); and development of respect for the natural environment (1[e]). Taking into account these educational requirements, obvious questions arise. Can a country teach its youth the superiority of a culture or the need to destroy another culture or people? Within the United States, a common idea taught to children is that the United States is the greatest country in the world. Leaving aside the fact that the United States has not signed the Convention on the Child, would this claim to superiority comply with these educational principles? Would the claim that "a holy war against Americans is acceptable under religious principles" meet these educational goals? Considering that practically every country in the world has ratified this convention, clearly laws concerning human rights have little meaning if the spirit and intent behind these laws become mired in a swamp of local emotions and politics.

A child belonging to an ethnic, religious, or linguistic minority, or a child of indigenous origin, shall be allowed to enjoy his or her own culture, to profess and practice his or her own religion, or use his or her own language (art. 30). This protection guards against children being deprived of important attributes to their development. For example, this right appears to prevent a child's parents from removing a child from an indigenous culture without the mature and knowing consent of the child. Another right apparently guaranteed under this provision is that of bilingual education. A child should be allowed to use his or her own language, which may not always be the prevalent language within a country.

A child has the right to rest and leisure, recreation, and participation in cultural and artistic life (art. 31). This right should be viewed in conjunction with age-specific activities, meaning that the activity must match the age of the child. This type of right clearly imposes challenges for countries that have few resources to devote to recreation and art.

States may not exploit children and must protect children from performing work likely to be hazardous or harmful to the child or work that interferes with the education of the child (art. 32). States must take measures to protect children from improper drug use and prevent the use of children in the illicit production and trafficking of prohibited drugs (art. 33). States undertake to protect the children from all forms of sexual exploitation and sexual abuse (art. 34). Sex trafficking of children, especially girls, is a problem worldwide and actually a common practice in some countries (Kawewe 1998). States shall take measures to prevent the abduction or sale of children for any purpose (art. 35). States shall protect the child against all other forms of exploitation prejudicial to the child's welfare (art. 36). All of these rights protecting the child seem self-evident, and few countries would disagree with any of these provisions.

No child shall be subjected to torture or other cruel, inhuman, or degrading treatment or punishment (art. 37[a]). Neither capital punishment nor life imprisonment without possibility of release shall be imposed for an offense committed by persons younger than 18 years of age (art. 37[a]). This provision causes difficulties for the United States where states impose sentences of life without parole or even the death penalty for convictions relating to offenses committed by persons younger than 18. Children in detention or "deprived of liberty" shall be separated from adults unless it is in the child's best interests not to do so (art. 37[c]). Children deprived of liberty shall have the right to maintain contact with his or her family through cor-

One of the most popular products enjoyed around the world is chocolate, much of which originates from cocoa farms in African countries. However, for years, not much attention arose as to who actually worked on those farms. Finally, in 1998 human rights groups reported that enslaved children were working on cocoa farms in the Ivory Coast and elsewhere in West Africa. A two-month investigation that began in April 2001 by a U.S. newspaper chain found that children as young as 11 were enslaved on some cocoa farms in the Ivory Coast (Knight Ridder 2001:A4).

The cocoa beans harvested by children are mixed with other beans and shipped to Europe and the United States, where they are made into chocolate and cocoa products found on grocery shelves. Other investigations have also uncovered evidence of young children laboring on the cocoa farms, with the children often forced to remain on the farms.

While outrage over this "cocoa slavery" has not led to a boycott of chocolate or cocoa beans (Levins 2001:B4), both producers and importers of the beans have taken steps to eliminate child slavery on the cocoa farms. This action demonstrates that uncovering violations of human rights and publicizing those violations can lead to positive results.

respondence and visits, unless exceptional circumstances exist to restrict this contact (art. 37[c]). Every child deprived of his or her liberty shall have the right to legal and other appropriate assistance (art. 37[d]).

States undertake to uphold and ensure respect for rules of international humanitarian law applicable to armed conflicts and relevant to the child (art. 38, para. 1). States must take all "feasible" measures to ensure that persons under 15 years of age do not directly participate in "hostilities" (art. 38, para. 2). States shall refrain from recruiting any person who has not attained the age of 15 into their armed forces (art. 38, para. 3). States shall take all feasible measures to protect children who are affected by armed conflict (art. 38, para. 4). While these provisions apply to States and their respective governments, rebel groups or nongovernmental forces have no qualms about recruiting children under 15 to fight in their conflicts. However, a State ratifying this convention has a duty to prevent this exploitation of the child. An obvious difficulty arises when the State government is fighting for its own survival, with no real power to enforce these provisions relating to children and armed conflict.

The United States encounters much criticism from European countries when it comes to capital punishment. European countries abolished executions years ago, while the United States continues to send convicted murderers to death row. In some U.S. states, this penchant for capital punishment also applies to those who commit crimes when they are juveniles or under the age of 18. Executing a person for a crime committed as a juvenile would violate article 37(*a*) of the Convention on the Rights of the Child, another reason the United States has not ratified that convention. Aside from the United States, other countries simply do not execute juveniles.

Why should juveniles not receive the death penalty? According to Ellen Marrus, a law professor in Texas, "Studies show that juveniles are still developing morally, emotionally, and intellectually at age 17, and can be more easily rehabilitated than adults" (Axtman 2001:3). Of course, for death penalty advocates, this argument holds little water. "We do not execute juveniles. We execute convicted capital murderers," says Dianne Clements, president of Justice for All, a national victims-advocate association based in Houston (3).

While twenty-three states in the United States allow the execution of juveniles, as sanctioned by the U.S. Supreme Court, clearly the norms of international law conflict with this practice. If the United States wants to apply customary international law principles against terrorism and other causes it supports, then it must also apply established international legal principles to the execution of juveniles and abolish this practice.

When a child is accused, or has been convicted, of violating a "penal law," States recognize the child's right to be treated with dignity and worth and the desirability of promoting the child's reintegration into society (art. 40, para. 1). The convention specifies a number of legal and other safeguards to ensure this right to dignity during penal proceedings (art. 40, para. 2 and 3). One of these safeguards is the presumption of innocence until proven guilty by law (article 40, para. 2[*b*][i]).

The final provision in part I of the convention notes that nothing in the convention shall affect any State laws that are more conducive to the realization of the rights of the child (art. 41). In other words, if a State has an existing law that would more likely ensure the fulfillment of a particular right of the child than provisions within the convention, the State's law should apply.

As can be seen, specific rights contained in the Convention on the Rights of the Child cover much territory. To ensure the fulfillment of those rights, States would clearly have to devote significant resources to this goal.

The above listing of substantive provisions follows the format of the convention itself. However, one criticism of part I of the Convention on the Child centers on the lack of a "conceptual model or logical sequence" in presenting the substantive rights of children (Korr, Fallon, and Brieland 1994: 333). But instead of an alleged hodgepodge, three categories actually summarize part I's provisions: entitlements, protections, and affirmative freedoms. Perceived this way, this "conceptual model" also enumerates the provisions in a developmental order. For example, under the category of entitlements, the rights of survival and development begin the list; health care, education, and social security follow. By presenting substantive provisions of the convention in different categories, students can possibly more easily grasp the actual content of the convention. In addition to introducing students to such a conceptual model, an attitude survey would measure the importance students place upon various rights (341–42). In one survey, students in Australia and the United States agreed most with the entitlement to health care and rated it most important, followed by survival and development, then parental responsibility (342).

While such a proposed conceptual model might help students better understand provisions within the convention, the model can, if not presented properly, be counterproductive to understanding the indivisibility of human rights. The conceptual model separates different human rights, possibly leading to a false impression that some rights are more important than others. This becomes especially problematic when followed by the proposed attitude survey, which actually asks students to rank the importance of rights. How can the entitlement to health care realistically be viewed as more important than the entitlement to survival or development? Yet when presented with a survey that requests a ranking of various rights, students are obviously compelled to make this type of judgment. An attitude of "less important versus more important" human rights would inevitably follow, which violates the key principle of indivisibility—that is, generally speaking, no human right is more important than another. Only after analyzing the particular circumstances of a given situation can social workers evaluate which human right might hold greater importance in that case.

Certainly, the sequence of substantive rights of the child as presented in the convention could be more logical. However, any attempt to categorize and rank those rights should always defer to indivisibility principles.

Part II

As is typical with conventions adopted by the United Nations, provisions exist in the Convention on the Rights of the Child to evaluate progress made by States party to the convention in realizing the obligations imposed by the convention. A Committee on the Rights of the Child consisting of "ten experts of high moral standing and recognized competence" in the field covered by the convention has the task of evaluating progress made by countries party to the convention (art. 43, para. 2). Every five years, States submit to the committee "reports on the measures they have adopted which give effect to the rights" under the convention and "on the progress made on the enjoyment of those rights" (art. 44, para. 1). These reports shall indicate factors and difficulties affecting fulfillment of the obligations under the convention (art. 44, para. 2). Reports shall also contain sufficient information to provide the committee with a comprehensive understanding of the implementation of the convention in the country concerned (art. 44, para. 1).

To promote effective implementation of the convention and to encourage international cooperation in the field covered by the convention, the United Nations Children's Fund and other United Nations organs may provide advice and reports to the committee (art. 45). The committee may make suggestions and recommendations based on the reports received by the States party to the convention. Those suggestions and recommendations are transmitted to the relevant State party and reported to the General Assembly of the United Nations, together with any comments from the State (art. 45[d]).

Clearly, any country ratifying the convention must make efforts to comply with its provisions. Of course, as with most United Nations conventions or treaties, enforcement rests within the individual country. If a country ratifies the convention but provides no means of legally enforcing provisions within the convention, the purpose of the convention becomes thwarted. The committee can report this noncompliance to the General Assembly with perhaps the affected country being shamed into doing better. However, no actual sanctions exist for countries that ratify the convention and then fail to enforce provisions.

Even without the ability to impose sanctions, the committee plays an important role in monitoring compliance with the terms of the convention. The establishment of this oversight at least provides a mechanism for reviewing how countries party to the convention are faring with putting into practice the rights of a child.

Part III

The final part of the Convention on the Rights of the Child concerns itself with ratification of or accession to the convention. At the time of ratification or accession, States may present "reservations" to the convention (art. 51). As previously noted, the purpose of a reservation is to allow a State the right to modify a provision or not to enforce a provision of the convention. However, any reservation incompatible with the object and purpose of the convention shall not be permitted (art. 51, para. 2). States may also propose amendments to the convention (art. 50).

Provisions in the convention on capital punishment and rights of a child to free expression undoubtedly meet opposition among U.S. politicians. The guarantee of health care to all children would also run afoul of the U.S. health care system, which does not treat health care as a right for anyone. Also, while the United States could ratify the treaty with reservations, any reservation would have to be compatible with the object and purpose of the convention. A reservation to guaranteeing health care to all children would most likely not be permitted.

Another factor likely inhibiting the United States from embracing the convention lies within the existing legal framework concerning children in the United States. U.S. states generally enact their own laws regarding children and are not under the thumb of the federal government. If the United States ratified the Convention on the Rights of the Child, the federal government would have to enact laws to ensure that each state complied with terms of the convention. In many States, laws affecting children already tend to be federal or uniform throughout the country (e.g., Australia, Germany). Undoubtedly, the U.S. federal government is reluctant to introduce a new set of laws that the states must then follow.

Yet the United States would still have much to gain by ratifying the Convention on the Child. At a minimum, government would have to pay more attention to children and their needs. While certainly the economic and social status of children in the United States is better than in many countries, among similarly situated countries the United States does not fare so well. The poverty and infant mortality rate of children in the United States is much higher than in other industrialized countries. Indeed, the infant mortality rate, meaning the death of children in the first year of their lives, is higher in the United States than in any other industrialized country (Health Division of the Children's Defense Fund 2000). And within the United States itself, disparity in infant mortality rates exists among racial groups, with African-American infants suffering a mortality rate more than twice that of non-Hispanic whites (U.S. Department of Health and Human Services 2000).

In addition to the Convention on the Child, the United Nations has issued other documents relating to children. In December 1986 the General Assembly of the United Nations adopted a declaration on foster placement and adoption proceedings involving children (United Nations 1986). This declaration states concern at the "large number of children who are abandoned or become orphans owing to violence, internal disturbance, armed conflicts, natural disasters, economic crises, or social problems" (preamble). Conscious of the need to "proclaim universal principles to be taken into account in cases where procedures are instituted relating to foster placement or adoption of a child, either nationally or internationally," the declaration lists principles to be followed in foster placement or adoption. The declaration makes it clear, though, that not all societies culturally accept foster placement or adoption. Various valuable alternative institutions do exist, such as the *kafalah* of Islamic law, which provide substitute care for children who cannot be cared for by their own parents. The declaration does not impose foster care and adoption on those cultures with alternative institutions.

Some specific provisions in the declaration follow.

- In placing a child outside the care of the child's own parents, the best interests of the child, particularly his or her need for affection and right to security and continuing care, should be the paramount consideration. (Article 5)
- Persons responsible for foster placement or adoption procedures should have professional or other appropriate training. (Article 6)
- Foster family care, though temporary in nature, may continue, if necessary until adulthood, but should not preclude either prior return to the child's own parents or adoption. (Article 11)
- In considering possible adoption placements, persons responsible for place-

ments should select the most appropriate environment for the child. (Article 14)

- The relationship between the child to be adopted and the prospective adoptive parents should be observed by child welfare agencies or services prior to the adoption. Legislation should ensure that the child is recognized in law as a member of the adoptive family and enjoys all rights relating to that relationship. (Article 16)
- Intercountry adoption may be considered when agencies cannot find a suitable foster care, adoptive, or other custodial relationship in the child's country of origin. (Article 17)
- Governments should establish policy, legislation, and effective supervision for the protection of children involved in intercountry adoption. (Article 18)
- In intercountry adoption, placements should be made through competent authorities or agencies with application of safeguards and standards equivalent to those existing in respect of national adoption. In no case should the placement result in improper financial gain for those involved in it. (Article 20)
- Where the nationality of the child differs from that of the prospective adoptive parents, all due weight shall be given to both the law of the State of which the child is a national and the law of the State of which the prospective adoptive parents are nationals. Due regard shall be given to the child's cultural and religious background and interests. (Article 24)

Certainly children whose parents are unable to care for them are entitled to special protection through laws and policies. While countries can easily ignore UN declarations, at least those declarations set a tone and provide guidance as to a universal standard. Often declarations address issues that a particular country may not have been aware of without the enormous international input that goes into UN declarations. For this reason alone, UN declarations on children have importance.

The social work profession in the United States has a historic commitment to child protection through comprehensive efforts to ensure the safety and healthy development of children (NASW 2000b:30). To promote these efforts, the profession supports these principles:

- Public and private agencies and systems that serve children and families should work collaboratively to maximize their resources and effectiveness in preventing child abuse and neglect.

- A comprehensive approach to the prevention of child abuse and neglect should include increased public awareness and availability of family support services, parenting education, and training for staff in the identification of risk factors for children and families. Community-based services to enhance and support healthy family life include day care, recreation and leisure activities, parent education, counseling, case management, job training, health and mental health services, and adequate financial support for families.
- Social work education and training should emphasize effective treatment for victims of child abuse and neglect, the psychological impact of trauma on a child's development, the specialized treatment needs of abused children, family-focused intervention, and community-based approaches toward prevention.
- Children are generally protected best by strengthening the child's family and kinship network.
- Services must recognize and address the special needs of vulnerable populations such as people with disabilities and very young children.

While many of these principles can also be found within the UN Convention on the Rights of the Child, policy statements by NASW do not specifically refer to the convention. In some respects, the convention goes further in providing children with various protections and rights, which could be viewed as going beyond the actual needs of a child.

PERSONS WITH DISABILITIES

Another vulnerable group that has received specific protection in the area of human rights is that of persons with disabilities, including mental illness. In 1975 the General Assembly of the United Nations adopted a Declaration on the Rights of Disabled Persons (United Nations 1975). Like many older documents from the United Nations, that declaration contains language that might now be frowned upon. For instance, some social workers no longer consider it correct to classify an individual as "disabled." Instead, they consider the correct terminology to be "a person with a disability." After all, it is not the person who is disabled. The person as a whole is not defined by disability. However, this contemporary view also has its detractors.

Some academics see disability as a social construct rather than a condition that is located with an individual (Gibson and DePoy 2002:155). The individual is disabled by a socially created set of circumstances and has the right to declare or define himself or herself as disabled by an environment rather than living with a disability. In other words, the social environment plays a large role in determining disability, not the individual. Consider the following example. Is a physical deficiency of nearsightedness any less of a hindrance to getting around than a physical inability to walk? Both conditions require corrective measures to overcome. Yet unless an individual is almost blind, U.S. society does not tend to classify the nearsighted individual as one with a disability, while the person unable to walk clearly has a disability. This social constructionist view determines whether a person is disabled.

In any case, for human rights purposes, it matters little whether we view disabilities as located with the individual or a social construct. This book takes the generally accepted contemporary view, which addresses a defined disability as connected to the individual. This focus centers on the disability and not some socially generalized imperfection of the individual.

Nonetheless, the 1975 declaration on persons with disabilities called needed attention to this vulnerable group. The declaration recognized the necessity of preventing physical and mental disabilities and of assisting persons with disabilities to develop their abilities in the most "varied fields of activities and of promoting their integration as far as possible in normal life" (United Nations 1975). Also aware that certain countries, at their present stage of development, could devote only limited efforts to that end, the declaration called for national and international action to ensure the protection of rights for persons with disabilities (United Nations 1975).

The declaration defines a person with a disability as "any person unable to ensure by himself or herself, wholly or partly, the necessities of a normal individual and/or social life, as a result of deficiency, either congenital or not, in his or her physical or mental capabilities" (para. 1). Specific provisions in the declaration for persons with disabilities include:

- "Inherent right to respect for their human dignity" (para. 3). Regardless of the seriousness of their disabilities, persons with disabilities have the same "fundamental rights as their fellow-citizens of the same age, which implies first and foremost the right to enjoy a decent life."
- Entitlement to measures designed to enable them to become as self-reliant as possible (para. 5).

- Right to medical, psychological, and functional treatment, including prosthetic and orthetic appliances (para. 6).
- Right to medical and social rehabilitation, education, vocational training and rehabilitation, counseling, placement services, and other services to assist in social integration (para. 6).
- Right to economic and social security and a decent level of living. People with disabilities have the right to secure and retain employment or to engage in a useful, productive, and remunerative occupation and to join trade unions (para. 7).
- Right to live with their families or with foster parents and to participate in all social, creative, or recreational activities (para. 9).
- Protection against exploitation and treatment of a discriminatory, abusive, or degrading nature (para. 10).
- Communication of rights contained in the declaration to persons with disabilities, their families, and communities (para. 13).

Many of the provisions in the declaration have become standard guidelines for policies concerning persons with disabilities. NASW advocates for the rights of people with disabilities to participate fully and equitably in society (NASW 2000e:247). These rights include the right to live independently, enjoy the rights of full societal membership, exercise self-determination, and have full participation in issues related to education, housing, transportation, work, health care, social services, and other public accommodations (247).

Other human rights documents addressing persons with disabilities include one entitled "Principles for the Protection of Persons with Mental Illness and the Improvement of Mental Care" (United Nations 1991). The General Assembly of the United Nations adopted this document in December 1991. This detailed document contains twenty-five principles concerning persons with mental illness, with an emphasis on providing guidelines for protecting the dignity and respect of persons with disabilities. Principle 1 lists the following fundamental freedoms and basic rights:

- All persons have the right to the best available mental health care, which shall be part of the health and social care system (para. 1).
- All persons with a mental illness shall be treated with humanity and respect for the inherent dignity of the human person (para. 2).

- All persons with a mental illness have the right to protection from economic, sexual, and other forms of exploitation, physical or other abuse, and degrading treatment (para. 3).
- There shall be no discrimination on the grounds of mental illness (para. 4).
- Persons with mental illness shall be provided with proper legal or other representation in matters concerning those individuals (para. 6).

Other principles (as numbered in the following) cover these specifics: guidelines for determining mental illness (4); the right to confidentiality (6); a proper standard of care (8); adequate treatment (9); rights of patients and proper conditions in regard to mental health facilities (13); admission guidelines, including involuntary admission (15 and 16); procedural safeguards (18); access to information (19); and criminal offenders (20). As with many UN declarations, the level of compliance among nations varies greatly. Political, cultural, economic, social, and other factors generally determine the degree of compliance.

As with most human rights issues, NASW has issued a detailed policy statement on mental health (NASW 2000d:226). NASW's position on mental health states that everyone residing in the United States shall be entitled to mental health care, which shall be provided in parity with treatment for other types of illnesses in all health care plans. Social workers play a key role in educating the public about mental illness as a means of fostering prevention, encouraging early identification and intervention, promoting treatment, and reducing the stigma associated with mental illness (227).

PERSONS WITH HIV-AIDS

One of the more troubling developments in the world since the early 1980s has been the spread of HIV-AIDS. This disease now afflicts all parts of the world, with particular severity in sub-Saharan Africa and regions of Asia. Persons with HIV-AIDS often encounter discrimination, especially because the disease is associated with homophobia and prostitutes.

Recognition that HIV-AIDS is now a world problem and that persons with the disease are deserving of protection came when the UN General Assembly adopted a resolution to combat AIDS in June 2001. Representatives from 189 nations participated in a historic three-day summit on racism that ended with adoption of the HIV-AIDS resolution (Swarns 2001). Drafters of the resolution walked a tightrope with some of the language within the HIV-AIDS resolution. Muslim nations had objected to initial language that named groups vulnerable to HIV-AIDS, including homosexuals and prostitutes. When Western nations "reluctantly agreed" to drop language specifically naming groups vulnerable to the disease, this answered such objections by Muslim nations. Further, instead of mentioning "men who have sex with men," the final draft of the resolution refers to "those who are at risk because of sexual practice." Prostitutes are referred to as those vulnerable to infection because of "livelihood," and prisoners as those made vulnerable through "institutional location" (Swarns 2001). With those changes, Muslim nations accepted the document.

Highlights of the HIV-AIDS resolution include the following proposals:

- By 2003, ensure national strategies and financing plans that confront stigma, silence and denial, and eliminate discrimination against people living with HIV-AIDS. These plans should incorporate partnerships with NGOs, businesses, and HIV-infected people.
- By 2003, integrate HIV-AIDS prevention, care, treatment, and support programs into the mainstream of development plans and national budgets.
- By 2003, establish national prevention targets, addressing factors leading to the spread of the epidemic, especially among groups with high infection rates.
- By 2003, develop policies to support orphans and children infected with HIV or AIDS and protect them from abuse, child trafficking, and loss of inheritance. Those policies should be implemented by 2005.
- By 2003, enact, strengthen, or enforce legislation, regulations, and other measures to eliminate all forms of discrimination against people living with HIV and AIDS. Eliminate discrimination against women and girls, including also violence, harmful traditional and customary practices, abuse, rape, battering, and trafficking.
- By 2005, strengthen the response to HIV-AIDS in the workplace and provide a supportive environment for HIV victims.
- By 2005, begin implementation of national, regional, and international strategies that facilitate access to HIV-AIDS prevention programs for migrants and mobile workers.
- By 2005, ensure that at least 90 percent of people ages 15 to 24 have access to information on the epidemic. By 2010, the figure should be at least 95 percent.
- By 2005, institute a wide range of prevention programs, aimed at encouraging

responsible sexual behavior, including abstinence and fidelity and expanded access to male and female condoms and sterile injecting equipment.

- By 2005, reduce the proportion of infants infected with HIV by 20 percent, and by 2010, 50 percent; and ensure that 80 percent of pregnant women have access to available services.

- By 2005, develop and make significant progress in implementing comprehensive care strategies required to provide access to affordable medicines, including antiretroviral drugs, diagnostics, and related technologies.

- By 2005, reach an overall target of annual expenditures of between $7 billion to $10 billion in low- and middle-income countries for care, treatment, and support for people living with HIV-AIDS.

- Support the rapid establishment of a much-needed global HIV-AIDS and health fund to finance an urgent response to the epidemic, particularly for the most severely affected countries in Africa and the Caribbean. (Neuffer 2001:B8)

The resolution to combat HIV-AIDS incorporates key concepts of human rights to assist a vulnerable group—international cooperation to provide adequate medical care while also seeking freedom from discrimination as well as freedom from violence. This use of human rights to acknowledge and address the suffering caused by a worldwide epidemic illustrates the attention that such an approach can bring to an issue.

Because HIV-AIDS has become a mainstream disease, the social work profession in the United States believes that the profession must take an active stand to mitigate the overwhelming psychological and social effects of the disease (NASW 2000a:5). This position should include efforts to mitigate the inequality of access to medical care and the lack of education and prevention in the United States and other countries (5). The profession should apply political pressure to elected officials to take action (5).

VICTIMS OF RACISM

Perhaps no violation of human dignity and human rights ranks so high as racism or racial prejudice. In November 1978 a branch of the United Nations, the United Nations Educational, Scientific, and Cultural Organization (UNESCO), adopted a Declaration on Race and Racial Prejudice (United Nations 1978). That declaration addressed the importance of acknowledging racial and cultural diversity as referenced in the preamble to UNESCO's own constitution, adopted in 1945:

The great and terrible war which has now ended was a war made possible by the denial of the democratic principles of the dignity, equality, and mutual respect of men, and by the propagation, in their place, through ignorance and prejudice, of the doctrine of the inequality of men and races.

Reference to the horrific events of World War II has continually provided a foundation for human rights principles, which had become increasingly significant by 1978 because, by that time, many new countries had come into existence through a decolonization process that found Western powers relinquishing control over their colonies in Africa and Asia. This "decolonization and other historical changes" created new opportunities for eradicating the "scourge of racism and of putting an end to its odious manifestations in all aspects of social and political life" (United Nations 1978: preamble). The 1978 declaration notes that "all human groups, whatever their composition or ethnic origin, contribute according to their own genius to the progress of the civilizations and cultures." However, "racism, racial discrimination, colonialism, and apartheid continue to afflict the world in ever-changing forms," a result of government and administrative practices "contrary to the principles of human rights." In addition, "injustice and contempt for human beings" leads to the "exclusion, humiliation, and exploitation, or to the forced assimilation, of the members of disadvantaged groups." To express "indignation" at those offenses against human dignity, UNESCO adopted the following provisions:

- All human beings belong to a single species and are descended from a common stock. They are born equal in dignity and rights and all form an integral part of humanity (United Nations 1978: art. 1, para. 1).
- All individuals and groups have the right to be different, to consider themselves as different, and to be regarded as such. However, the diversity of lifestyles and the right to be different may not, in any circumstances, serve as a pretext for racial prejudice; they may not justify any discriminatory practice, nor provide a ground for the policy of apartheid, which is the extreme form of racism (para. 2).
- Differences between achievements of the different peoples are entirely attributable to geographical, historical, political, economic, social, and cultural factors. Such differences can in no case serve as a pretext for any rank-ordered classification of nations or peoples (para. 5).

The intent behind these provisions is clear: *No race or group may elevate it-self over another.* This laudable principle is clearly easier to state than carry out. For example, what about patriotic slogans? Should Americans go around saying that their country is the greatest on earth? Does not this common expression by Americans violate the rule against using different achievements to serve as a pretext to rank their nation as "number one"?

Further provisions of the UNESCO declaration attack racial theories that promote an inherent superiority or inferiority of particular racial or ethnic groups. These theories have no "scientific foundation" and are "contrary to the moral and ethical principles of humanity" (art. 2, para. 1). Racial preju-dice, historically linked with inequalities in power and reinforced by eco-nomic and social differences between individuals and groups, has no justi-fication (art. 2, para. 3). Racial segregation and apartheid "constitute crimes against the conscience and dignity of mankind and may lead to political ten-sions and gravely endanger international peace and security" (art. 4, para. 3).

The declaration also addresses culture as a means to allow women and men to affirm that they are born equal in dignity and rights and to recog-nize that they should respect the right of all groups to their own cultural identity (art. 5, para. 1). In a controversial statement, the declaration notes that it "rests with each group to decide in complete freedom on the mainte-nance, and if appropriate, the adaptation or enrichment of the values which it regards as essential to its identity" (art. 5, para. 1). Does this mean that, for example, if a culture approves the practice of clitorectomy in young girls, other cultures should not contest this practice as cruel and degrading treat-ment? What about the practice of spouse battering? Or of infanticide? Or the death penalty? At some point, a balance between culture and human rights has to be achieved. But where do cultures draw the line between human rights violations and culturally acceptable practices that infringe upon generally accepted human rights provisions? This dilemma is more fully explored in chapter 7 under cultural relativism.

States have a responsibility to see that the educational resources of all countries are used to combat racism (art. 5. para. 2). Mass media are urged to promote understanding, tolerance, and friendship among individuals and groups within "due regard to the principles embodied in the Universal Declaration of Human Rights, particularly the principle of freedom of ex-pression" (para. 3).

The declaration also places the "prime responsibility for ensuring human rights and fundamental freedoms" for all individuals and groups onto the State (art. 6, para. 1). States should take steps to prohibit and eradicate racism and to encourage dissemination of knowledge and the findings of appropriate research on the causes and prevention of racial prejudice and racist attitudes (para. 2). These steps should include legislation where appropriate and with due regard to principles embodied in the Universal Declaration of Human Rights and the International Covenant on Civil and Political Rights (para. 2).

The UNESCO declaration makes no pretenses about merely relying upon laws to fight racial prejudice and racism. "Since laws prohibiting racial discrimination are not in themselves sufficient," States must supplement them with

- administrative machinery for the systematic investigation of instances of racial discrimination;
- acomprehensive framework of legal remedies against acts of racial discrimination;
- broadly based education and research programs designed to combat racial prejudice and racial discrimination; and
- programs of positive political, social, educational, and cultural measures calculated to promote genuine mutual respect among groups (para. 3).

Where circumstances warrant, States should undertake programs to promote the advancement of disadvantaged groups and, in the case of nationals, to ensure their effective participation in the decision-making processes of the community (para. 3).

States should also adopt laws against propaganda or practices put forward by any organization or group that are based on ideas or theories referring to the alleged superiority of racial or ethnic groups or which seek to justify or encourage racial hatred and discrimination (art. 7). Individuals and groups must conform to this legislation and "use all appropriate means to help the population as a whole to understand and apply it" (art. 7). In some countries, especially the United States, this type of legislation could be ruled unconstitutional because of the limitations on States to prohibit free speech. In the United States, unless speech is aimed at producing imminent lawless action and is likely to result in that action, an individual generally can make any type of racist statement he or she wants (*Brandenburg v. Ohio*, 395 US 444 [1969]).

Individuals have duties toward fellow human beings and are obligated to promote harmony among peoples, to combat racism and racial prejudice, and to assist in eradicating racial discrimination (art. 8, para 1). Researchers should ensure that their scientific findings are objective and are not racially misinterpreted (art. 8, para. 1–2). States and individuals should pay particular attention to racial or ethnic groups that are socially or economically disadvantaged and ensure their protection against discrimination in social measures such as housing, employment, and health (art. 9, para. 2). Population groups of foreign origin within countries should be treated with dignity, and efforts should be made to facilitate their adaptation to the host environment (para. 3). Children of immigrants should have the opportunity to be taught in their mother tongue (para. 3).

In another controversial statement, the UNESCO declaration notes that existing "disequilibria" in international economic relations contribute to the exacerbation of racism and racial prejudice; all States should consequently endeavor to contribute to the restructuring of the international economy on a more equitable basis (para. 4). This particular statement appears to be aimed squarely at the United States and European countries. The haves, meaning the Western nations, contribute to racism and racial prejudice by excluding the have-nots.

Finally, international organizations are called upon to cooperate and assist in the full and complete implementation of principles set out in the declaration, thus contributing to the legitimate struggle of all men, born equal in dignity and rights, against the tyranny and oppression of racism, racial segregation, apartheid, and genocide, so that all peoples of the world may be forever delivered from these scourges (art. 10). This statement appears especially grandiose. If only organizations would follow the principles of the UNESCO declaration, a major step would be achieved in forever ridding the world of racism, segregation, apartheid, and genocide.

More than twenty years after UNESCO adopted its declaration against racism, the United Nations in September 2001 held a World Conference Against Racism to acknowledge racial prejudice in the contemporary world and the pernicious legacy of slavery (Swarns 2001). As with the original 1978 UNESCO declaration, statements issued at the world conference emphasized that nations must never forget the Holocaust. Other statements, however, encountered criticism from the United States, especially those attacking Israel and its treatment of Palestinians (Swarns 2001).

Aside from the Israel and Palestinian issues, the World Conference Against Racism issued statements about slavery and colonialism:

> We acknowledge that slavery and the slave trade, including the trans-Atlantic slave trade, were appalling tragedies in the history of humanity not only because of their abhorrent barbarism but also in terms of their magnitude, organized nature, and especially their negation of the essence of victims. . . .
>
> We also acknowledge that slavery and the slave trade are a crime against humanity and should always have been so, especially the trans-Atlantic slave trade. . . .
>
> Slavery and the slave trade are among the major sources and manifestations of racism, racial discrimination, xenophobia, and related intolerance, and that Africans and people of African descent, Asians and people of Asian descent, and indigenous peoples were victims of these acts and continue to be victims of their consequences. . . .
>
> The World Conference also recognizes that colonialism has led to racism, racial discrimination, xenophobia, and related intolerance, and that Africans and people of African descent, and people of Asian descent, and indigenous peoples were victims of colonialism and continue to be victims of its consequences. The World conference, aware of the moral obligation on the part of all concerned States, calls on these states to take appropriate and effective measures to halt and reverse the lasting consequences of those practices. (Associated Press 2001)

While the above wording may appear harsh to those who trace their roots to colonial ancestors, some Africans felt the wording did not go far enough: they demanded an explicit apology and specific promises of compensation from Europe to make up for past wrongs (Swarns 2001). The Europeans refused to apologize explicitly, fearing this might open the door to lawsuits, and in addition they refused to endorse either unconditional debt cancellation or compensatory foreign aid.

Clearly, issues of racism also resonate throughout the social work profession. Social workers everywhere will inevitably face this ugly phenomenon. The profession supports an inclusive society in which racial, ethnic, social, sexual orientation, and gender differences are valued and respected (NASW 2000f:264). NASW advocates policies aimed at reducing racism—policies focusing on education, employment, housing and community, health care and mental health services, public welfare services, social services, criminal justice, and political activity (264–65). The profession should develop guidelines to emphasize social work as a calling that strives to empower those oppressed and hampered because of racial or ethnic identification (265).

GAYS AND LESBIANS

At present, no human rights document exists that specifically addresses issues involving gays and lesbians, other than in the context of HIV-AIDS. Protection from abuse has remained elusive for lesbians, gay men, and bisexual or transgendered people, despite the premise in the Universal Declaration of Human Rights that, "All people are born free and equal in dignity and rights" (United Nations 1948). In virtually every country of the world, people suffer from discrimination based on their actual or perceived sexual orientation or gender identity (489). Sexual minorities have been persecuted in a significant number of countries and in many different ways, including application of the death penalty or long prison sentences for private sexual acts between consenting adults (489).

Even in the United States, "prejudice against lesbians, bisexual people, and gay men remains prevalent" (NASW 2000c:195). Discrimination based on sexual orientation in critical areas of employment and housing remains lawful in most jurisdictions and appears to be widespread (195). NASW takes the position that "same-gender sexual orientation should be afforded the same respect and rights as other-gender orientation. Discrimination and prejudice directed against any group are damaging to the social, emotional, and economic well-being of the affected group and of society as a whole" (197).

The irony concerning gays and lesbians is that the United Nations generally tends to be in the forefront in promoting human rights for various segments of society. However, this is not the case concerning this vulnerable group. While some countries, especially those of northern Europe, appear to actively promote rights of gays and lesbians, many countries actively persecute this vulnerable group. Religious and cultural practices in many countries frown or even condemn homosexuality. Countries often claim that homosexuality is simply against religion and culture and, therefore, not entitled to protection under any human rights theory. Certainly, though, as stated above, the Universal Declaration emphasizes that *all* people are born free and equal in dignity and rights. How, then, can a country, group, or individual justify discrimination against gays and lesbians without violating human rights? The response seems to rest upon the elevation of religion and culture over any broad-based interpretation of the Universal Declaration. This issue will undoubtedly receive further attention from human rights activists in future years.

OLDER PERSONS

A major and growing vulnerable group is that of older persons. For the year 2000, the United Nations estimated that the world had 590 million people aged 60 years or older (Whrnet 2001). Since the entire world population in 2000 was about six billion people (UNFPA 2000), the percentage of persons 60 years or older is about 10 percent. By 2025, the number of persons 60 years or older is expected to exceed one billion.

The United Nations has addressed human rights issues related to older persons in the Universal Declaration of Human Rights, the International Covenant on Civil and Political Rights, and the International Covenant on Economic, Social, and Cultural Rights. While provisions in those documents usually do not address issues specifically related to older persons, in 1999 the UN General Assembly issued a document known as "Principles for the Older Person" (United Nations 1999). This document aimed to ensure that "priority attention will be given to the situation of older persons" with reference to the following areas:

- *Independence*—Older persons should have access to adequate food, water, shelter, clothing, and health care through the provision of income, family and community support, and self-help. Older persons should have the opportunity to work and to participate in determining when to retire. Older persons should be able to reside at home for as long as possible.
- *Participation*—Older persons should remain integrated in society, participate actively in the formulation and implementation of policies that directly affect their well-being, and share their knowledge and skills with younger generations. Older persons should be able to serve as volunteers in positions appropriate to their interests and capabilities and to form associations.
- *Care*—Older persons should benefit from family and community care and have access to adequate and appropriate health care. Older persons should have access to social and legal services to enhance their autonomy, protection, and care.

When residing in any shelter, care, or treatment facility, older persons should be able to enjoy human rights and fundamental freedoms.

- *Self-fulfillment*—Older persons should be able to pursue opportunities for the full development of their potential. Older persons should have access to the educational, cultural, spiritual, and recreational resources of society.
- *Dignity*—Older persons should be able to live in dignity and security and be free of exploitation and physical or mental abuse. Older persons should be treated fairly regardless of age, gender, racial or ethnic background, disability or other status, and be valued independently of their economic contribution. (United Nations 1999)

The importance of human rights to older persons will increase as their population increases. The social work profession supports a number of policies that promote the well-being of older adults, including the promotion of health care, income resources, and government oversight of older persons (NASW 2000g:284–85).

The continual growth and importance of human rights becomes clear when considering the many areas in which the United Nations has already addressed specific human rights. The UN has frequently supported vulnerable groups through declarations and other statements. While many of these statements can appear utopist or simply unrealistic, the intent is to raise awareness of particular groups or issues. Over time, greater attention to vulnerable groups can lead to improved conditions and relations within the overall society.

QUESTIONS

1. Suppose that you are treating a sexually abused child. The child initially disclosed facts about the abuse but now says the abuse never happened. Does this situation have any connection with provisions of the Convention on the Rights of the Child?
2. Millions of children in the United States do not have health care coverage. Discuss this in regard to the Convention on the Rights of the Child?
3. Should the United States ratify the Convention on the Rights of the Child? State reasons for your position.
4. How does the Convention on the Rights of the Child view child labor in developing countries?

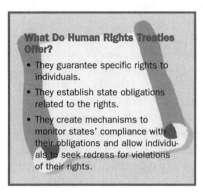

What Do Human Rights Treaties Offer?

- They guarantee specific rights to individuals.
- They establish state obligations related to the rights.
- They create mechanisms to monitor states' compliance with their obligations and allow individuals to seek redress for violations of their rights.

FIGURE 6.1

5. In your opinion, does the Convention on the Rights of the Child adequately balance the role of a child's parents in the child's upbringing with the right of the child to his or her own development?

6. How do United Nations documents on persons with disabilities expand the concept of human rights contained in the Universal Declaration of Human Rights?

7. How does the fight against HIV-AIDS fit under the umbrella of human rights?

8. If discrimination against gays and lesbians is not viewed as a violation of their human rights, do you believe that countries will devote the same attention and effort to combating this type of discrimination?

9. Is it reasonable to devote the same level of resources to those individuals over age 60 as to those individuals under age 18? Base your reasons on human rights principles.

REFERENCES

Angelou, M. 1986. *All God's Children Need Traveling Shoes*. New York: Vintage.

Associated Press. 2001. Excerpts from the documents adopted by the World Conference Against Racism. *St. Louis Post-Dispatch* (September 9): A1, 10.

Axtman, K. 2001. Teen murderer searches for fairness in court. *Christian Science Monitor* (October 22): 3.

Gibson, S. F. and E. DePoy. 2002. Theoretical approaches to disability content in social work education. *Journal of Social Work Education* 38.1: 153–65.

Health Division of the Children's Defense Fund. 2000. *See* www.npnd.org. mortality.htm.

Illinois Department of Children and Family Services. 2001. Fostering Illinois: Linking families together for children's futures. *Our Kids* (September) 5: 3.

Kawewe, S. 1998. The inability of the United Nations to reform world practices that endanger Third World children. *New Global Development: Journal of International and Comparative Social Welfare* 14: 46–62.

Knight Ridder. 2001. Chocolate makers now want to help rid cocoa farms of child slavery. *St. Louis Post-Dispatch* (July 1): A4.

Korr, S., B. Fallon, and D. Brieland. 1994. UN Convention on the Rights of the Child: Implications for social work education. *International Social Work* 37.4: 333–45.

Levins, H. 2001. Outrage over cocoa slavery hasn't led to calls for boycott. *St. Louis Post-Dispatch* (July 8): B4.

Mahmoody, B. and W. Hoffer. 1987. *Not Without My Daughter*. New York: St. Martin's.

National Association of Social Workers (NASW). 2000a. Acquired immunodeficiency syndrome and immunodeficiency virus. In *Social Work Speaks: National Association of Social Workers Policy Statements, 2000–2003*, 3–7. 5th ed. Washington, D.C.: NASW Press.

———. 2000b. Child abuse and neglect. In *Social Work Speaks*, 27–31. 5th ed. Washington, D.C.: NASW Press.

———. 2000c. Lesbian, gay, and bisexual issues. In *Social Work Speaks*, 193–204. 5th ed. Washington, D.C.: NASW Press.

———. 2000d. Mental health. In *Social Work Speaks*, 222–28. 5th ed. Washington, D.C.: NASW Press.

———. 2000e. People with disabilities. In *Social Work Speaks*, 244–50. 5th ed. Washington, D.C.: NASW Press.

———. 2000f. Racism. In *Social Work Speaks*, 261–66. 5th ed. Washington, D.C.: NASW Press.

———. 2000g. Senior health, safety, and vitality. In *Social Work Speaks*, 280–86. 5th ed. Washington, D.C.: NASW Press.

Neuffer, E. 2001. Anti-AIDS plan sets out a strategy, but "the real work only starts now." *St. Louis Post-Dispatch* (June 28):B8.

Reichert E. and R. McCormick. 1997. Different approaches to child welfare: United States and Germany. *Journal of Law and Social Work* 7.1: 17–33.

Rosemond, J. 2002. Children's rights should include hearing "no" frequently. *Southern Illinoisan* (March 17): D5.

Swarns, R. 2001. Conference calls for reversing consequences of slavery: UN meeting on racism ends in controversy. New York Times News Service in *St. Louis Post-Dispatch* (September 9): A1, A10.

UNFPA (United Nations Population Fund). 2000. *See* www.unfpa.org/swp/2000/ English/boxes_3.html (box 3).

United Nations. 1948. *Universal Declaration of Human Rights.* Adopted December 10, 1948. GA. Res. 217 AIII. United Nations Document a/810. New York: UN.

——. 1975. General Assembly. *Declaration on the Rights of Disabled Persons.* Res. 3447(XXX), December 9, 1975. *See* www.unhchr.ch/html1/menu3/b/72.htm.

——. 1978. *Declaration on Race and Racial Prejudice.* United Nations Educational, Scientific, and Cultural Organization. November 27, 1978. *See* www.unhchr.ch/html1/menu3/b/d_prejud.htm.

——. 1986. Declaration of Foster Placement and Adoption. *See* www.unhchr.ch/html.

——. 1989. UN General Assembly. *Convention on the Rights of the Child* (U.N. Document A/Res/44/23). New York: UN.

——. 1991. General Assembly. *Principles for the Protection of Persons with Mental Illness and the Improvement of Mental Health Care.* Res/46/119. December 17, 1991. *See* www.unhchr.ch/html1/menu3/b/68.htm.

——. 1999. *Principles for the Older Person. See* www.un.org.

U.S. Department of Health and Human Services, Centers for Disease Control. 2000. Fact Sheet. *See* www.cdc.gov.nchs/releases/00facts/infantmo.htm.

Whrnet (Women's human rights net). 2001. *See* www.whrnet.org.

7

International Aspects of Human Rights

The future of our earth may depend on the ability of all [of us] to identify and develop new . . . patterns of relating across difference. The old definitions have not served us, nor the earth that supports us.

—*Audre Lorde (1995:502)*

So far, the focus of the preceding chapters in this book has been on human rights and social work in the United States. Since most social workers in the United States will not be working in other countries, it may seem that knowledge about human rights in a global perspective would have little importance. However, nothing could be further from reality.

At the international level, the social work profession places great importance on the concept of human rights (Staub-Bernasconi 1998; Ife 2001). The International Federation of Social Workers (IFSW) states that "social workers respect the basic human rights of individuals and groups as expressed in the United Nations Universal Declaration of Human Rights and other international conventions derived from that Declaration" (IFSW 2000:7). The achievement of human rights for all people is a fundamental prerequisite for a caring world

(5). Social workers believe that attainment of basic human rights requires positive action by individuals, communities, and nations as well as international groups, and that it one's clear duty not to inhibit those rights (5).

The Universal Declaration of Human Rights contemplates international cooperation and knowledge-sharing as a means of realizing human rights for everyone. By recognizing the international aspect of human rights, social workers can establish connections to foreign counterparts and frequently gain important knowledge about common social work issues.

THE THIRD GENERATION OF HUMAN RIGHTS

Discussion about the international aspects of human rights principles includes what is often called the third generation of human rights. Human rights do not exist in a vacuum or simply within a particular country. When considering human rights, it matters what occurs in other countries because human rights do not stop at the borders of individual countries. What occurs in South Africa has relevance to the exercise of human rights in the United States, just as what occurs in the United States has relevance to South Africa.

Specific human rights provisions that address this interconnectedness are found in the Universal Declaration: "Everyone is entitled to a social and international order in which the rights and freedoms set forth in this Declaration can be fully realized" (art. 28). In other words, the entitlement to a social and international order in which human rights can be fully realized imposes obligations upon all member countries of the United Nations. Countries must do what they can to promote human rights and create conditions in which human rights can flourish. As a member of the United Nations, the United States has a duty to help establish international norms which allow the exercise of human rights. With its enormous economic, military, and technological strength, the United States is better positioned than most countries to help accomplish this goal.

In addition to the entitlement to a social and international order that promotes human rights, the Universal Declaration states that, "Everyone, as a member of society, has the right to social security and is entitled to realization, through national effort and international co-operation and in accordance with the organization and resources of each State, of the economic, social, and cultural rights indispensable for his dignity and the free development of his personality" (art. 22). Here, the key terms are "international co-operation" and "in accordance with the organization and resources of each State." The United States, with its greater resources, has a duty to cooperate with other countries in bringing about everyone's "social security" and "economic, social, and cultural rights indispensable" for "dignity" and "free development" of the personality.

Perhaps more than any other provision of the Universal Declaration, the right to social security and an international order in which human rights can occur poses the greatest challenges to social workers. Many social workers do not involve themselves with international issues. However, as a human rights profession, social work inevitably crosses paths with global concerns. Increasing contacts between governments and individuals of other countries have created significant areas of international responsibility for social work, as well as new challenges, by reshaping the social work environment in the following ways:

- International social forces and events—most dramatically, the movement of populations—have changed the makeup of social agency caseloads and affected domestic practice in many countries, including the United States.
- Both more and less economically developed countries now share social problems far more often than in previous decades, making mutual work and exchange increasingly desirable.
- The actions of one country—politically, economically, and socially—now affect other countries' social and economic well-being as well as the overall social health of the planet.
- Rapidly advancing technological developments in areas such as communications provide enhanced opportunities for the international sharing and exchanging of information and experiences. (Healy 2001)

The changing social work environment provides numerous opportunities for social workers to reshape the profession into a more diverse and internationally oriented field. The NASW's *Code of Ethics* specifically notes that social workers should promote conditions that encourage respect for cultural and social diversity both within the United States and "globally" (NASW 1996:6.04c). Other ethical responsibilities clearly require social

WORLDS APART

Groucho Marx said he would never join any club that would have him as a member. Governments of the world's 49 least developed countries shared that sentiment at their third U.N. conference, held last month [May 2001] in Brussels. The gathering was aimed at tackling their endemic poverty and marginalization in an increasingly prosperous global economy. It produced more talk about the poorest people in the world and little results.

Membership of the least developed countries group is dominated by sub-Saharan Africa, but stretches from Haiti to Bangladesh and Cambodia. Almost half of the total LDC population—around 300 million people—survives on less than $1 a day. The LDC reality demolishes the myth that globalization is narrowing the gap between rich and poor. Twenty years ago, the ratio of average income in least developed countries to income in the developed countries was 1 to 87. Today, it is 1 to 98, and the gap is widening.

With 11 percent of the world's population, LDCs account for 0.5 percent of world income, and an even smaller share of world trade. Ten years ago, at the last U.N. conference on LDCs, rich countries promised decisive action. However commitment has fallen shamefully short, and nowhere more so than on trade. Ministers from industrialized countries used the Brussels conference to talk up the generous preferences offered to poor-country exports in the form of lower tariff barriers. In reality, these preferences amount to a disguised form of highway robbery. While average tariffs are low, they are exceptionally high in sectors such as agriculture, textiles, and other labor-intensive manufacturing sectors where poor countries might have a competitive edge. Rich countries are three times more likely to impose high tariffs on LDC exports than they are on exports from other industrialized countries.

According to World Bank estimates, LDCs lose about $2.5 billion a year because of market access restrictions in rich countries. The worst offender is the United States. For every $1 that Bangladesh receives in American aid, it loses another $7 thanks to restrictions on textile imports. This means lower wages and reduced employment opportunities for thousands of women textile workers. Early evidence shows the Africa Growth and Opportunity Act, passed by Congress last year [2000], is working as planned—bumping up African textile exports—but not enough to threaten U.S. producers, and with the Customs Service interpreting its provisions very strictly.

The view from Europe isn't much better. Last October, the European Union trade commissioner Pascal Lamy proposed unrestricted market ac-

(continued)

cess for all LDC exports. Everything but Arms, as the proposal was dubbed, would have created new export opportunities. More important, it would have given the EU a claim to international leadership in projecting LDC interests on to the international trade agenda. Unfortunately, the Lamy proposal became the target of an ill-informed attack by the familiar coalition of big farm and agribusiness interests, led in this case by British farmers. EU trade ministers promptly postponed the opening of European agricultural markets until 2006. What started out as Everything but Arms has ended up as Everything but Farms, destroying the credibility of any EU claim to leadership in helping the poor. The response of some EU states in placing powerful vested interests before the interests of the world's poor highlights the gulf separating rhetoric and policy.

The sheer chutzpah of Europe and the United States in demanding liberalization in poor countries while subsidizing their own producers to the tune of $1 billion a day defies credibility. If anything, the record on aid and debt relief has been even less inspiring than on trade. Having promised more 10 years ago, rich countries have cut aid to LDCs by $3.5 billion, or by almost one-third. And while some LDCs are benefiting from the international debt relief initiative, saving $1 billion this year, this falls far short of what is needed.

Rich countries could have used the LDC conference to support widening the benefits of global prosperity. They could have started with a tariff bonfire, and a timetable for delivering on the commitment to increased aid and debt relief. The G8—the richest countries in the history of the world—meet in July [2001] in Italy. The poorest countries will still need more debt relief, help fighting AIDS, and a breakthrough on market access. (Offenheiser 2001:B7)

workers to extend their efforts to assist diverse populations both within and outside the United States.

The increasing relevance of international issues to the social work profession creates a need for social work students to learn more about the international aspect of the profession. Human rights play a significant role in this area of study.

RIGHT TO DEVELOPMENT

Historically, there has been strong resistance to the idea of a collective right to development—the right of people in poorer countries to a fairer share of global wealth and resources (Whrnet 2001). The right to development means that wealthier countries as well as international development agencies and financial institutions are held accountable for the impact of poverty on human rights. Increasingly, the right to development is also understood to encompass the rights of people in poor and marginalized communities within developed countries (1).

Perhaps issues concerning the right to development can be illustrated in concrete terms by this fact: On September 11, 2001, the day terrorists attacked the World Trade Center and the Pentagon, "more than 35,000 of the world's children died of starvation. A similar number have perished from hunger every day since then in developing countries" (Ford 2001:7). In an attempt to find the root causes of terrorism, wealthy countries cannot avoid examining poverty and injustice in the less developed countries. As stated by British Prime Minister Tony Blair in November 2001, "One illusion has been shattered on 11 September: that we can have the good life of the West, irrespective of the state of the rest of the world" (7). Acknowledging that a self-centered West can no longer ignore the rest of the world is at least a start in tackling human rights issues of the third generation.

Ironically, when the threat of widespread anthrax attacks occurred in the United States after the September 11 terrorist attacks, the U.S. government considered ways to economically obtain drugs to fight anthrax, including circumventing a patent on a key anthrax drug held by a German company. Yet the U.S. government had not been so magnanimous in its position on allowing poorer countries the right to obtain cheap anti–HIV-AIDS drugs. Curiously, after September 11, 2001, the "United States and its allies finally gave in to Third World demands that poor countries facing epidemics such as AIDS should be allowed to sidestep international patent law so as to make or buy cheap generic drugs" (10).

Unless the haves of the world pay more attention to the have-nots, a system of "global apartheid" may be inevitable (Booker and Minter 2001:11). Global apartheid refers to an "international system of minority rule whose attributes include: differential access to basic human rights; wealth and power structured by race and place; structural racism, embedded in global

AID TO OTHER NATIONS HELPS U.S. IN LONG RUN

Listening to Southern Illinois residents talk about the uprooting of families during the Great Flood of 1993 can only arouse sympathy. Many people lost their possessions and homes.

The government helped many flood victims, but didn't respond adequately to others. The relief effort simply did not satisfy every person's needs, as is frequently the case when disaster strikes.

In questioning the government's failure to do more for flood victims, a woman from Grand Tower asked me: "Why does our government help people in Somalia and Bosnia before it does something for its own? I'm not against aid to other countries, but let's take care of our own people first." As a former Peace Corps volunteer in Cameroon, Africa, I could not help but take note of this plea.

Why do we seemingly fail to direct enough attention to our local problems before sending billions of dollars in aid overseas? We hear this question often, but rarely do we receive any response.

Certainly, some residents failed to receive adequate compensation for their flood losses. To help fill this shortfall in flood relief, should our government have diverted funds from its foreign aid budget? No. Foreign aid dollars do not benefit only the recipient. The giver of those dollars will often receive just as great a benefit as the recipient.

If we look at foreign aid in purely economic terms, the United States has reaped a bountiful harvest by plowing dollars into distant lands. Our government has helped areas like Europe and Asia develop into regions favorable for U.S. investments. Americans make lots of money by selling products overseas. Without having established contacts with countries through foreign aid programs, we would have a much more closed and unproductive economy.

The United States also has gained an important stature in the world through foreign aid. We must continue our foreign aid if we want to remain a positive force in world events. Without a significant U.S. presence abroad, circumstances could be much worse, forcing more of our resources to be devoted to defense spending rather than items like flood relief.

Finally, there is the humanitarian aspect of foreign aid. Sure, we have problems in the United States. But when tragedy strikes in other parts of the world, whether due to civil war or natural disasters, national borders disappear. A child in Africa evokes just as much concern as a child in Illinois—and isn't this only right? After all, the life of a human being is precious, regardless of national origin.

(continued)

Foreign assistance is not always a one-way street, either. During the Mississippi floods, the continually flood-ravaged country of Bangladesh actually sent tea to the flood victims of the United States. This may seem insignificant, but the cost of that aid would have been substantial to Bangladesh.

I am not saying that our government couldn't have done more for the Mississippi flood victims. But foreign aid is an important item of spending for all Americans. And, on a per-capita basis, Americans have already cut foreign spending to a level well below that of other industrialized nations.

When it comes to helping our own, I am all for it. But cutting into the foreign aid budget will not accomplish this goal. We need to look elsewhere if we are truly serious about helping Americans. McCormick 1994:A6)

economic processes, political institutions, and cultural assumptions; and the international practice of double standards that assume inferior rights to be appropriate for certain 'others,' defined by location, origin, race or gender" (11). Seven of the most wealthy countries in the world have only 12 percent of the world's population but use over 70 percent of its resources in cash terms and dominate all major decision-making bodies (Alexander 1996). With this discrepancy in the distribution of resources, it is probably not a question of if, but when, voices of the have-nots become much louder.

Human rights principles require attention to the plight of the Third World and to obligations that wealthy countries have to the Third World. A right to development in a fair and equitable global system lies at the heart of human rights. In 1986 the General Assembly of the United Nations adopted a Declaration on the Right to Development (United Nations 1986). That declaration highlighted the human right of everyone to participate in economic, social, cultural, and political development. In addition, the declaration outlined obligations that countries have in creating national and international conditions favorable to the right to development.

The introduction to the Declaration on the Right to Development refers to article 28 of the Universal Declaration of Human Rights, which states that everyone is entitled to a social and international order in which human rights can be realized. Specific articles of the right to development declaration provide that

- The right to development is an inalienable human right (art. 1, para. 1).
- The right to development implies the full realization of peoples to self-determination, including the right to full sovereignty over natural wealth and resources (para. 2).
- The human person is the central subject of development and should be the active participant and beneficiary of the right to development (art. 2, para. 1).
- All human beings have a responsibility for development, and they should promote and protect an appropriate political, social, and economic order for development (para. 2).
- States have the primary responsibility for the creation of national and international conditions favorable to the right to development (art. 3, para. 1).
- States have a duty to co-operate with each other in ensuring development and obstacles to development. States should promote a new international order based on sovereign equality, interdependence, mutual interest, and co-operation. States should encourage the observance and realization of human rights (para. 3).
- States have a duty to take steps to formulate international development policies that facilitate the right to development (art. 4, para. 1).
- Sustained action is necessary to promote more rapid development of developing countries (para. 2).
- States shall take steps to eliminate massive and flagrant violations of human rights resulting from apartheid, racism, racial discrimination, colonialism, foreign domination and occupation, and aggression (art. 5).
- All human rights are indivisible and interdependent; States should give equal attention and urgent consideration to promotion of civil, political, economic, social, and cultural rights (art. 6, para. 2).
- All States should promote international peace and security and do their utmost to accomplish a complete disarmament under effective international control (art. 7).
- States shall ensure equality of opportunity for all concerning access to basic resources, education, health services, food, housing, employment, and the fair distribution of income. Effective measures should be undertaken to ensure that women have an active role in the development process (art. 8, para. 1).

Responsibilities contained within the Declaration on the Right to Development tend to be general and difficult to measure. For instance, the statement that "sustained action is necessary to promote more rapid development of developing countries" does not specify what action should be taken. Likewise, "effective international control" does little to illuminate what steps countries should take in establishing cooperation. International aid programs often do little to improve the conditions of developing countries. Yet a wealthy country providing international aid may believe that it is actually undertaking sustained and effective efforts in the development of other countries.

While few could object to provisions contained in the Declaration on the Right to Development, difficulties arise in actually measuring progress toward development. Generally accepted statistics—such as the gross national product—used by international development agencies do not adequately measure distribution and access to resources. Inequality of resources could be rampant within a country even though the GNP of that country ranks high among developing countries. "Measures of success must go beyond the transformation of international institutions to redress the social, economic, and environmental consequences of global separate development" (Alexander 1996:272). To better indicate success in world development and an end to global apartheid, the following ten targets provide specific measures toward this goal:

1. Everyone has enough to eat.
2. Everyone has access to clean water and sanitation.
3. Average life expectancy is equal, wherever you are born.
4. Everyone has access to adequate housing, learning, and health care.
5. Adult literacy is universal for men and women.
6. Everyone has an income sufficient to sustain life; income inequality is less than 1:15 worldwide—in other words, nobody earns more than 15 times what another person earns on a worldwide basis.
7. Average annual carbon dioxide emissions are below the sustainable level, estimated to be between 0.46 and 1.7 tons per person in every country.
8. All adults have a say in their government and equal representation in international institutions.

Human Rights In the United Nations System

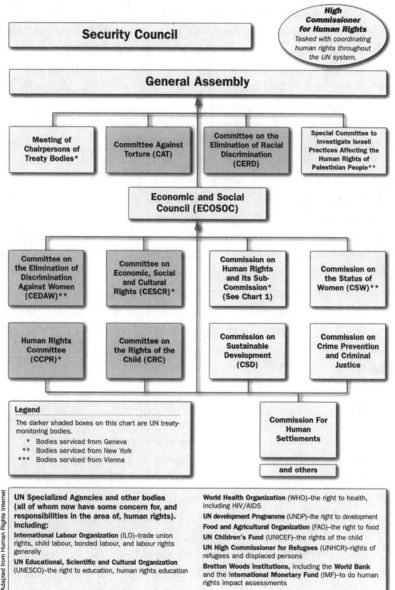

FIGURE 7.1

UN Commission on Human Rights and its Subcommission

Office of the High Commissioner for Human Rights/UN Centre for Human Rights
(Services all bodies on this chart)

UN Commission on Human Rights

Sub-Commission on Prevention of Discrimination and Protection of Minorities

Special Procedures

Working Groups

- Enforced or involuntary disappearances
- Arbitrary detention
- Situations of gross violations (Res. 1503)
- Structural adjustment programmes and economic, social and cultural rights
- Right to development
- Drafting a declaration on human rights defenders

- Drafting an optional protocol to the Torture Convention
- Drafting an optional protocol to the Convention on the Rights of the Child, on children in armed conflict
- Drafting an optional protocol to the Convention on the Rights of the Child, on sale of children, child prostitution and child pornography

Special Rapporteurs (Thematic)

- Summary or arbitrary execution
- Torture
- Religious intolerance
- Mercenaries
- Sales of children, child prostitution and child pornography
- Freedom of opinion and expression

- Violence against women
- Racism, racial discrimination and xenophobia
- Internally displaced persons
- Independence of the judiciary
- Illicit movement & dumping of toxic and dangerous products

Special Rapporteurs or Representatives (Country-specific)

Afghanistan	Guatemala	Occupied Territories *(Palestine)*
Burundi	Haiti	
Cambodia	Iran	Somalia
Cuba	Iraq	Sudan
Equatorial Guinea	Myanmar	Zaire
Former Yugoslavia		

Advisory Services, training, fellowships, and promotional activities for:

- National plans of action
- Constitutions
- Free and fair elections
- Legislative reform
- National and regional human rights institutions

- Human rights in law enforcement
- The judiciary and the legal professions
- Human rights in prisons
- Human rights and the armed forces
- Internal conflict resolution

- Parliament and human rights
- Curriculum development and human rights in education
- Treaty reporting and international obligations
- Strengthening NGOs and the mass media

Working Groups

- Communications on gross violations
- Detention
- Indigenous populations
- Contemporary forms of slavery
- Minorities

Special Rapporteurs & Studies

- Traditional practices affecting health of women and children
- Cultural property of indigenous peoples
- Compensation to victims of gross violations
- Impunity of perpetrators of violations of human rights
- Discrimination against HIV- or AIDS-infected people
- Right to adequate housing
- Right to fair trial
- States of emergency
- Human rights in extreme poverty
- Treaties with indigenous peoples
- Human rights & population transfers
- Administration of justice
- Conscientious objection
- Forced evictions
- Human rights and income distribution
- Realization of economic, social and cultural rights
- Solution of problems involving minorities
- Privatization of prisons
- Human rights and the environment
- Peace and human rights
- Independence of the judiciary

The Special Rapporteurs/Special Representatives and Working Groups change according to resolutions of the Commission and Sub-Commission. This chart is intended to be illustrative, not definitive.

Adapted from Human Rights Internet

FIGURE 7.2

9. All have equal protection of the law.

10. All have equal freedom of movement worldwide. (Alexander 1996:272)

Instead of relying upon impersonal and misleading economic figures to measure a country's development, the above measures provide a more complete picture of how a society is doing. In terms of economic performance, the United States always comes out on top or close to the top when measured by such traditional yardsticks as the gross national product. However, how does the United States perform when measured by the above ten targets? Certainly, the United States meets many of those goals—but not all. When measured on a worldwide basis, the above targets appear almost impossible to achieve. Yet the targets themselves remain commendable and worthy of consideration.

The danger of not seriously addressing human development issues lies in the consequences of this neglect: famine, disease, violence, civil war, terrorism, and many other ills have roots within the global apartheid mentioned above. Social workers in the United States have great incentive to broaden their interests and devote attention to international development. The social work profession has much to offer in this area.

INTERNATIONAL HUMAN RIGHTS ISSUES RELATING TO SOCIAL WORK

In contrast to the broad issues of economic and social development, specific international human rights issues relating to the social work profession include globalization, cultural relativism, self-determination, and social exclusion. This list of issues is by no means complete, and social workers can encounter all types of circumstances that involve cross-cultural issues of human rights. However, by understanding concepts such as globalization and cultural relativism, social workers are better positioned to address other international human rights issues.

Globalization

One of the most talked-about issues relating to human rights is that of globalization. Although the term is not well-defined, globalization is widely used to connote a process of global integration in which diverse peoples, economies, cultures, and political processes are increasingly subjected to international influences.

> People in small American towns watch television news reports about conflicts in Africa, make international calls to family members on vacation in Europe, drive cars manufactured in Japan, or go out to eat foods originating in other countries without even thinking about it. Exposure to international events is not limited to the Western industrial nations. Today, rural villagers in India are familiar with the latest trends in European pop music, know about sensational murder trials in the United States, and are in regular communication with family members who work in other countries. (Midgley 1997:xii)

Clearly, many governments and people have benefited from globalization. However, the key human rights issue concerning globalization involves questions as to who benefits the most from globalization and who defines the goals or rules of globalization?

Assume that a shoe company in the United States decides to shift production to China. The U.S. company has made this decision because of lower costs and fewer workplace regulations in China than in the United States. On the surface, China benefits from this new investment because the inflow of funds to establish a shoe factory creates jobs. In a similar superficial fashion, by paying workers less and not being subject to strict employment conditions, the U.S. company benefits. However, a downside can also exist with this type of investment. The U.S. company takes advantage of less stringent employment and environmental laws and low wages. By allowing the U.S. company to invest in its country, China may experience increased pollution and abuses in the workplace that do not occur in the United States. In the United States, those who worked at the company lose their jobs and most likely health care, pension, and other benefits. The bottom line is that globalization often creates both winners and losers. The winners in the above example would be executives and possibly shareholders of the U.S. company and those in China who receive profits from the establishment of the factory. Chinese workers at the factory may now have employment, but if working conditions are hazardous or abusive, the health of the workers may suffer. Losers would definitely include employees at the now closed U.S.

factory and, as noted, possibly Chinese workers if employment conditions affect their health.

In addition to assessing the question as to who benefits from aspects of globalization, a parallel question arises as to who defines the goals or rules of globalization? In the above example, the Chinese government defines the rules of foreign operations within its jurisdiction. The decision to locate a U.S. factory in China belongs to the executives of the U.S. company. In neither instance do workers play a significant role in the decision.

Does the establishment of the U.S. shoe factory in China meet human rights principles, whereby everyone is entitled to a social order that promotes human rights contained in the Universal Declaration? Unless the U.S. company assists its employees in finding alternative employment and continues benefits until the employees find other work, then the closing of the factory would not promote human rights for those employees. Also, unless the Chinese government required the U.S. company to provide a safe working environment, a nondiscriminatory hiring procedure, and fair wages, then the establishment of the factory in China would not promote human rights for Chinese workers. If China allows the U.S. company to pollute the environment, then this would be another violation of human rights.

In addition to the IMF and the World Bank, another example of economic globalization is provided by the World Trade Organization (WTO). And just like the IMF and the World Bank, this multinational agency establishes rules for its members, who must then comply with those rules to receive benefits. For instance, the World Trade Organization sets rules concerning international trade. Before a country can become a member of the WTO, that country must agree to abide by those particular rules. Today, most countries of the world belong to the WTO. Yet, while the WTO may appear to bring order and stability to the global trading system, its rules can also violate human rights. "Public health is a stark example. Diseases that are under control in the developed world cause millions of premature deaths in the developing world. One of the main reasons is a group of WTO patent-protection laws that have had a substantial impact on the price of drugs within the developing world where people's need for drugs is great and their ability to pay is not" (Booker and Minter 2001; Levinson 2001:5). Currently, the HIV-AIDS crisis in Africa best illustrates how the WTO's patent rules can benefit wealthy countries and punish developing countries. Under these rules, all WTO member states are required to grant at least a twenty-year

Two international organizations that have recently come under fire from many sides are the International Monetary Fund (IMF) and the World Bank. These two global institutions, created in the aftermath of World War II, are designed in large part to help developing countries out of financial crises and overcome poverty (KNT 2000: C2). However, not everyone believes that these organizations have adhered to this initial idea. Critics of the IMF and World Bank say that these institutions support development projects that degrade the environment and force countries to adopt policies that keep wages down and curtail spending on health care, including AIDS, and other social programs (C2). Some view these institutions as nothing more than powerful instruments of the West whose policies are designed to further the interests of Western countries over other countries.

In response to such complaints, these organizations claim they are trying to change and improve their business methods. In this view, the IMF and World Bank should be revamped, not shut down, especially at a time when poverty remains a major challenge facing humanity (C2).

Clearly, international assistance raises many issues. Cooperation between countries is an ongoing process and a learning experience. Benefits can evolve from working together and listening to differing viewpoints. This aspect of human rights has more importance now than ever before.

patent-protection period in all fields of technology, including drugs. These rules prevent other member countries from producing or importing low-cost generic copies of otherwise patented drugs. If a country violates those rules, then harsh penalties could be imposed against the violating country (Levinson 2001). With HIV-AIDS, where most cases are now running rampant in the developing countries (and especially Africa), the inability to afford drugs for treating HIV-AIDS literally becomes a life-or-death matter. However, if countries with insufficient funds to purchase high-cost patented drugs for treatment are not allowed to produce those drugs or to import generic substitutes without incurring a severe penalty, then most likely no treatment will occur. The result is a knowing complicity in the deaths of literally millions of HIV-AIDS victims just for the sake of protecting the profits of Western drug companies that own the patents to these desperately needed drugs. Recently, in a concession to this criticism of protecting patents, Western drug companies have agreed to provide needed HIV-AIDS drugs to African nations at substantially reduced prices. However, even at the reduced prices, many countries may not be able to afford the drugs without financial assistance.

From a human rights position, the inventor of a drug is of course entitled to patent protection. However, the Universal Declaration also requires international cooperation in bringing social security to everyone. If a WTO rule prevents a country from treating its citizens with HIV-AIDS drugs because of that country's inability to purchase costly patented drugs, should some kind of exception exist that allows the country to produce or purchase the less expensive generic drugs? Or should the companies owning the patents be required to either relinquish the patent or lower the cost of patented drugs in cases where many lives are at stake? The response to that question possibly depends upon who sets or defines the rules concerning international cooperation in regard to trade.

Clearly, though, developing countries that participate in international trade organizations generally do increase the overall wealth of their citizens (*Economist* 2001:67). In countries that have not "globalized" their economies as much as others, income per head has shrunk, and the number of people in poverty has risen. In countries that increased their international trade, income per head rose, as did levels of life expectancy and schooling. However, these comparisons can also be misleading because they do not address progress among specific groups, such as women or minorities. Increased national wealth may not be a reliable indicator of a uniform benefit to society since certain groups can fall through the cracks in the distribution of that wealth.

The above examples illustrate why globalization presents the social work profession with significant human rights and ethical challenges. Globalization can bring many benefits to all countries. At the same time, however, globalization can be disruptive and lead to the human rights violations of many individuals and communities.

Cultural Relativism

Human rights concepts promote the idea of universality, which, in its extreme form, essentially means that human rights apply to every country and individual without exception. However, difficulties can arise in applying or interpreting human rights in a particular cultural setting. Obviously, not all cultures are the same, which presents the dilemma of determining the role culture should play in promoting human rights. If the cultural norm in a country prevents women from holding political offices, should human rights principles of nondiscrimination overrule that cultural norm and allow women into those positions? Supporters of cultural relativism would claim that culture should prevail over any universal application of human rights. Yet the Platform for Action adopted by the United Nations in 1995 elevates human rights above cultural norms when those norms inhibit or negatively impact on the human rights of women (United Nations 1996). For example, it is a human right that women not be discriminated against on the basis of gender in the workplace and participation in government. Therefore, if local custom frowns on women holding political positions, then enforcement of this custom would be a human rights violation.

In discussing cultural relativism, a key question to ask would be: Who defines culture and cultural norms? (Rao 1995). Whose voices contribute or are allowed to contribute to the definition of culture and activities appropriate within that culture? Using the above example of not allowing women to participate in policy-making, some might claim that no harm or human rights violation occurs to women under this cultural norm. However, exclusion from a vital societal function can lead to a sense of disenfranchisement, which does violate human rights principles. The claim that women have not participated in policy-making for centuries or decades does not necessarily justify this cultural norm, especially if women have never been allowed to voice their opinions concerning this specific cultural norm in the first place.

Here are other examples of dilemmas social workers could encounter in the cultural relativism versus universality debate on human rights:

- A female Cambodian refugee living in a U.S. city asks for help at a shelter for battered women. The local Cambodian Mutual Assistance Association criticizes the shelter, charging that its focus on counseling the woman on her rights and on preparations for independence are destroying the fabric of Cambodian family and social life.
- Iranian social work educators were instrumental in bringing family planning services to Iran in the 1970s. Were the mullahs right that this represented a fundamental threat to the Islamic way of life, or was it essential practice to meet the needs of women and their families?

Since September 11, 2001, many Americans are thinking more broadly and redefining their concept of culture, especially in light of how the United States differs from Arab and Islamic cultures (Farah 2002:15–17). However, the trend today goes against treating all cultures as equal and downplaying the concept of universal values—what has been called cultural relativism. Now the aim is to examine a culture and to evaluate aspects of that culture, even if it means saying that one culture is "better" than another.

Opponents say cultural relativism is flawed in two ways. First, it contradicts itself: to state that no one should judge other cultures, or that all cultures should be equally defended, is itself a judgment (17). Then there's the problem of the slippery slope. When anthropologists first embraced relativism early in the twentieth century, it was in the spirit of scientific rigor: the way to understand another culture, they argued, was to abandon one's own values and assumptions. But relativism seeped into other contexts, until all ethics became relative. Radical relativists were even willing to defend female genital mutilation in some societies (17).

Of course, by discarding cultural relativism, individuals and governments must then adopt a set of universal values as guidelines. "The most popular option currently may be the UN Declaration of Human Rights, but some anthropologists resist even that as a Western import" (17).

It would be a mistake to simply ignore the concept of cultural relativism when considering social work and other issues. The need not only to tolerate but respect cultural differences is crucial in today's world. However, extreme cultural relativism should be tempered by a set of universal values. While the UN Declaration of Human Rights has its deficiencies, that document still represents a valuable tool in limiting the excesses of cultural relativism.

- West Indian politicians in a U.S. city speak out against the child protection agency's investigations of child abuse in families using corporal punishment, asserting that West Indians don't want their children to grow up undisciplined.
- Local community development workers in Bangladesh encounter a group of enraged local leaders, charging that their micro-enterprise and literacy programs for women are destroying family roles and violating the Koran (Qur'an).
- Efforts to ensure nondiscriminatory treatment for gays and lesbians encounter

hostility in Jamaica, Zimbabwe, the United States, and elsewhere. (Healy 2001:153)

For a Western-oriented social worker, positions on the above situations may seem obvious. Of course, men should not beat women; women should have family-planning information available if desired; parents should not beat children as a form of discipline; women should be able to obtain literacy and allowed to have their own businesses; and gays and lesbians should be protected from discrimination. Yet even when human rights principles seem clear, social workers should consider and learn about the cultural aspect of any given particular situation. To do this, a knowledge of the culture becomes crucial.

Like universality, cultural relativism has limits. The balancing of divergent interests plays a key role in addressing these key concepts of human rights.

Self-determination

The concept of self-determination appears prominently in the Universal Declaration of Human Rights and the two International Covenants. In the context of human rights and the individual, self-determination refers to the right of an individual to freely develop his or her own personality and essentially make his or her own choices in life (United Nations 1948:art. 22). However, in the field of human rights, self-determination also refers to the right of "peoples" to "freely determine their political status and freely pursue their economic, social, and cultural development" (United Nations 1948:art. 1, para. 1). "All peoples have the right of self-determination. By virtue of that right they freely determine their political status and freely pursue their economic, social, and cultural development" (see appendix B).

Social workers frequently encounter self-determination issues with individuals. For example, NASW advocates client self-determination in "end-of-life" decisions (NASW 2000:41–44). The social work profession strives to enhance the quality of life; to encourage the exploration of life options; and to advocate for access to options, including providing all information to make appropriate choices. Competent individuals should have the opportunity to make their own choices, but only after being informed of all options and consequences (43). While self-determination in this situation focuses

HOW FOREIGNERS SEE AMERICANS

During a recent trip to Australia, I dared mention to the elderly owner of a snack bar that he sounded English and not Australian, a distinction obvious to locals but not so apparent to those from afar, like Americans.

No, no, no, responded the proprietor, in an accent that I would swear had at least a hint of Queen's English. He was Australian. We dislike the English, he said. Australians like Americans. After all, where would Australia be without the Americans? The Yanks saved Australia from the Japanese in World War II.

I should have been flattered, with swirls of pride gushing throughout, but a previous residence of seven years in Australia helped nip any thoughts of nationalistic bombast.

True, the snack bar owner had made a valid point. In the ominous days of Japanese expansion during World War II, Australia found itself imperiled by a possible Japanese invasion of its territory. England, the traditional protector of Australia, was too preoccupied in the European sector of the war to lend a hand to Australia. Only the United States, with its vast arsenal of soldiers and weapons, offered hope of salvation.

On Dec. 27, 1941, the Australian Prime Minister John Curtin announced that without "inhibitions of any kind," Australia would now look "to America" for help in meeting its defense needs. The rest is history. After having been driven out of the Philippines by the Japanese, U.S. General Douglas MacArthur proclaimed in Melbourne, Australia, that he would "return" to stop Japanese military expansion in Asia. The general and his army kept their promise. Yet, no matter how much Americans did to save Australia from the martial aims of the Japanese, anyone attaching contemporary importance to this circumstance should proceed carefully.

No self-respecting Australian born after the war would ever state that the United States saved Australia from the Japanese. And, I suspect that even the snack bar owner concocts a similarly fawning spiel for English tourists, which probably goes something likes this: "Those bloody Yanks think they own the place, don't they? Thank God you're English."

Regardless of nationality, a trip abroad provides a person with an ideal opportunity to discover the uniqueness of his or her background. As Americans, we inevitably carry mental baggage that shapes the way we view others. The flip-side is that being American also shapes the way others view us.

Ever since World War II, Americans have lorded over world affairs. The immensely successful U.S. Marshall Plan assisted France, West Germany, and other European countries, in overcoming the devastation of war. Americans also helped the Japanese rebuild their country after the war.

(continued)

Our postwar assistance to Europe, Japan, and other areas helped shape a contemporary world conducive to U.S. ideals and objectives. Even former communistic countries have succumbed to the design of a world significantly influenced by U.S. economic and cultural developments.

When Americans travel abroad, we cannot help but notice countless, familiar icons of U.S. society that have found niches in the foreign setting. People all over the world watch American films, listen to American music, eat American-inspired hamburgers, and wear American-style clothes. Without much thought, we could assume that, because elements of our society have caught on overseas, foreigners prefer our way of life to theirs, thus supporting a view of national greatness.

Yet, a foreign penchant for U.S. items does not translate into cultural superiority. Japanese who eat at McDonalds are not indicating they prefer the American way of life to theirs, just as Americans who buy Japanese televisions or eat sushi do not become more Japanese.

Sorting out the role and perceptions of the United States overseas is a complex task. The U.S. clearly occupies a dominant position in the world today, and it is unlikely that this position will change in the near future. Yet, for many of us, the import of this leadership role may not become evident until a crisis occurs and the dispatch of American troops ensues.

However, the U.S. presence overseas extends well beyond the latest hot spot. Our foreign interests encompass education, business, media, tourism, and numerous other areas of life abroad. How well Americans manage and understand the complexities of these international exchanges carries much more importance than crisis intervention.

An elderly snack bar owner in Australia seemingly celebrates the Yank presence Down Under because of what Americans did over 50 years ago. A young Australian eagerly purchases the latest Michael Jordan sporting item but protests American politics.

While such actions may seem insignificant, emotions lurking behind those actions form the essence of international relations. (McCormick 1997) on the individual, human rights issues of self-determination tend to focus on groups or countries.

On a group level, peoples have the right to freely determine their political status and freely pursue their economic, social, and cultural development. Social workers may encounter a minority group within a State that feels totally estranged from the majority. How much freedom should the minority group have in determining their political status? Should every minority group be allowed to secede from a country and set up a separate state? In the United States and other countries, governments have given indigenous and aboriginal peoples some authority to develop their own political entities and to create a nation within a particular area. To some extent, Native Americans have been allowed to determine their own policies within what is known as a reservation. However, while Native Americans may be allowed to "freely pursue" their economic, social, and cultural development upon a reservation, economic and social conditions on the reservations frequently result in high unemployment and alcoholism (Van Wormer 1997). The reservation concept might appear to be a proper method of achieving self-determination, but Native Americans might also feel trapped on the reservation. Native Americans, especially younger ones, may view the reservation as nothing more than a sop to appease Native Americans and a cruel trick played upon them by the U.S. government.

Taken literally, the human rights concept of self-determination could result in any group qualifying as a "people" and being allowed to establish their own country or self-governing unit. Palestinians, Macedonians, Albanians, Native Hawaiians, French Canadians, and numerous other ethnic groups the world over could all claim the human right to determine their own political status and freely pursue their economic, social, and cultural development.

The logic of this human right is compelling but also seems to challenge the universality principle. Clearly, merit exists in granting political status to individuals and groups that share common ancestry, religion, language, history, and other attributes that create different peoples. However, if human rights apply to all, regardless of origin or culture, then should self-determination occupy a primary role in human rights? Should not the focus be on ensuring the economic, social, and cultural rights of everyone rather than encouraging "peoples" to separate themselves from mainstream society? Should not government policy encourage Native Americans to adopt the customs and language of the dominant culture, a policy that would most likely facilitate their achievement of economic, social, and political rights? If only the minority group would become more like the dominant group, then human rights would become much less messy. Cultural relativism concerns would diminish, and universality would become much easier to accomplish.

Of course, the detriment in ignoring the issue of self-determination becomes evident. While all peoples are entitled to economic and social human rights, without self-determination those in authority can belittle or diminish the importance of individuals and minority groups. Drafters of human rights documents clearly recognized the danger in promoting a dominant culture over a less prominent group. Self-determination, on both an individual and group level, contains important human rights principles in international social work.

Social Exclusion

Another social work concept closely linked to human rights involves *social exclusion*, a term describing segments of the population who no longer participate in the opportunities available in society (Gore 1995). Social exclusion can lead to destructive consequences if allowed to fester.

The term originated in France in the 1970s and was originally applied to disadvantaged or marginalized social groups, such as people with mental illness, drug problems, or family difficulties (Healy 2001:273). In the 1980s, social exclusion evolved to refer to the new poverty associated with technological change and economic restructuring (Gore 1995:1–2; Healy 2001). Social exclusion expresses the loss of social solidarity, as part of the population no longer participates in significant opportunities available in the society (Gore 1995). Social exclusion can occur at any level of society, both nationally or globally:

> The growing gap in wealth between the richest and poorest nations and between the richest and poorest segments of the population within nations is a major indicator of social exclusion. Refugees, migrants, and the displaced are often excluded from all benefits of citizenship—sometimes for their lifetimes and even the lifetimes of their children. Within the globalization of economies and institutions, social exclusion can be applied to analysis of trade, aid, migration, debt policies, and so on. The concept also links to other critical con-

> The development of the world into different societies poses extraordinary challenges for both current and future generations of social workers. Perhaps the term that best encompasses these challenges is that of *global apartheid*:
>
> > Global apartheid, stated briefly, is an international system of minority rule whose attributes include: differential access to basic human rights; wealth and power structured by race and place; structural racism, embedded in global economic processes, political institutions, and cultural assumptions; and the international practice of double standards that assume inferior rights to be appropriate for certain "others," defined by location, origin, race, or gender. (Booker and Minter 2001:11)
>
> The concept of global apartheid brings home underlying issues prevalent in international social work. Is one society or culture more deserving than another? What obligations do those in relatively wealthy countries have in respect to less wealthy countries? Clearly, from a human rights perspective, social workers have a duty to learn about social issues affecting other cultures and societies. The social work profession has an obligation to work toward a cooperative world society, one in which global apartheid plays little or no role.

cepts; for example, the socially excluded include those who are excluded from human rights and those who are excluded from security. (Healy 2001:274)

Social exclusion represents the opposite of what human rights mean. The goal of human rights is to provide everyone with a minimum basis for existence, which includes economic security and human dignity, political participation in society, and protection of the minority culture. Social exclusion violates all of those human rights.

Consequences of social exclusion on an international basis can be devastating. Individuals who have no outlet to voice grievances or who receive inadequate compensation for their labor can never lead full lives. Some individuals may turn to violence as a reaction to their exclusion from society. In any case, those who fail to obtain a stake in the fruits of society will always lead a marginal existence.

Social workers should examine circumstances of social exclusion. "The social work profession needs to work cross-nationally to determine if the concept of social exclusion adds important insight to existing concepts, such as poverty and marginality, and to further specify its social work applications" (Healy 2001:274). Viewing social exclusion in a human rights context can also help social workers understand the actual and potential harm caused by this phenomenon. As previously stated, human rights aim to provide everyone with political, economic, social, and cultural rights that ensure the participation of marginal individuals and groups within society. Social exclusion violates the entire premise of human rights. By promoting human rights, social workers inevitably challenge circumstances of social exclusion.

SUMMARY

Most social workers will probably not work outside their own country of origin. However, all the above concepts—globalization, cultural relativism, self-determination, and social exclusion—address issues common to human rights. Understanding these concepts is crucial in establishing a familiarity with human rights.

While this chapter has focused on the international perspective of human rights, it is also true that viewing human rights as an international concept simply misses the point. No distinction should be made between human rights in the United States and human rights somewhere else. Differences in culture may require diverse applications of human rights. However, the underlying significance of human rights transcends borders and cultures. Human rights belong to everyone, wherever they live.

QUESTIONS

1. Why is the distinction between international social work and national social work artificial?
2. What is the third generation of human rights? How does this generation of rights relate to social work practice?
3. What does the term *global apartheid* symbolize?
4. Why is it difficult to measure "development?"
5. What are some of the negative aspects of globalization? What are some of the positive aspects of globalization?

6. Should cultural practices take precedence over human rights principles?
7. Why is self-determination a human rights concept?
8. Why does social exclusion conflict with human rights?
9. The *International Code of Ethics* specifically refers to human rights, while NASW's *Code of Ethics* makes no mention of human rights. What reasons might exist for the presence of human rights in the international code and the absence of human rights in NASW's code?
10. Why is it important for social workers to learn about social work in other countries?

REFERENCES

Alexander, T. 1996. *Unravelling Global Apartheid. An Overview of World Politics.* Cambridge, Eng.: Polity Press.

Booker S. and W. Minter. 2001. Global apartheid. *The Nation* (July 9): 11–17.

Economist, The. 2001. Globalisation and prosperity: Going global. (December 8–14): 67.

Farah, S. 2002. Cultural lens: judging you, judging me. Confronted with terror, Americans are rethinking their "I'm OK, you're OK" culture. *Christian Science Monitor* (March 14): 15–17.

Ford, P. 2001. Injustice seen as fertile soil for terrorists. *Christian Science Monitor* (November 28): 7, 10.

Gore, C. 1995. Introduction: Markets, citizenship, and social exclusion. In G. Rodgers, C. Gore, and J. B. Figueiredo, eds., *Social Exclusion: Rhetoric, Reality, Responses,* 1–40. Geneva: International Labor Organization/International Institute for Labor Studies.

Healy, L. 2001. *International Social Work: Professional Action in an Interdependent World.* New York: Oxford University Press.

Ife, J. 2001. *Human Rights and Social Work: Towards Rights-based Practice.* Cambridge: Cambridge University Press.

International Federation of Social Workers (IFSW). 2000. *See* www.ifsw.org/ 4.5.6.pub.html.

Kawewe, S. 2001. The impact of gender disempowerment on the welfare of Zimbabwean women. *International Social Work* 44.4: 471–85.

KNT. 2000. IMF and World Bank response to complaints. *Southern Illinoisan* (April 15): C2.

Levinson, M. 2001. Mismanaging globalizaiton. *Dissent* (Fall): 5–7.

Lorde, A. 1995. Age, race, class, and sex: Women redefining difference. In M. C. Anderson and P. H. Collins, eds., *Race, Identity, Class, and Gender: An Anthology,* 502. New York: Wadsworth.

McCormick, R. 1994. Aid to other nations helps U.S. in long run. *Southern Illinoisan* (January 4): A6.

——. 1997. How foreigners see Americans. *Southern Illinoisan* (March 16): D2

Midgley, J. 1997. *Social Welfare in Global Context*. Thousand Oaks, Calif.: Sage.

National Association of Social Workers (NASW). 1996. *Code of Ethics*. Washington, D.C: NASW Press.

——. 2000. *Social Work Speaks: National Association of Social Workers Policy Statements, 2000–2003*. 5th ed. Washington, D.C.: NASW Press.

Offenheiser, R. 2001. Worlds apart. The actions of the rich don't follow their promises. *St. Louis Post-Dispatch* (June 28): B7.

Rao, A. 1995. The politics of gender and culture in international human rights discourse. In J. Peters and W. Wolper, eds., *Women's Rights, Human Rights: International Feminist Perspectives*, 167–75. New York: Routledge.

Staub-Bernasconi, S. 1998. Soziale Arbeit als Menschenrechtsprofession. In A. Woehrle, ed., *Profession und Wissenschaft Sozialer Arbeit: Positionen in einer Phase der generellen Neuverortnung und Spezifika*, 305–32. Pfaffenweiler, Ger.: Cenaurus.

UNFPA (United Nations Population Fund). 2000. *See* www.unfpa.org/swp/2000/english/boxes_3.html (box 3).

United Nations. 1948. *Universal Declaration of Human Rights*. Adopted December 10, 1948. GA. Res. 217 AIII. United Nations Document a/810. New York: UN.

——. 1986. *Declaration on the Right to Development. See* www/un/org.

——. 1996. *The Beijing Declaration and the Platform for Action*. 4th World Conference on Women, Beijing, China, September 4–15, 1995. New York: UN Department of Public information.

Van Wormer, K. 1997. *Social Welfare: A World View*. Chicago: Nelson-Hall.

Whrnet (Women's human rights net). 2001. *See* www.whrnet.org/textv/issues/14htm.

8

Applying Human Rights to the Social Work Profession

The mortal choice which every German had to make—whether or not he knew he was making it—is a choice which we Americans have never had to confront. But personal and professional life confronts us with the same kind of choice, less mortally, to be sure, every day.

—Milton Mayer (1955:94)

The preceding chapters of this book have examined the concept of human rights and various documents that seek to guarantee the application of those rights by governments. Certainly, without government and other support of human rights, little progress can be made in actually incorporating human rights into the policies and practices of everyday life. However, in order to apply human rights to social work policies and practices, social workers should understand that knowledge alone will not provide a sufficient tool with which to apply human rights. In addition to acquiring specific knowledge of the terms and definitions used in human rights, social workers need to understand how to translate human rights into the social work profession. This ability requires an understanding of government agencies, clients, and social work concepts.

EVERYBODY SUPPORTS HUMAN RIGHTS

A curious aspect of human rights is that few governments or individuals would openly oppose human rights or denigrate the importance of human rights. No president of the United States would ever state, in public at least, any opposition to human rights. The head of a social work agency would never want to be accused of violating an individual's human rights. Certainly, social workers do not want to violate the human rights of their colleagues or clients. The NASW's policy statement on human rights mandates the adoption of human rights as a foundation principle upon which all of social work theory and applied knowledge rests: "In a world where increasingly there is a serious questioning of the responsibility of society to ensure that peoples' civil, political, cultural, social, and economic needs are met, social workers should be absolutely clear about where they stand" (NASW 2000:181). Social workers "must speak out against inhumane treatment of people in whatever form it exits" (181). According to NASW:

- Social workers should promote U.S. ratification of the Universal Declaration of Human Rights as well as critical UN treaties such as the International Covenant on Economic, Social, and Cultural Rights, the Convention on the Elimination of All Forms of Discrimination Against Women (CEDAW), and the Convention on the Rights of the Child.
- Social workers must be especially vigilant about human rights violations related to children's rights and exploitation such as child labor, child prostitution, and other crimes of abuse and take leadership in developing public and professional awareness regarding these issues.
- Social workers must advocate for the rights of vulnerable people and must condemn policies, practices, and attitudes of bigotry, intolerance, and hate that put any person's human rights in grave jeopardy. The violation of human rights based on race, ethnicity, gender, sexual orientation, age, disability, immigration status, or religion provide a few examples.
- Social workers should publicize opposition to the death penalty and work toward its abolition, recognizing that the death penalty has not been found to be a deterrent to violent crime and that it provides inhumane and degrading punishment.

- When entitlements are nonexistent or inadequately implemented, social workers must work in collaboration with governmental and nongovernmental organizations and other groups of people in the community to become a leading force for the health and welfare of all people, including the world's most vulnerable.
- Social workers must become partners with the United Nations in advancing human development and human rights, including economic human rights, and work toward closing the economic gap.
- In all fields of social work practice, whether with individuals or families, with groups, communities, domestic institutions, or nations, social work must be grounded in human rights.
- Recognizing that social workers who advocate on behalf of human rights can become subject to reprisal, NASW should ensure that social workers who are threatened are given the full support of the profession. (NASW 2000:181–82)

In summary, NASW states that the "appalling prevalence of wars, genocide, ethnic cleansing; discrimination and social exclusion, gender inequality, battering, rape, and the sale of women; sweatshops, child labor, and enslavement; and the suppression of human rights, demonstrates that the struggle for human rights remains a high priority for the social work profession in the 21st century" (NASW 2000:182). Unquestionably, human rights play a major role in the social work profession.

The stigma attached to violating human rights looms large in the public consciousness, even if many individuals do not fully understand the concepts and definitions of human rights. However, when it comes to actually applying human rights to everyday existence, all types of obstacles arise to prevent the exercise of human rights. To effectively apply human rights to social work practice, social workers must be aware of these obstacles and develop methods to avoid merely giving lip service to human rights.

The following example illustrates the difficulty in defining a human right and subsequently realizing that right. Human rights instruments state that government must not discriminate against individuals on the basis of gender, race, age, religion, and other standards. Discrimination in all its forms presents a formidable barrier to the application of human rights. To realize this human right of an existence free from discrimination, governments generally enact laws prohibiting discrimination on the basis of gender, race, age, religion, and other standards, especially in respect to the workplace. Yet how effective are those laws in accomplishing a neutral, nondiscriminatory workplace or other environment?

To give substance to antidiscrimination laws existing in the United States, federal and state governments have established watchdog agencies such as the Equal Employment and Opportunity Commission and various Departments of Human Rights to investigate complaints of discrimination. Yet filing a complaint with one of these entities can be intimidating and, without adequate legal resources, futile. An employer will usually devote significant resources to contest any complaint of discrimination. After all, discrimination is bad business and creates a negative impression among staff and the public. Even if an employee can weather the storm and convince the government investigator that evidence of discrimination exists, the employer can then offer to settle the matter and escape any consequence whatsoever. The charge of discrimination generally is obliterated from governmental files after a relatively short period of time, usually one year. In other words, to avoid any finding of a human rights violation, the employer simply offers the victim recompense that should have been provided in the first place, after which all is forgotten. A settlement can even be less than what the employer should have been providing, in which case the employer often ends up benefiting from the investigative process.

Of course, many astute government leaders, social workers, and other individuals *do* take human rights obligations seriously and consciously try to prevent discriminatory practices from ever occurring. However, lack of education, resources, and the inclination to value a profitable bottom line over substantive human rights practices can easily blur the desire or need for ensuring human rights. All of these factors can impact on social workers as they apply human rights to practice.

FOUNDATION OF THE SOCIAL WORK PROFESSION

Historically, the social work profession has challenged inequities among individuals and groups. Social work originates from humanitarian and democratic ideas, which prompt the profession to challenge discrimination and the unequal distribution of resources. This core value of challenging inequities and promoting democratic ideals now forms part of the social worker's code of ethics (NASW 1996).

The profession focuses on both the individual (or group) and her or his environment with the acknowledgment that environment plays a key role in the fulfillment of an individual's needs (Compton and Galaway 1994; Kirst-Ashman and Hull 1993; Germain and Gitterman 1996). Not only do social workers attempt to assist individuals, but they also attempt to bring about change on a broader, more global level (Goldstein 1992). This dual focus distinguishes the social work profession from other helping professions, like psychology and nursing, which generally address individual issues but without a mandate to challenge environmental impediments in resolving those issues.

Because the foundation of the social work profession centers on assisting vulnerable populations and others in need, the profession has developed interventions for that assistance. These interventions are closely tied to the field of human rights.

MAJOR INTERVENTIONS IN THE SOCIAL WORK PROFESSION

The social work profession has established various interventions for social workers in promoting the dual focus of the profession: assisting individuals and attempting to bring about global change. These interventions include challenging oppression; empowerment; and strengths perspective. By understanding these interventions, social workers can more easily recognize the link between their profession and human rights.

Challenging Oppression

Social workers have traditionally considered the oppressed and marginalized as being part of their constituencies. Oppression relates to an unjust use of authority or power over an individual or group. Different forms of oppression exist, including oppression based on race, ethnicity, class, gender, age, and sexual orientation. Each form of oppression creates a unique injustice and an inequitable power structure that allows the oppression both to exist and perpetuate. However, common to each form is the individual's or group's social reality (Appleby, Colon, and Hamilton 2001). Oppression, like racism or sexism, frequently manifests itself both in individual and institutional acts.

Repeated exposure to oppression may lead to internalized oppression whereby a person or group has internalized negative self-images projected by the external oppressor. Individuals often experience rage from internalized oppression. Repression of this rage can lead to self-destructive behavior or destructive behavior toward others (Shulman 1999).

Social workers have the responsibility to challenge individual and social relations that create and maintain oppression (Pinderhughes 1989). Social workers aim to reduce oppressive power structures, which requires both micro- and macro-level skills (Solomon 1976; Gutierrez 1990; Lee 1994; Simon 1994).

Challenging oppression clearly relates to the exercise of human rights. Humanitarian and democratic ideals are anathema to oppression, which stems from inequitable distributions of power. In the struggle to reduce oppression, social workers inevitably promote human rights.

Empowerment

Another intervention used by social workers and tied to human rights is that of empowerment. This intervention examines circumstances that contribute to differential treatment concerning ethnicity, age, class, national origin, religion, and sexual orientation. The empowerment tradition responds to the individual's and group's experiences of oppression (Saleebey 2002). Empowerment focuses on how an individual is treated in society and how an individual has access to resources and power (Cowger 1994; Roche and Dewees 2001). Reducing inequitable power structures forms a key foundational basis for empowerment (Solomon 1976; Gutierrez 1990; Lee 1994; Simon 1994).

Two interdependent and interactive dynamics characterize empowerment (Cowger 1994). Personal empowerment resembles the clinical notion of self-determination, whereby clients give direction to the helping process, take charge and control of their personal lives, get their "head straight," learn new ways to think about their situation, and adopt new behaviors that give them more satisfying and "rewarding outcomes" (Cowger 1994:263). Personal empowerment also relates to opportunity, for without opportunity the process of self-determination becomes difficult. For instance, an individual who has no medical coverage and no legal or economic means to obtain that coverage will find it difficult, with his or her own resources, to adequately meet health care needs.

The social empowerment dynamic recognizes that an individual's characteristics cannot be separated from the context in which the individual exists (Cowger 1994). An individual's behavior or traits are connected to those of others through social involvement (Falck 1988). An individual with resources and an opportunity to play an important role in his or her own environment can more easily shape outcomes. An individual who has influence in the community may persuade medical practitioners to provide low-cost or free medical services to those without health care benefits. Without that contextual influence, however, an individual would most likely find it difficult to encourage medical practitioners to provide those services.

Personal empowerment and social empowerment are mutually inclusive. When an individual achieves personal empowerment, that individual also achieves social empowerment (Cowger 1994). Assisting individuals and groups to empower themselves to overcome inequitable treatment forms a key part of the social work profession. This empowerment tradition goes hand in hand with the achievement of human rights, which center on equitable treatment for everyone, regardless of status.

Strengths Perspective

Strengths perspective is another social work intervention closely related to human rights. Strengths perspective states that an individual's or group's strengths are central to the helping relationship. This intervention acknowledges that structural injustices have isolated many individuals and groups from necessary resources and fair treatment. Strengths perspective focuses on resiliency and ways in which people cope, in spite of many obstacles and injustices. Without the strengths perspective, social workers may fall into the trap of viewing an individual or group as being pathological and may focus on "what is wrong" with that individual or group.

Certainly, by acknowledging the strengths of individuals and groups, social workers are better poised to tie human rights principles to a particular situation. For example, when confronted with an individual who is HIV-positive and has been injecting heroin with used needles, a social worker using the strengths perspective would focus on other elements of the individual's circumstances. By learning about the individual's background and own personal obstacles, the social worker would inevitably look for strengths exhibited by the individual. Within this framework, the social worker could then address human rights issues related to the individual's circumstances.

Ethnic-sensitive Practice

Ethnic-sensitive practice aims to raise a social worker's awareness of racism in the wider society. Social conditions related to powerlessness are integral to the experiences of persons of different ethnic backgrounds (Van Wormer 1997). Ethnic-sensitive practice emphasizes the significance of race and ethnicity as a mediator of people's day-to-day objective experience and of their subjective sense of self. This intervention restores an appreciation to people for their particular cultural experience and identity (Devore-Schlesinger, 1996; McGoldrick, Giordano, and Pearce 1996; Swenson 1998).

Feminist Practice

Feminist practice focuses on a critique of power relations characterized primarily by gender domination and subordination. This intervention suggests an alternative way of understanding and using power based on collaboration and cooperation rather than on competition (Van Den Bergh and Cooper 1986; Bricker-Jenkins, Hooeyman, and Gottlieb 1991). For instance, although feminist practice emphasizes gendered patterns of power, it also addresses practices that disempower or oppress anyone, whether on the basis of race, religion, sexual orientation, or other category.

Cultural Competence

Cultural competence entails the recognition of different prejudices—ethnocentrism, sexism, classism, heterosexism, and racism—and then understanding that society as a whole possesses and indeed acts on many of those prejudices. This intervention requires continuous effort on part of the social worker to increase knowledge about the client's culture, including its norms, vocabulary, symbols, and strengths (Van Wormer 1997:209).

Interventions within the social work profession are essential tools in promoting the link between the social work profession and human rights. The interventions described above are in no way the only interventions that promote human rights. All interventions within the social work profession relate to human rights issues and address ways in which to apply human rights to practice. However, in addition to understanding interventions and their role in human rights, another method exists by which social workers can relate human rights to practice. This method focuses on the connection between the code of ethics followed by the National Association of Social Workers and human rights.

THE MISSION OF THE SOCIAL WORK PROFESSION

The primary mission of the social work profession is to enhance human well-being and help meet the basic human needs of all people, with particular attention to the needs and empowerment of all people who are vulnerable, oppressed, and living in poverty.—NASW (1996:1)

A paradox of the social work profession lies in the statement that social work is a human rights profession (Staub-Bernasconi 1998; International Federation of Social Workers 2000; Ife 2001). While the statement rings true, a clear link between social work and human rights often escapes the profession in the United States, as evidenced by the dearth of literature on this topic (Witkin 1998; Reichert 2001a, 2001b). The elusive nature of equating social work with human rights appears to arise from the absence of a clear point of departure for social workers wishing to embrace human rights in their practice. If social work is a human rights profession, then where do social workers begin in applying human rights to practice? Where is the human rights compass to guide social workers?

Clearly, in applying human rights to practice, social workers must understand the concept of human rights and have knowledge about human rights documents, particularly the Universal Declaration of Human Rights (Center for Human Rights 1994; NASW 2000). However, in addition to human rights documents, another significant instrument exists to help social workers better understand the connection between their profession and human rights. That document is the *Code of Ethics*, drafted by the National Association of Social Workers (NASW 1996). While many provisions of that code relate to individual conduct, such as confidentiality and personal interaction with clients, other provisions contain numerous examples of human rights. Because the vast majority of social workers in the United States refer to the NASW's *Code of Ethics* for guidance (Loewenberg and Dolgoff 1992; Reamer 1995, 1998; Congress 1999;), this code can serve as the point of departure for connecting the profession to human rights.

By relating a code of ethics followed by most U.S. social workers to specific human rights, social workers in the United States can better apply human rights to their practice and promote the primary mission of the profession. Provisions contained in the code entreat social workers to work toward fulfilling the human rights of clients. While the code never mentions the term *human rights* as such, language in the code nonetheless resembles that of important human rights documents, especially the Universal Declaration. Provisions of the code essentially require adherence to human rights principles, without actually using the term *human rights*. By identifying the code as a human rights document, social workers can better understand why their profession is a human rights profession and can better apply human rights to practice.

THE NASW'S *CODE OF ETHICS*

Professional ethics are at the core of social work. The profession has an obligation to articulate its basic values, ethical principles, and ethical standards. The NASW Code of Ethics sets forth these values, principles, and standards to guide social workers' conduct. The Code is relevant to all social workers and social work students, regardless of their professional functions, the settings in which they work, or the population they serve.—NASW (1996:2)

Ethics are a set of "moral principles and the rules of conduct recognized in respect of a particular class of human action or a particular group" (*Webster's* 1989). Ethics also have to do with determining the "right" course of action, or what is morally necessary in a particular situation considering all aspects of that situation (Loewenberg and Dolgoff 1992; Reamer 1995; Mannig 1997; Mattison 2000).

The development of the first social work code of ethics finds its roots in 1915, when the Flexner Report raised the concern that social work could not be considered a profession unless it had a code. Credit goes to Mary Richmond for having developed in 1920 the first experimental code of ethics for caseworkers. A chapter of the American Association of Social Workers developed the first code of ethics. This organization was the NASW's predecessor. The first NASW code, ratified in 1960, was only one page long and included fourteen broadly worded "proclamations" (Congress 1999). For example, certain proclamations included every social worker's duty to give precedence to professional responsibility over personal interests; respect the privacy of clients; and give appropriate professional service in public.

In 1979, amendments to the NASW code addressed responsibility to clients, colleagues, the profession, and society (Loewenberg and Dolgoff 1992). Also for the first time, the code incorporated procedures to enforce certain parts of the code, with social workers now being required to cooperate in implementing the code and abiding by any disciplinary rulings. The code required social workers to cooperate in its implementation and abide by any disciplinary rulings (Congress 1999). As part of its revision in 1996, the NASW code expanded ethical responsibilities of social workers to the broader society (NASW 1996). The 1996 code also adopted an international perspective by stating that "social workers should promote conditions that encourage respect for cultural and social diversity within the Untied States and globally" (NASW 1996:27).

Provisions of the NASW Code

While the NASW's *Code of Ethics* (as revised in 1996) does not provide a detailed set of guidelines for every situation encountered by social workers, the code does provide guidance in handling numerous situations. The code also explains responsibilities arising from ethical obligations. Without noting any specific connection to human rights, the code embodies human rights issues that social workers have an obligation or responsibility to pursue. As with the Universal Declaration, the code has also generated criticism. Among these criticisms is the notion that those in power have written the code in order to regulate conduct with clients (Witkin 2000; Ife 2001). Because those in power can dictate enforcement and interpretations of the code, clients may not receive adequate consideration when ethical issues arise. Another criticism concerns the focus on individuals without including broader religious, ethnic, or other group perspectives (Allen 1993; Abramson 1996; Witkin 2000).

Certainly, the NASW's *Code of Ethics* has drawbacks. Yet by linking the code to human rights, social workers can find that the code provides a worthy frame of reference for the profession.

Ethical Principles

The code encompasses and affirms six values, each of which translates into a separate and worthy ethical principle:

- The value of *service* translates into the ethical principle that a social worker's primary goal is to help people in need and to address social problems.
- The value of *social justice* translates into the ethical principle that social workers should challenge social injustice. Efforts by social workers to effect social change focus primarily on issues of poverty, unemployment, discrimination, and other forms of social injustice. Challenging social injustice promotes sensitivity to and knowledge about oppression in the context of cultural and ethnic diversity.
- The value of *the dignity and worth of the person* translates into the ethical principle that social workers should respect the inherent dignity and worth of every single individual. Social workers should treat each person in a caring and respectful fashion, with special consideration given for an individual's differences in the light of cultural and ethnic diversity.
- The value of *the importance of human relationships* translates into the ethical principle that social workers should recognize the central importance of meaningful human relationships in everyone's life.
- The value of *integrity* translates into the ethical principle that social workers should behave in a trustworthy manner. Social workers should act honestly and responsibly while promoting worthwhile ethical practices on the part of the organizations with which they are affiliated.
- The value of *competence* translates into the ethical principle that social workers should develop and enhance their professional expertise and competence to the best of their abilities within their own areas of social work practice.

From the above six values and implied ethical principles derive concrete ethical standards which apply to the professional activities of all social workers. The code expresses these standards as ethical responsibilities social workers have to various groups: to clients; to colleagues; to the social work profession itself; and to the broader society (NASW 1996).

The ethical responsibilities of social workers include both those that are enforceable and those that are aspirational (NASW 1996). Ethical responsibilities that relate to human rights tend to be aspirational and are not specifically enforceable. The aspirational nature of ethical responsibilities concerning human rights correlates to the more general difficulty of legally enforcing human rights. The basis for fulfilling human rights relies to a great extent on education and good will. Even with supportive laws, human rights remain tenuous and dependent upon the aspirations of individuals.

CONNECTING THE NASW CODE TO HUMAN RIGHTS

Connecting the NASW's *Code of Ethics* with human rights can best be illustrated by citing an ethical responsibility encompassed by the code and matching that responsibility with a relevant provision from the Universal Declaration of Human Rights. The Universal Declaration directs attention to the human rights of individuals and groups, with few references to governments or States and their obligations to enforce human rights. The Universal Declaration is itself an aspirational document, with little attention given to the actual enforcement of human rights. Nonetheless, many countries have now adopted treaties to enforce specific human rights as contained in the declaration. Therefore, the Universal Declaration embodies the essence of human rights and provides the best frame of reference in linking social work practice to human rights.

Ethical Responsibilities

Under the NASW's *Code of Ethics*, social workers have an ethical responsibility to clients that includes understanding culture and its function in human behavior and society. Social workers should be informed and knowledgeable in regard to their clients' cultures and be able to demonstrate competence in providing services that are sensitive to the differences among people and cultural groups. Social workers should seek to understand the reality of social diversity and the nature of oppression, especially in respect to race, ethnicity, national origin, color, sex, sexual orientation, age, marital status, political belief, religion, and mental or physical disability (NASW 1996:1.05). These ethical guidelines incorporate a number of provisions from the Universal Declaration, which include the human right to cultural

The importance of social workers acting ethically cannot be understated. In their pursuit of human rights or social justice, social workers must create an environment in which ethics flourish. In this context, individual virtues may actually take a backseat to the overall professional situation in which social workers find themselves.

According to Randy Cohen, who has studied ethics, group dynamics can often dictate how the individual acts:

> In his profound and moving book, *The Face of Battle*, the British military historian John Keegan considers the question of why, when faced with the horror and suffering of combat, most soldiers don't simply run away. He concludes that they are motivated not by high ideals of patriotism, not by ideology, not by anything one would identify as ethics. Keegan sees these soldiers standing fast so as not to be the least worthy among those assembled. And by that, he does not mean the entire army, but those few men nearby. Keegan suggests that even under the most extreme and appalling conditions, most of us will behave about as well as our neighbors." (Cohen 2002:22)

The same tendency to act as the neighbors could also lead to soldiers running from battle, if that is what other, nearby soldiers are doing.

According to Cohen, something "similar has been observed in the early careers of police officers. If a rookie cop is assigned to a corrupt station house, he stands a good chance of being corrupted himself. Put the same young officer in a clean station, and there's a very good chance he'll turn out to be an honest cop. His or her personal ethics hardly come into it" (22).

Cohen's point is that individual ethics generally are insufficient to create an ethical environment:

> Just as individual ethics can be understood only in relation to the society within which it is practiced, it is also true that individual ethical behavior is far likelier to flourish within a just society. It might be argued that to lead an ethical life one must work to build a just society. . . . Every community is dynamic—Sparta or the precinct house. We not only live in it, but by our actions we create it. And as important, our community exists not only in the world but in our minds. It forms our values even as we shape its structures. (Cohen 2002:22)

Attention to ethics clearly relates to the pursuit of human rights. However, the focus of ethics should be on the environment, as well as the individual.

life (art. 27), cultural development (art. 22), freedom of political belief (art. 19), freedom of religion (art. 18), and entitlement to human rights without discrimination (art. 2) (United Nations 1948).

The ethical guidelines that caution social workers not to practice, condone, or collaborate with any form of discrimination on the basis of race, ethnicity, national origin, color, sex, and other categories also correlates to various human rights principles. The Universal Declaration views everyone as equal before the law without any discrimination (art. 7). Everyone is entitled to human rights without distinctions based on race, color, sex, language, religion, political or other opinion, national or social origin, property, birth, or other status (art. 2) (United Nations 1948).

While many ethical responsibilities of a social worker correlate to human rights, one entire category of responsibilities in NASW's *Code of Ethics* appears based on the Universal Declaration: the ethical responsibilities of social workers to the broader society (NASW 1996:6). Under this category, social workers should

- Promote the general welfare of society and advocate for living conditions conducive to the fulfillment of basic human needs (6.01);
- Facilitate informed participation by the public in shaping social policies and institutions (6.02);
- Provide appropriate professional services in public emergencies to the greatest extent possible (6.03);
- Engage in social and political action that seeks to ensure that all people have equal access to employment and resources (6.04a);
- Act to expand choice and opportunity for all people, with special regard for vulnerable, disadvantaged, oppressed, and exploited people and groups (6.04b);
- Promote conditions that encourage respect for cultural and social diversity within the United States and globally (6.04c); and
- Act to prevent and eliminate domination of, exploitation of, and discrimination against any person, group, or class (6.04d).

This wide-ranging category of ethical responsibilities contains within itself a mini–Universal Declaration. The language is uncanny in its resemblance to the spirit of the declaration.

APPLYING ETHICAL RESPONSIBILITIES TO HUMAN RIGHTS—A CASE STUDY

After recognizing the strong connection of human rights to ethical standards of the social work profession, social workers can then take the crucial step of applying human rights to the profession through ethical principles. Because social workers practice in many different settings with diverse individuals and groups, analysis of the particular setting is important. The following case study illustrates this point.

CASE STUDY

Maya is 40 years old with three children ages five, seven, and eleven and has been living with a white Anglo male for the past three years. Maya immigrated to the United States from an Asian country four years ago. The children's father has little contact with them. One of Maya's children has a serious illness, and Maya has incurred large medical debts from the cost of treatment for the illness. Maya has worked regularly as a secretary, earning $25,000 a year, but Maya is now unemployed. Maya's partner has become physically abusive, but Maya has stayed in her relationship with him, partly for economic reasons. However, Maya has recently gone to a women's shelter with her children because she fears the partner. Maya now feels that she has few options. If she returns to the partner, she fears for her safety and that of her children. However, if she does not return, she has nowhere else to go and insufficient resources with which to obtain shelter on her own.

In analyzing the above situation in a human rights context, a social worker initially identifies the relevant human rights issues. After identifying these, the social worker connects these human rights to ethical responsibilities as outlined in social work practice. Upon making this connection of human rights to ethical responsibilities, the social worker can then form an appropriate intervention with the client.

Human Rights Issues

- "No one shall be subjected to torture or to cruel, inhuman, or degrading treatment or punishment" (United Nations 1948:art. 5). The physical abuse of Maya clearly falls within the prohibition against cruel and degrading treatment.
- "Everyone has the right to life, liberty, and the security of person" (art. 3). Maya

should feel safe as a person. Maya does not, yet she has a human right to that safety.

- "Everyone has the right to a standard of living adequate for the health and well-being of himself and of his family, including food, clothing, housing and medical care, and necessary social services, and the right to security in the event of unemployment, sickness, disability, widowhood, old age, or other lack of livelihood in circumstances beyond his control" (art. 25). Maya should be provided with medical care, food, and housing. Maya does not have health insurance for her children. Currently, she does have food for herself and her children because she is staying at the shelter. However, Maya's stay at the shelter will be limited, and Maya needs housing away from the partner.

Maya's circumstances involve the above human rights. The next step crucially connects those human rights with a social worker's ethical responsibilities as relating to Maya's situation.

Ethical Responsibilities

- Social workers have an ethical responsibility to clients that includes understanding culture and its function in human behavior and society (NASW 1996:1.05a). A social worker should familiarize herself with, and be sensitive to, cultural issues relating to Maya's Asian background.
- Social workers have an ethical responsibility to promote the general welfare of society and advocate for living conditions conducive to the fulfillment of basic human needs (6.01). A social worker should advocate for Maya's basic human needs, as outlined above under the human rights section.
- Social workers have an ethical responsibility to prevent and eliminate domination of, exploitation of, and discrimination against any person or group based on national origin, sex, or ethnicity (6.04d). In Maya's situation, a social worker should intervene to protect Maya against physical abuse from her partner, as this abuse has overtones of gender and ethnicity issues.
- Social workers have an ethical responsibility to improve social conditions in order to meet basic human needs and promote social justice and to promote conditions that encourage respect for cultural and social diversity within the United States and globally (6.04c). A social worker viewing Maya's circumstances can view the situation not simply as one involving individual issues but also as one with broader structural issues. This also provides the client with a

larger framework, one that establishes its relevance at a national and even global level, not just an individual one.

This case study illustrates the connection between human rights and ethics. By seeing and analyzing the particular circumstances of any given situation through the prism of human rights principles and ethical responsibilities, social workers can readily recognize the importance of human rights to their profession. Thus understood, one comes to realize that, frequently, human rights principles mirror ethical responsibilities as stated in the NASW's *Code of Ethics*.

ADDITIONAL CASE STUDIES

The following case studies all raise issues involving human rights and ethical responsibilities. Questions posed at the end of each case study provide guidance in helping to identify and analyze those issues.

CASE STUDY #1

Stephanie, age 86, lives by herself in a home she has occupied for fifty years. Stephanie now finds it difficult to take care of herself. However, she does not want to leave her home. Stephanie's grown children are now considering placing her in a nursing home. As a social worker, you have been asked to assess Stephanie's ability to remain at home and outside the nursing home.

Questions and Exercises

1. What human rights issues are relevant to this case study? Cite specific provisions within human rights instruments, including the Universal Declaration of Human Rights and international conventions. List issues for both Stephanie and the children.
2. What ethical issues are involved? Cite specific provisions within NASW's *Code of Ethics*.
3. Is there a link between the ethical issues and the human rights issues? If so, what is that link?
4. What controversy or conflict might arise from the human rights and ethical issues relevant to the case study?

5. How would you explain these relevant human rights issues to Stephanie and to Stephanie's children?

6. As a social worker, what approach would you take in this case?

CASE STUDY #2

Raymond, currently age 15, joined a gang at the age of 10. The gang is involved in all types of criminal activities, including the dealing of drugs. Recently, police arrested Raymond, and Raymond was convicted as an adult of a serious drug offense. Raymond is now serving a ten-year prison sentence in an adult facility. As a social worker employed at the prison where Raymond is serving his sentence, you provide counseling for Raymond.

1. What human rights issues are relevant to this case study? Cite specific provisions within human rights instruments, including the Universal Declaration of Human Rights and international conventions.

2. What ethical issues are involved? Cite specific provisions within NASW's *Code of Ethics*.

3. Is there a link between the ethical issues and the human rights issues? If so, what is that link?

4. What controversy or conflict might arise from the human rights and ethical issues relevant to the case study?

5. Do you believe that Raymond's human rights have been violated? If so, how? Cite specific examples.

CASE STUDY #3

Reah has recently gotten off welfare and now works at two different jobs. She has three children, ages 4, 5, and 7 years. While Reah earns more income than she received from welfare, her overall welfare benefits, including housing and health care, were greater. Reah and her children live in a low-income area with a high crime rate. Schools in the area have significantly fewer resources than those in most other areas. Reah has begun counseling with you to help cope with depression.

1. What human rights issues are relevant to this case study? Cite specific provisions within human rights instruments, including the Universal Declaration of Human Rights and international conventions.

2. What ethical issues are involved? Cite specific provisions within NASW's *Code of Ethics*.

3. Is there a link between the ethical issues and the human rights issues? If so, what is that link?

4. What controversy or conflict might arise from the human rights and ethical issues relevant to Reah's situation?

CASE STUDY #4

Jenny and Alice are a lesbian couple. They would like to adopt a child. As a social worker, you have performed a home study and recommended approval of the proposed adoption. However, during the legal adoption proceedings, the judge refuses to allow the adoption, saying that he did not believe homosexuals could be fit parents.

1. What human rights issues are relevant to this case study? Cite specific provisions within human rights instruments, including the Universal Declaration of Human Rights and international conventions.

2. What ethical issues are involved? Cite specific provisions within NASW's *Code of Ethics*.

3. Is there a link between the ethical issues and the human rights issues? If so, what is that link?

4. What controversy or conflict might arise from the human rights and ethical issues relevant to Jenny and Alice's situation?

CASE STUDY #5

Mark has lost his job and is currently unemployed. Mark is 57 years old and has few prospects for new employment. Mark has a spouse, Judith, but the couple has no children living at home. Mark currently receives $300 every two weeks in unemployment benefits but has no health care. Judith has only a part-time job with no benefits. The couple has always relied on Mark's health care benefits from his employment to cover their medical needs. Judith has diabetes and needs regular medical care. As a social worker, you are employed with the local public benefits office. Mark and Judith come to your office for assistance.

1. What human rights issues are relevant to this case study? Cite specific provisions within human rights instruments, including the Universal Declaration of Human Rights and international conventions.

2. What ethical issues are involved? Cite specific provisions within NASW's *Code of Ethics*.

3.   Is there a link between the ethical issues and the human rights issues? If so, what is that link?

4.   What controversy or conflict might arise from the human rights and ethical issues relevant to Mark and Judith's situation?

5.   How could you best help Mark and Judith?

CASE STUDY #6

Anna is a Hispanic woman employed as an accountant by a large accounting firm. For the past three years, Anna has received significantly lower merit increases than all her colleagues. Anna files a complaint with the Equal Employment and Opportunity Commission against her employer on the basis of discrimination. Anna and her employer settle the complaint, but six months later Anna's employer dismisses her, saying that she did not work as hard as the others. As a social worker who does counseling, you are approached by Anna to take her case.

1.   What human rights issues are relevant to this case study? Cite specific provisions within human rights instruments, including the Universal Declaration of Human Rights and international conventions.

2.   What ethical issues are involved? Cite specific provisions within NASW's *Code of Ethics*.

3.   Is there a link between the ethical issues and the human rights issues? If so, what is that link?

4.   What controversy or conflict might arise from the human rights and ethical issues relevant to Anna's situation?

CASE STUDY #7

A 6-year-old Cuban boy, Fidel, and his mother attempt to flee Cuba on a small boat to the United States. During the trip to the United States, the boat capsizes and Fidel's mother drowns. A fisherman rescues Fidel and takes him to Miami where the boy has distant relatives. Those relatives begin caring for Fidel. However, Fidel's father in Cuba files a petition in U.S. courts to request custody of Fidel. Fidel's relatives dispute that petition and file a counterpetition seeking custody of Fidel. The father and Fidel have a close relationship, but Fidel's relatives claim that Cuba is a dictatorship and Fidel would have no future life in that country. As a social worker, you are requested to submit to the court an assessment of which course of action would be in Fidel's best interests.

1. What human rights issues are relevant to this case study? Cite specific provisions within human rights instruments, including the Universal Declaration of Human Rights and international conventions.
2. What ethical issues are involved? Cite specific provisions within NASW's *Code of Ethics*.
3. Is there a link between the ethical issues and the human rights issues? If so, what is that link?
4. What controversy or conflict might arise from the human rights and ethical issues relevant to Fidel's situation?

CASE STUDY #8

Azza, an Ethiopian immigrant who moved to the United States thirteen years ago and now lives in Florida, plans to take her 10-year-old American-born daughter back to Ethiopia in a few months to have her circumcised. "They say it helps us control our emotions" she says. The 35-year-old mother is confused about whether or not she wants to put her daughter through the procedure, first saying that she and her husband are not sure what they are going to do, and finally saying that it is up to him and the Ethiopian doctors to decide.

1. What human rights issues are relevant to this case study? Cite specific provisions within human rights instruments, including the Universal Declaration of Human Rights and international conventions.
2. What ethical issues are involved? Cite specific provisions within NASW's *Code of Ethics*.
3. What is the link between the human rights issues and ethical issues?
4. Discuss the issue between the right to culture and human rights.

CONCLUSION

Human rights issues, such as freedom from physical abuse and a right to medical care and housing, clearly fall within the ethical responsibilities of social workers. By emphasizing the human rights aspect of social work, social workers can enhance their own fulfillment of ethical responsibilities.

Social workers who connect human rights issues with ethical principles can also better identify issues that go beyond individual circumstances. For instance, from a human rights perspective, a social worker would not view domestic violence as simply an issue involving the dynamics of the individual or couple but also as an issue that operates on a national or international scale. If it is a human right to be safe and secure, then this right would apply to everyone at any place anytime, irrespective of circumstances. Ethical principles in the social work profession support this view of domestic violence as a structural issue that social workers should address on a broad scale.

Individuals alone may not always be capable of overcoming oppression, especially when obstacles arise from broader structural difficulties. Adopting a human rights and ethics perspective can help social workers more readily identify structural difficulties in planning appropriate interventions. By recognizing structural difficulties as human rights and ethical issues, social workers can only enhance the primary mission of their profession.

QUESTIONS

1. Discuss a human rights issue you have experienced in social work practice.
2. How do human rights principles relate to different interventions used in social work practice?
3. Why is it important to analyze power structures when applying human rights to a particular situation?
4. How are NASW's *Code of Ethics* and the Universal Declaration of Human Rights similar? How are they different?
5. What difficulties exist in applying human rights to social work practice?
6. Discuss the human rights concept of universality in relation to social work ethics? Is universality compatible with social work ethics?
7. Why is the social work profession different from other helping professions?
8. How might antidiscrimination laws actually promote discrimination?
9. What reasons might account for why NASW's *Code of Ethics* does not mention the term *human rights*?
10. Can social work practice benefit from a human rights perspective?

REFERENCES

Abramson, M. 1996. Toward a more holistic understanding of ethics in social work. *Social Work in Health Care* 23.2: 1–15.
Allen, J. A. 1993. The constructivist paradigm: Values and ethics. *Journal of Teaching in Social Work* 8: 31–54.

Appleby, G., E. Colon, and J. Hamilton. 2001. *Diversity, Oppression, and Social Functioning: Person In-Environment Assessment and Intervention.* Boston: Allyn and Bacon.

Bricker-Jenkins, M., N. Hooeyman, and N. Gottlieb, eds. 1991. *Feminist Social Work Practice in Clinical Settings.* Newbury Park, Calif.: Sage.

Center for Human Rights. 1994. *Human Rights and Social Work: A Manual for Schools of Social Work and the Social Work Profession.* Training Series no. 1. Geneva: United Nations.

Cohen, R. 2002. The politics of ethics. *The Nation* (April 8): 21–23.

Compton, B. R. and B. Galaway. 1994. *Social Work Processes.* 5th ed. Belmont, Calif.: Wadsworth.

Congress, E. 1999. *Social Work Values and Ethics: Identifying and Resolving Professional Dilemmas.* Chicago: Nelson-Hall.

Cowger, C. 1994. Assessing client strengths: Clinical assessment for client empowerment. *Social Work: Journal of the National Association of Social Workers* 39.3: 262–67.

Devore, W. and E. Schlesinger. 1996. *Ethnic-sensitive Social Work Practice.* 5th ed. Boston. Allyn & Bacon.

Falck, H. 1988. *Social Work: The Membership Perspective.* New York: Springer.

Germain, C. B. and A. Gitterman. 1996. *The Life Model of Social Work Practice.* 2d ed. New York: Columbia University Press.

Goldstein, H. 1992. "If social work hasn't made progress as a science, might it be an art?" *Families in Society: Journal of Contemporary Human Services* (January): 48–55.

Gutierrez, L. M. 1990. Working with women of color: An empowerment perspective. *Social Work: Journal of the National Association of Social Workers* 35: 149–53.

Ife, J. 2001. *Human Rights and Social Work: Towards Rights-based Practice.* Cambridge: Cambridge University Press.

International Federation of Social Workers (IFSW). 2000. *See* www.ifsw.org/publication/4.5.3 pub.html.

Loewenberg, F. M. and R. Dolgoff. 1992. *Ethical Decisions for Social Work Practice.* Itasca, Ill.: Peacock.

Krist-Ashman, K. K. and G. H. Hull. 1993. *Understanding Generalist Practice.* Chicago: Nelson-Hall.

Lee, J. 1994. *The Empowerment Approach to Social Work Practice.* New York: Columbia University Press.

Mannig, S. 1997. The social worker as a moral citizen: Ethics in action. *Social Work: Journal of the National Association of Social Workers* 42.3: 223–30.

Mattison, M. 2000. Ethical Decision-making: The person in the process. *Social Work: Journal of the National Association of Social Workers* 45.3: 201–12.

Mayer, M. 1955. *They Thought They Were Free: The Germans, 1933–1955.* Chicago: University of Chicago Press.

McGoldrick, M., J. Giordano, and J. Pearce, eds. 1996. *Ethnicity and Family Therapy.* 2d ed. New York: Guilford.

National Association of Social Workers (NASW). 1996. *Code of Ethics*. Washington, D.C: NASW Press.

——. 2000. *Social Work Speaks: National Association of Social Workers Policy Statements, 2000–2003*. 5th ed. Washington, D.C.: NASW Press.

Pinderhughes, E. 1989. *Understanding Race, Ethnicity, and Power: The Key to Efficacy in Clinical Practice*. New York: Free Press.

Reamer, F. 1995. *Social Work Values and Ethics*. New York: Columbia University Press.

——. 1998. *Ethical Standards in Social Work: A Critical Review of the NASW Code of Ethics*. Washington, D.C.: NASW Press.

Reichert, E. 2001a. Move from social justice to human rights provides new perspective. *Professional Development: The International Journal of Continuing Social Work Education* 4.1: 5–13.

——. 2001b. Placing human rights at the center of the social work profession. *Journal of Intergroup Relations* 28.1 (Spring): 43–50.

Roche, S. and M. Dewees. 2001. Teaching About Human Rights in Social Work. *Journal of Teaching in Social Work* 21.1–2: 137–55.

Saleebey, D., ed. 2002. *The Strengths Perspective in Social Work Practice*. 3d ed. Boston: Allyn and Bacon.

Shulman, L. 1999. *Skills of Helping Individuals and Groups*. 4th ed. Itasca, Ill.: Peacock.

Simon, B. 1994. *The Empowerment Tradition in American Social Work*. New York: Columbia University Press.

Solomon, B. 1976. *Black Empowerment: Social Work in Oppressed Communities*. New York: Columbia University Press.

Staub-Bernasconi, S. 1998. Soziale Arbeit als Menschenrechtsprofession. In A. Woehrle, ed., *Profession und Wissenschaft Sozialer Arbeit: Positionen in einer Phase der generellen Neuverortnung und Spezifika*, 305–32. Pfaffenweiler, Ger.: Cenaurus.

Swenson, C. 1998. Clinical social work's contribution to a social justice perspective. *Social Work: Journal of the National Association of Social Workers* 43.6: 527–37.

United Nations. 1948. *Universal Declaration of Human Rights*. Adopted December 10, 1948. GA. Res. 217 AIII. United Nations Document a/810. New York: UN.

Van Den Bergh, N. and L. B. Cooper, eds. 1986. *Feminist Visions for Social Work*. Silver Spring, Md.: NASW.

Van Wormer, K. 1997. *Social Welfare: A World View*. Chicago: Nelson-Hall.

Webster's. 1989. [*Webster's*] *Encyclopedia: An Unabridged Dictionary of the English Language*. New York: Portland House.

Witkin, S. 1998. Human rights and social work. *Social Work: Journal of the National Association of Social Workers* 43: 197–201.

——. 2000. Ethics-R-Us. *Social Work: Journal of the National Association of Social Workers* 45.3: 197–200.

Conclusion

For too long, the social work profession in the United States has avoided specific integration of human rights documents and provisions into the study of social work. Yet human rights concepts permeate all aspects of social work practice and policy.

Possibly no other profession cries out for the integration of human rights as does social work. The value of human rights to the profession lies in a relatively concrete framework from which to present social work principles. While a useful concept, social justice simply does not provide a similar framework upon which to guide social work practice and policy. Social justice has become more of a buzzword than a body of principles that can be cited and incorporated into the profession.

Of course, human rights present their own challenges when applying these rights to social work practice and policy. How can human rights apply to everyone if that means questioning long-standing cultural or religious norms? Even when a consensus exists on the application of a human right, what happens if no enforcement of that right occurs?

Human rights are continually evolving, especially at the grassroots level, as illustrated by the 4th UN World Conference on Women (Beijing, 1995), which led in turn to the accompanying NGO Forum on Women. Tensions brought about by differing viewpoints over human rights will always exist. Likewise, issues of culture, religion, and power will always be part of the struggle for human rights. But while the struggle for human rights focuses primarily on the commonality of individuals and groups throughout the world, it cannot help but recognize that people are also different.

Social workers everywhere have a unique role to play in promoting human rights. As members of a human rights profession, social workers can make a significant contribution to the development of human rights.

The ultimate goal of this book is to prompt students, educators, and professionals to further their knowledge about human rights and develop techniques for applying human rights to the profession. This book can serve only as a starting point in the study of human rights and their application to the social work profession. My hope is that others will build on the premise of this book and work to expand the connection between social work and human rights.

APPENDIX A

Universal Declaration of Human Rights

PREAMBLE

Whereas recognition of the inherent dignity and of the equal and inalienable rights of all members of the human family is the foundation of freedom, justice, and peace in the world,

Whereas disregard and contempt for human rights have resulted in barbarous acts which have outraged the conscience of mankind, and the advent of a world in which human beings shall enjoy freedom of speech and belief and freedom from fear and want has been proclaimed as the highest aspiration of the common people,

Whereas it is essential, if man is not to be compelled to have recourse, as a last resort, to rebellion against tyranny and oppression, that human rights should be protected by the rule of law,

Whereas it is essential to promote the development of friendly relations between nations,

Whereas the peoples of the United Nations have in the Charter reaffirmed their faith in fundamental human rights, in the dignity and worth of the human person and in the equal rights of men and women and have determined to promote social progress and better standards of life in larger freedom,

Whereas Member States have pledged themselves to achieve, in cooperation with the United Nations, the promotion of universal respect for and observance of human rights and fundamental freedoms,

Whereas a common understanding of these rights and freedoms is of the greatest importance for the full realization of this pledge,

Now, therefore,
The General Assembly
Proclaims this Universal Declaration of Human Rights as a common standard of achievement for all peoples and all nations, to the end that every individual and every organ of society, keeping this Declaration constantly in mind, shall strive by teaching and education to promote respect for these rights and freedoms and by progressive measures, national and international, to secure their universal and effective recognition and observance, both among the peoples of Member States themselves and among the peoples of territories under their jurisdiction.

Article 1
All human beings are born free and equal in dignity and rights. They are endowed with reason and conscience and should act towards one another in a spirit of brotherhood.

Article 2
Everyone is entitled to all the rights and freedoms set forth in this Declaration, without distinction of any kind, such as race, colour, sex, language, religion, political or other opinion, national or social origin, property, birth or other status.

Furthermore, no distinction shall be made on the basis of the political, jurisdictional or international status of the country or territory to which a person belongs, whether it be independent, trust, non-self-governing or under any other limitation of sovereignty.

Article 3
Everyone has the right to life, liberty, and the security of person.

Article 4
No one shall be held in slavery or servitude; slavery and the slave trade shall be prohibited in all their forms.

Article 5
No one shall be subjected to torture or to cruel, inhuman, or degrading treatment or punishment.

Article 6
Everyone has the right to recognition everywhere as a person before the law.

Article 7
All are equal before the law and are entitled without any discrimination to equal protection of the law. All are entitled to equal protection against any discrimination in violation of this Declaration and against any incitement to such discrimination.

Article 8
Everyone has the right to an effective remedy by the competent national tribunals for acts violating the fundamental rights granted him by the constitution or by law.

Article 9
No one shall be subjected to arbitrary arrest, detention, or exile.

Article 10
Everyone is entitled in full equality to a fair and public hearing by an independent and impartial tribunal, in the determination of his rights and obligations and of any criminal charge against him.

Article 11
1. Everyone charged with a penal offence has the right to be presumed innocent until proved guilty according to law in a public trial at which he has had all the guarantees necessary for his defence.

2. No one shall be held guilty of any penal offence on account of any act or omission which did not constitute a penal offence, under national or international law, at the time when it was committed. Nor shall a heavier penalty be imposed than the one that was applicable at the time the penal offence was committed.

Article 12
No one shall be subjected to arbitrary interference with his privacy, family, home or correspondence, nor to attacks upon his honor and reputation. Everyone has the right to the protection of the law against such interference or attacks.

Article 13
1. Everyone has the right to freedom of movement and residence within the borders of each State.

2. Everyone has the right to leave any country, including his own, and to return to his country.

Article 14
1. Everyone has the right to seek and to enjoy in other countries asylum from persecution.

2. This right may not be invoked in the case of prosecutions genuinely arising from non-political crimes or from acts contrary to the purposes and principles of the United Nations.

Article 15
1. Everyone has the right to a nationality.

2. No one shall be arbitrarily deprived of his nationality nor denied the right to change his nationality.

Article 16

1. Men and women of full age, without any limitation due to race, nationality, or religion, have the right to marry and to found a family. They are entitled to equal rights as to marriage, during marriage and at its dissolution.

2. Marriage shall be entered into only with the free and full consent of the intending spouses.

3. The family is the natural and fundamental group unit of society and is entitled to protection by society and the State.

Article 17

1. Everyone has the right to own property alone as well as in association with others.

2. No one shall be arbitrarily deprived of his property.

Article 18

Everyone has the right to freedom of thought, conscience, and religion; this right includes freedom to change his religion or belief, and freedom, either alone or in community with others and in public or private, to manifest his religion or belief in teaching, practice, worship, and observance.

Article 19

Everyone has the right to freedom of opinion and expression; this right includes freedom to hold opinions without interference and to seek, receive, and impart information and ideas through any media and regardless of frontiers.

Article 20

1. Everyone has the right to freedom of peaceful assembly and association.

2. No one may be compelled to belong to an association.

Article 21

1. Everyone has the right to take part in the government of his country, directly or through freely chosen representatives.

2. Everyone has the right of equal access to public service in his country.

3. The will of the people shall be the basis of the authority of government; this will shall be expressed in periodic and genuine elections which shall be by universal and equal suffrage and shall be held by secret vote or by equivalent free voting procedures.

Article 22

Everyone, as a member of society, has the right to social security and is entitled to realization, through national effort and international co-operation and in accordance with the organization and resources of each State, of the economic, social, and cultural rights indispensable for his dignity and the free development of his personality.

Article 23

1. Everyone has the right to work, to free choice of employment, to just and favourable conditions of work and to protection against unemployment.

2. Everyone, without any discrimination, has the right to equal pay for equal work.

3. Everyone who works has the right to just and favourable remuneration ensuring for himself and his family an existence worthy of human dignity, and supplemented, if necessary, by other means of social protection.

4. Everyone has the right to form and to join trade unions for the protection of his interests.

Article 24

Everyone has the right to rest and leisure, including reasonable limitation of working hours and periodic holidays with pay.

Article 25

1. Everyone has the right to a standard of living adequate for the health and well-being of himself and of his family, including food, clothing, housing and medical care, and necessary social services, and the right to security in the event of unemployment, sickness, disability, widowhood, old age, or other lack of livelihood in circumstances beyond his control.

2. Motherhood and childhood are entitled to special care and assistance. All children, whether born in or out of wedlock, shall enjoy the same social protection.

Article 26

1. Everyone has the right to education. Education shall be free, at least in the elementary and fundamental stages. Elementary education shall be compulsory. Technical and professional education shall be made generally available and higher education shall be equally accessible to all on the basis of merit.

2. Education shall be directed to the full development of the human personality and to the strengthening of respect for human rights and fundamental freedoms. It shall promote understanding, tolerance, and friendship among all nations, racial or religious groups, and shall further the activities of the United Nations for the maintenance of peace.

3. Parents have a prior right to choose the kind of education that shall be given to their children.

Article 27

1. Everyone has the right freely to participate in the cultural life of the community, to enjoy the arts, and to share in scientific advancement and its benefits.

2. Everyone has the right to the protection of the moral and material interests resulting from any scientific, literary, or artistic production of which he is the author.

Article 28

Everyone is entitled to a social and international order in which the rights and freedoms set forth in this Declaration can be fully realized.

Article 29

1. Everyone has duties to the community in which alone the free and full development of his personality is possible.

2. In the exercise of his rights and freedoms, everyone shall be subject only to such limitations as are determined by law solely for the purpose of securing due recognition and respect for the rights and freedoms of others and of meeting the just requirements of morality, public order, and the general welfare in a democratic society.

3. These rights and freedoms may in no case be exercised contrary to the purposes and principles of the United Nations.

Article 30

Nothing in this Declaration may be interpreted as implying for any State, group, or person any right to engage in any activity or to perform any act aimed at the destruction of any of the rights and freedoms set forth herein.

APPENDIX B

International Covenant on Civil and Political Rights

PREAMBLE

The States Parties to the present Covenant,

Considering that, in accordance with the principles proclaimed in the Charter of the United Nations, recognition of the inherent dignity and of the equal and inalienable rights of all members of the human family is the foundation of freedom, justice, and peace in the world,

Recognizing that these rights derive from the inherent dignity of the human person,

Recognizing that, in accordance with the Universal Declaration of Human Rights, the ideal of free human beings enjoying civil and political freedom and freedom from fear and want can only be achieved if conditions are created whereby everyone may enjoy his civil and political rights, as well as his economic, social, and cultural rights,

Considering the obligation of States under the Charter of the United Nations to promote universal respect for, and observance of, human rights and freedoms,

Realizing that the individual, having duties to other individuals and to the community to which he belongs, is under a responsibility to strive for the promotion and observance of the rights recognized in the present Covenant,

Agree upon the following articles:

PART I

Article 1

1. All peoples have the right of self-determination. By virtue of that right they freely determine their political status and freely pursue their economic, social, and cultural development.

2. All peoples may, for their own ends, freely dispose of their natural wealth and resources without prejudice to any obligations arising out of international economic co-operation, based upon the principle of mutual benefit, and international law. In no case may a people be deprived of its own means of subsistence.

3. The States Parties to the present Covenant, including those having responsibility for the administration of Non-Self-Governing and Trust Territories, shall promote the realization of the right of self-determination, and shall respect that right, in conformity with the provisions of the Charter of the United Nations.

PART II

Article 2

1. Each State Party to the present Covenant undertakes to respect and to ensure to all individuals within its territory and subject to its jurisdiction the rights recognized in the present Covenant, without distinction of any kind, such as race, colour, sex, language, religion, political or other opinion, national or social origin, property, birth, or other status.

2. Where not already provided for by existing legislative or other measures, each State Party to the present Covenant undertakes to take the necessary steps, in accordance with its constitutional processes and with the provisions of the present Covenant, to adopt such legislative or other measures as may be necessary to give effect to the rights recognized in the present Covenant.

3. Each State Party to the present Covenant undertakes:

(*a*) To ensure that any person whose rights or freedoms as herein recognized are violated shall have an effective remedy, notwithstanding that the violation has been committed by persons acting in an official capacity;

(*b*) To ensure that any person claiming such a remedy shall have his right thereto determined by competent judicial, administrative, or legislative authorities, or by any other competent authority provided for by the legal system of the State, and to develop the possibilities of judicial remedy;

(*c*) To ensure that the competent authorities shall enforce such remedies where granted.

Article 3

The States Parties to the present Covenant undertake to ensure the equal right of men and women to the enjoyment of all civil and political rights set forth in the present Covenant.

Article 4

1. In time of public emergency which threatens the life of the nation and the existence of which is officially proclaimed, the States Parties to the present Covenant may take measures derogating from their obligations under the present Covenant to the extent strictly required by the exigencies of the situation, provided that such measures are not inconsistent with their other obligations under international law and do not involve discrimination solely on the ground of race, colour, sex, language, religion, or social origin.

2. No derogation from articles 6, 7, 8 (paragraphs 1 and 2), 11, 15, 16, and 18 may be made under this provision.

3. Any State Party to the present Covenant availing itself of the right of derogation shall immediately inform the other States Parties to the present Covenant, through the intermediary of the Secretary-General of the United Nations, of the provisions from which it has derogated and of the reasons by which it was actuated. A further communication shall be made, through the same intermediary, on the date on which it terminates such derogation.

Article 5

1. Nothing in the present Covenant may be interpreted as implying for any State, group, or person any right to engage in any activity or perform any act aimed at the destruction of any of the rights and freedoms recognized herein or at their limitation to a greater extent than is provided for in the present Covenant.

2. There shall be no restriction upon or derogation from any of the fundamental human rights recognized or existing in any State Party to the present Covenant pursuant to law, conventions, regulations, or custom on the pretext that the present Covenant does not recognize such rights or that it recognizes them to a lesser extent.

PART III

Article 6

1. Every human being has the inherent right to life. This right shall be protected by law. No one shall be arbitrarily deprived of his life.

2. In countries which have not abolished the death penalty, sentence of death may be imposed only for the most serious crimes in accordance with the law in force at the time of the commission of the crime and not contrary to the provisions of the present Covenant and to the Convention on the Prevention and Punishment of the Crime of Genocide. This penalty can only be carried out pursuant to a final judgement rendered by a competent court.

3. When deprivation of life constitutes the crime of genocide, it is understood that nothing in this article shall authorize any State Party to the present Covenant to derogate in any way from any obligation assumed under the provisions of the Convention on the Prevention and Punishment of the Crime of Genocide.

4. Anyone sentenced to death shall have the right to seek pardon or commutation

of the sentence. Amnesty, pardon, or commutation of the sentence of death may be granted in all cases.

5. Sentence of death shall not be imposed for crimes committed by persons below eighteen years of age and shall not be carried out on pregnant women.

6. Nothing in this article shall be invoked to delay or to prevent the abolition of capital punishment by any State Party to the present Covenant.

Article 7

No one shall be subjected to torture or to cruel, inhuman, or degrading treatment or punishment. In particular, no one shall be subjected without his free consent to medical or scientific experimentation.

Article 8

1. No one shall be held in slavery; slavery and the slave-trade in all their forms shall be prohibited.

2. No one shall be held in servitude.

3. (*a*) No one shall be required to perform forced or compulsory labour;

(*b*) Paragraph 3(*a*) shall not be held to preclude, in countries where imprisonment with hard labour may be imposed as a punishment for a crime, the performance of hard labour in pursuance of a sentence to such punishment by a competent court;

(*c*) For the purpose of this paragraph the term "forced or compulsory labour" shall not include:

(i) Any work or service, not referred to in subparagraph (*b*), normally required of a person who is under detention in consequence of a lawful order of a court, or of a person during conditional release from such detention;

(ii) Any service of a military character and, in countries where conscientious objection is recognized, any national service required by law of conscientious objectors;

(iii) Any service exacted in cases of emergency or calamity threatening the life or well-being of the community;

(iv) Any work or service which forms part of normal civil obligations.

Article 9

1. Everyone has the right to liberty and security of person. No one shall be subjected to arbitrary arrest or detention. No one shall be deprived of his liberty except on such grounds and in accordance with such procedure as are established by law.

2. Anyone who is arrested shall be informed, at the time of arrest, of the reasons for his arrest and shall be promptly informed of any charges against him.

3. Anyone arrested or detained on a criminal charge shall be brought promptly before a judge or other officer authorized by law to exercise judicial power and shall be entitled to trial within a reasonable time or to release. It shall not be the general rule that persons awaiting trial shall be detained in custody, but release may be subject to guarantees to appear for trial, at any other stage of the judicial proceedings, and, should occasion arise, for execution of the judgement.

4. Anyone who is deprived of his liberty by arrest or detention shall be entitled to take proceedings before a court, in order that that court may decide without delay on the lawfulness of his detention and order his release if the detention is not lawful.

5. Anyone who has been the victim of unlawful arrest or detention shall have an enforceable right to compensation.

Article 10
1. All persons deprived of their liberty shall be treated with humanity and with respect for the inherent dignity of the human person.

2. (*a*) Accused persons shall, save in exceptional circumstances, be segregated from convicted persons and shall be subject to separate treatment appropriate to their status as unconvicted persons;

(*b*) Accused juvenile persons shall be separated from adults and brought as speedily as possible for adjudication.

3. The penitentiary system shall comprise treatment of prisoners the essential aim of which shall be their reformation and social rehabilitation. Juvenile offenders shall be segregated from adults and be accorded treatment appropriate to their age and legal status.

Article 11
No one shall be imprisoned merely on the ground of inability to fulfil a contractual obligation.

Article 12
1. Everyone lawfully within the territory of a State shall, within that territory, have the right to liberty of movement and freedom to choose his residence.

2. Everyone shall be free to leave any country, including his own.

3. The above-mentioned rights shall not be subject to any restrictions except those which are provided by law, are necessary to protect national security, public order (*ordre public*), public health or morals or the rights and freedoms of others, and are consistent with the other rights recognized in the present Covenant.

4. No one shall be arbitrarily deprived of the right to enter his own country.

Article 13
An alien lawfully in the territory of a State Party to the present Covenant may be

expelled therefrom only in pursuance of a decision reached in accordance with law and shall, except where compelling reasons of national security otherwise require, be allowed to submit the reasons against his expulsion and to have his case reviewed by, and be represented for the purpose before, the competent authority or a person or persons especially designated by the competent authority.

Article 14

1. All persons shall be equal before the courts and tribunals. In the determination of any criminal charge against him, or of his rights and obligations in a suit at law, everyone shall be entitled to a fair and public hearing by a competent, independent, and impartial tribunal established by law. The Press and the public may be excluded from all or part of a trial for reasons of morals, public order (ordre public), or national security in a democratic society, or when the interest of the private lives of the parties so requires, or to the extent strictly necessary in the opinion of the court in special circumstances where publicity would prejudice the interests of justice; but any judgement rendered in a criminal case or in a suit at law shall be made public except where the interest of juvenile persons otherwise requires or the proceedings concern matrimonial disputes or the guardianship of children.

2. Everyone charged with a criminal offence shall have the right to be presumed innocent until proved guilty according to law.

3. In the determination of any criminal charge against him, everyone shall be entitled to the following minimum guarantees, in full equality:

(*a*) To be informed promptly and in detail in a language which he understands of the nature and cause of the charge against him;

(*b*) To have adequate time and facilities for the preparation of his defence and to communicate with counsel of his own choosing;

(*c*) To be tried without undue delay;

(*d*) To be tried in his presence, and to defend himself in person or through legal assistance of his own choosing; to be informed, if he does not have legal assistance, of this right; and to have legal assistance assigned to him, in any case where the interests of justice so require, and without payment by him in any such case if he does not have sufficient means to pay for it;

(*e*) To examine, or have examined, the witnesses against him and to obtain the attendance and examination of witnesses on his behalf under the same conditions as witnesses against him;

(*f*) To have the free assistance of an interpreter if he cannot understand or speak the language used in court;

(*g*) Not to be compelled to testify against himself or to confess guilt.

4. In the case of juvenile persons, the procedure shall be such as will take account of their age and the desirability of promoting their rehabilitation.

5. Everyone convicted of a crime shall have the right to his conviction and sentence being reviewed by a higher tribunal according to law.

6. When a person has by a final decision been convicted of a criminal offence and when subsequently his conviction has been reversed or he has been pardoned on the ground that a new or newly discovered fact shows conclusively that there has been a miscarriage of justice, the person who has suffered punishment as a result of such conviction shall be compensated according to law, unless it is proved that the nondisclosure of the unknown fact in time is wholly or partly attributable to him.

7. No one shall be liable to be tried or punished again for an offence for which he has already been finally convicted or acquitted in accordance with the law and penal procedure of each country.

Article 15
1. No one shall be held guilty of any criminal offence on account of any act or omission which did not constitute a criminal offence, under national or international law, at the time when it was committed. Nor shall a heavier penalty be imposed than the one that was applicable at the time when the criminal offence was committed. If, subsequent to the commission of the offence, provision is made by law for the imposition of a lighter penalty, the offender shall benefit thereby.

2. Nothing in this article shall prejudice the trial and punishment of any person for any act or omission which, at the time when it was committed, was criminal according to the general principles of law recognized by the community of nations.

Article 16
Everyone shall have the right to recognition everywhere as a person before the law.

Article 17
1. No one shall be subjected to arbitrary or unlawful interference with his privacy, family, home, or correspondence, nor to unlawful attacks on his honour and reputation.

2. Everyone has the right to the protection of the law against such interference or attacks.

Article 18
1. Everyone shall have the right to freedom of thought, conscience, and religion. This right shall include freedom to have or to adopt a religion or belief of his choice, and freedom, either individually or in community with others and in public or private, to manifest his religion or belief in worship, observance, practice, and teaching.

2. No one shall be subject to coercion which would impair his freedom to have or to adopt a religion or belief of his choice.

3. Freedom to manifest one's religion or beliefs may be subject only to such limi-

tations as are prescribed by law and are necessary to protect public safety, order, health, or morals, or the fundamental rights and freedoms of others.

4. The States Parties to the present Covenant undertake to have respect for the liberty of parents and, when applicable, legal guardians to ensure the religious and moral education of their children in conformity with their own convictions.

Article 19

1. Everyone shall have the right to hold opinions without interference.

2. Everyone shall have the right to freedom of expression; this right shall include freedom to seek, receive, and impart information and ideas of all kinds, regardless of frontiers, either orally, in writing, or in print, in the form of art, or through any other media of his choice.

3. The exercise of the rights provided for in paragraph 2 of this article carries with it special duties and responsibilities. It may therefore be subject to certain restrictions, but these shall only be such as are provided by law and are necessary:

(*a*) For respect of the rights or reputations of others;

(*b*) For the protection of national security or of public order (*ordre public*), or of public health or morals.

Article 20

1. Any propaganda for war shall be prohibited by law.

2. Any advocacy of national, racial, or religious hatred that constitutes incitement to discrimination, hostility, or violence shall be prohibited by law.

Article 21

The right of peaceful assembly shall be recognized. No restrictions may be placed on the exercise of this right other than those imposed in conformity with the law and which are necessary in a democratic society in the interests of national security or public safety, public order (ordre public), the protection of public health or morals, or the protection of the rights and freedoms of others.

Article 22

1. Everyone shall have the right of freedom of association with others, including the right to form and join trade unions for the protection of his interests.

2. No restrictions may be placed on the exercise of this right other than those which are prescribed by law and which are necessary in a democratic society in the interests of national security or public safety, public order (*ordre public*), the protection of public health or morals, or the protection of the rights and freedoms of others. This article shall not prevent the imposition of lawful restrictions on members of the armed forces and of the police in their exercise of this right.

3. Nothing in this article shall authorize States Parties to the International Labour

Organisation Convention of 1948 concerning Freedom of Association and Protection of the Right to Organise to take legislative measures which would prejudice, or to apply the law in such a manner as to prejudice, the guarantees provided for in that Convention.

Article 23

1. The family is the natural and fundamental group unit of society and is entitled to protection by society and the State.

2. The right of men and women of marriageable age to marry and to found a family shall be recognized.

3. No marriage shall be entered into without the free and full consent of the intending spouses.

4. States Parties to the present Covenant shall take appropriate steps to ensure equality of rights and responsibilities of spouses as to marriage, during marriage and at its dissolution. In the case of dissolution, provision shall be made for the necessary protection of any children.

Article 24

1. Every child shall have, without any discrimination as to race, colour, sex, language, religion, national or social origin, property or birth, the right to such measures of protection as are required by his status as a minor, on the part of his family, society, and the State.

2. Every child shall be registered immediately after birth and shall have a name.

3. Every child has the right to acquire a nationality.

Article 25

Every citizen shall have the right and the opportunity, without any of the distinctions mentioned in article 2 and without unreasonable restrictions:

(a) To take part in the conduct of public affairs, directly or through freely chosen representatives;

(b) To vote and to be elected at genuine periodic elections which shall be by universal and equal suffrage and shall be held by secret ballot, guaranteeing the free expression of the will of the electors;

(c) To have access, on general terms of equality, to public service in his country.

Article 26

All persons are equal before the law and are entitled without any discrimination to the equal protection of the law. In this respect, the law shall prohibit any discrimination and guarantee to all persons equal and effective protection against discrimination on any ground such as race, colour, sex, language, religion, political or other opinion, national or social origin, property, birth, or other status.

Article 27

In those States in which ethnic, religious, or linguistic minorities exist, persons belonging to such minorities shall not be denied the right, in community with the other members of their group, to enjoy their own culture, to profess and practise their own religion, or to use their own language.

PART IV

Article 28

1. There shall be established a Human Rights Committee (hereafter referred to in the present Covenant as the Committee). It shall consist of eighteen members and shall carry out the functions hereinafter provided.

2. The Committee shall be composed of nationals of the States Parties to the present Covenant who shall be persons of high moral character and recognized competence in the field of human rights, consideration being given to the usefulness of the participation of some persons having legal experience.

3. The members of the Committee shall be elected and shall serve in their personal capacity.

Article 29

1. The members of the Committee shall be elected by secret ballot from a list of persons possessing the qualifications prescribed in article 28 and nominated for the purpose by the States Parties to the present Covenant.

2. Each State Party to the present Covenant may nominate not more than two persons. These persons shall be nationals of the nominating State.

3. A person shall be eligible for renomination.

Article 30

1. The initial election shall be held no later than six months after the date of the entry into force of the present Covenant.

2. At least four months before the date of each election to the Committee, other than an election to fill a vacancy declared in accordance with article 34, the Secretary-General of the United Nations shall address a written invitation to the States Parties to the present Covenant to submit their nominations for membership of the Committee within three months.

3. The Secretary-General of the United Nations shall prepare a list in alphabetical order of all the persons thus nominated, with an indication of the States Parties which have nominated them, and shall submit it to the States Parties to the present Covenant no later than one month before the date of each election.

4. Elections of the members of the Committee shall be held at a meeting of the States Parties to the present Covenant convened by the Secretary-General of the

United Nations at the Headquarters of the United Nations. At that meeting, for which two thirds of the States Parties to the present Covenant shall constitute a quorum, the persons elected to the Committee shall be those nominees who obtain the largest number of votes and an absolute majority of the votes of the representatives of States Parties present and voting.

Article 31

1. The Committee may not include more than one national of the same State.

2. In the election of the Committee, consideration shall be given to equitable geographical distribution of membership and to the representation of the different forms of civilization and of the principal legal systems.

Article 32

1. The members of the Committee shall be elected for a term of four years. They shall be eligible for re-election if renominated. However, the terms of nine of the members elected at the first election shall expire at the end of two years; immediately after the first election, the names of these nine members shall be chosen by lot by the Chairman of the meeting referred to in article 30, paragraph 4.

2. Elections at the expiry of office shall be held in accordance with the preceding articles of this part of the present Covenant.

Article 33

1. If, in the unanimous opinion of the other members, a member of the Committee has ceased to carry out his functions for any cause other than absence of a temporary character, the Chairman of the Committee shall notify the Secretary-General of the United Nations, who shall then declare the seat of that member to be vacant.

2. In the event of the death or the resignation of a member of the Committee, the Chairman shall immediately notify the Secretary-General of the United Nations, who shall declare the seat vacant from the date of death or the date on which the resignation takes effect.

Article 34

1. When a vacancy is declared in accordance with article 33 and if the term of office of the member to be replaced does not expire within six months of the declaration of the vacancy, the Secretary-General of the United Nations shall notify each of the States Parties to the present Covenant, which may within two months submit nominations in accordance with article 29 for the purpose of filling the vacancy.

2. The Secretary-General of the United Nations shall prepare a list in alphabetical order of the persons thus nominated and shall submit it to the States Parties to the present Covenant. The election to fill the vacancy shall then take place in accordance with the relevant provisions of this part of the present Covenant.

3. A member of the Committee elected to fill a vacancy declared in accordance

with article 33 shall hold office for the remainder of the term of the member who vacated the seat on the Committee under the provisions of that article.

Article 35

The members of the Committee shall, with the approval of the General Assembly of the United Nations, receive emoluments from United Nations resources on such terms and conditions as the General Assembly may decide, having regard to the importance of the Committee's responsibilities.

Article 36

The Secretary-General of the United Nations shall provide the necessary staff and facilities for the effective performance of the functions of the Committee under the present Covenant.

Article 37

1. The Secretary-General of the United Nations shall convene the initial meeting of the Committee at the Headquarters of the United Nations.

2. After its initial meeting, the Committee shall meet at such times as shall be provided in its rules of procedure.

3. The Committee shall normally meet at the Headquarters of the United Nations or at the United Nations Office at Geneva.

Article 38

Every member of the Committee shall, before taking up his duties, make a solemn declaration in open committee that he will perform his functions impartially and conscientiously.

Article 39

1. The Committee shall elect its officers for a term of two years. They may be re-elected.

2. The Committee shall establish its own rules of procedure, but these rules shall provide, inter alia, that:

(*a*) Twelve members shall constitute a quorum;

(*b*) Decisions of the Committee shall be made by a majority vote of the members present.

Article 40

1. The States Parties to the present Covenant undertake to submit reports on the measures they have adopted which give effect to the rights recognized herein and on the progress made in the enjoyment of those rights:

(*a*) Within one year of the entry into force of the present Covenant for the States Parties concerned;

(*b*) Thereafter whenever the Committee so requests.

2. All reports shall be submitted to the Secretary-General of the United Nations, who shall transmit them to the Committee for consideration. Reports shall indicate the factors and difficulties, if any, affecting the implementation of the present Covenant.

3. The Secretary-General of the United Nations may, after consultation with the Committee, transmit to the specialized agencies concerned copies of such parts of the reports as may fall within their field of competence.

4. The Committee shall study the reports submitted by the States Parties to the present Covenant. It shall transmit its reports, and such general comments as it may consider appropriate, to the States Parties. The Committee may also transmit to the Economic and Social Council these comments along with the copies of the reports it has received from States Parties to the present Covenant.

5. The States Parties to the present Covenant may submit to the Committee observations on any comments that may be made in accordance with paragraph 4 of this article.

Article 41

1. A State Party to the present Covenant may at any time declare under this article that it recognizes the competence of the Committee to receive and consider communications to the effect that a State Party claims that another State Party is not fulfilling its obligations under the present Covenant. Communications under this article may be received and considered only if submitted by a State Party which has made a declaration recognizing in regard to itself the competence of the Committee. No communication shall be received by the Committee if it concerns a State Party which has not made such a declaration. Communications received under this article shall be dealt with in accordance with the following procedure:

(*a*) If a State Party to the present Covenant considers that another State Party is not giving effect to the provisions of the present Covenant, it may, by written communication, bring the matter to the attention of that State Party. Within three months after the receipt of the communication, the receiving State shall afford the State which sent the communication an explanation or any other statement in writing clarifying the matter, which should include, to the extent possible and pertinent, reference to domestic procedures and remedies taken, pending, or available in the matter.

(*b*) If the matter is not adjusted to the satisfaction of both States Parties concerned within six months after the receipt by the receiving State of the initial communication, either State shall have the right to refer the matter to the Committee, by notice given to the Committee and to the other State.

(*c*) The Committee shall deal with a matter referred to it only after it has ascertained that all available domestic remedies have been invoked and exhausted in the matter, in conformity with the generally recognized principles of international law. This shall not be the rule where the application of the remedies is unreasonably prolonged.

(*d*) The Committee shall hold closed meetings when examining communications under this article.

(*e*) Subject to the provisions of subparagraph (*c*), the Committee shall make available its good offices to the States Parties concerned with a view to a friendly solution of the matter on the basis of respect for human rights and fundamental freedoms as recognized in the present Covenant.

(*f*) In any matter referred to it, the Committee may call upon the States Parties concerned, referred to in subparagraph (*b*), to supply any relevant information.

(*g*) The States Parties concerned, referred to in subparagraph (*b*), shall have the right to be represented when the matter is being considered in the Committee and to make submissions orally and/or in writing.

(*h*) The Committee shall, within twelve months after the date of receipt of notice under subparagraph (*b*), submit a report:

(i) If a solution within the terms of subparagraph (*e*) is reached, the Committee shall confine its report to a brief statement of the facts and of the solution reached;

(ii) If a solution within the terms of subparagraph (*e*) is not reached, the Committee shall confine its report to a brief statement of the facts; the written submissions and record of the oral submissions made by the States Parties concerned shall be attached to the report.

In every matter, the report shall be communicated to the States Parties concerned.

2. The provisions of this article shall come into force when ten States Parties to the present Covenant have made declarations under paragraph 1 of this article. Such declarations shall be deposited by the States Parties with the Secretary-General of the United Nations, who shall transmit copies thereof to the other States Parties. A declaration may be withdrawn at any time by notification to the Secretary-General. Such a withdrawal shall not prejudice the consideration of any matter which is the subject of a communication already transmitted under this article; no further communication by any State Party shall be received after the notification of withdrawal of the declaration has been received by the Secretary-General, unless the State Party concerned has made a new declaration.

Article 42
1. (*a*) If a matter referred to the Committee in accordance with article 41 is not resolved to the satisfaction of the States Parties concerned, the Committee may, with

the prior consent of the States Parties concerned, appoint an *ad hoc* Conciliation Commission (hereinafter referred to as the Commission). The good offices of the Commission shall be made available to the States Parties concerned with a view to an amicable solution of the matter on the basis of respect for the present Covenant;

(*b*) The Commission shall consist of five persons acceptable to the States Parties concerned. If the States Parties concerned fail to reach agreement within three months on all or part of the composition of the Commission, the members of the Commission concerning whom no agreement has been reached shall be elected by secret ballot by a two-thirds majority vote of the Committee from among its members.

2. The members of the Commission shall serve in their personal capacity. They shall not be nationals of the States Parties concerned, or of a State not party to the present Covenant, or of a State Party which has not made a declaration under article 41.

3. The Commission shall elect its own Chairman and adopt its own rules of procedure.

4. The meetings of the Commission shall normally be held at the Headquarters of the United Nations or at the United Nations Office at Geneva. However, they may be held at such other convenient places as the Commission may determine in consultation with the Secretary-General of the United Nations and the States Parties concerned.

5. The secretariat provided in accordance with article 36 shall also service the commissions appointed under this article.

6. The information received and collated by the Committee shall be made available to the Commission and the Commission may call upon the States Parties concerned to supply any other relevant information.

7. When the Commission has fully considered the matter, but in any event not later than twelve months after having been seized of the matter, it shall submit to the Chairman of the Committee a report for communication to the States Parties concerned:

(*a*) If the Commission is unable to complete its consideration of the matter within twelve months, it shall confine its report to a brief statement of the status of its consideration of the matter;

(*b*) If an amicable solution to the matter on the basis of respect for human rights as recognized in the present Covenant is reached, the Commission shall confine its report to a brief statement of the facts and of the solution reached;

(*c*) If a solution within the terms of subparagraph (*b*) is not reached, the Commission's report shall embody its findings on all questions of fact relevant to the issues between the States Parties concerned, and its views on the possibilities of an amicable solution of the matter. This report shall also contain the written submissions and a record of the oral submissions made by the States Parties concerned;

(*d*) If the Commission's report is submitted under subparagraph (*c*), the States Parties concerned shall, within three months of the receipt of the report, notify the Chairman of the Committee whether or not they accept the contents of the report of the Commission.

8. The provisions of this article are without prejudice to the responsibilities of the Committee under article 41.

9. The States Parties concerned shall share equally all the expenses of the members of the Commission in accordance with estimates to be provided by the Secretary-General of the United Nations.

10. The Secretary-General of the United Nations shall be empowered to pay the expenses of the members of the Commission, if necessary, before reimbursement by the States Parties concerned, in accordance with paragraph 9 of this article.

Article 43
The members of the Committee, and of the ad hoc conciliation commissions which may be appointed under article 42, shall be entitled to the facilities, privileges, and immunities of experts on mission for the United Nations as laid down in the relevant sections of the Convention on the Privileges and Immunities of the United Nations.

Article 44
The provisions for the implementation of the present Covenant shall apply without prejudice to the procedures prescribed in the field of human rights by or under the constituent instruments and the conventions of the United Nations and of the specialized agencies and shall not prevent the States Parties to the present Covenant from having recourse to other procedures for settling a dispute in accordance with general or special international agreement in force between them.

Article 45
The Committee shall submit to the General Assembly of the United Nations, through the Economic and Social Council, an annual report on its activities.

PART V

Article 46
Nothing in the present Covenant shall be interpreted as impairing the provisions of the Charter of the United Nations and of the constitutions of the specialized agencies which define the respective responsibilities of the various organs of the United Nations and of the specialized agencies in regard to the matters dealt with in the present Covenant.

Article 47

Nothing in the present Covenant shall be interpreted as impairing the inherent right of all peoples to enjoy and utilize fully and freely their natural wealth and resources.

PART VI

Article 48

1. The present Covenant is open for signature by any State Member of the United Nations or member of any of its specialized agencies, by any State Party to the Statute of the International Court of Justice, and by any other State which has been invited by the General Assembly of the United Nations to become a party to the present Covenant.

2. The present Covenant is subject to ratification. Instruments of ratification shall be deposited with the Secretary-General of the United Nations.

3. The present Covenant shall be open to accession by any State referred to in paragraph 1 of this article.

4. Accession shall be effected by the deposit of an instrument of accession with the Secretary-General of the United Nations.

5. The Secretary-General of the United Nations shall inform all States which have signed this Covenant or acceded to it of the deposit of each instrument of ratification or accession.

Article 49

1. The present Covenant shall enter into force three months after the date of the deposit with the Secretary-General of the United Nations of the thirty-fifth instrument of ratification or instrument of accession.

2. For each State ratifying the present Covenant or acceding to it after the deposit of the thirty-fifth instrument of ratification or instrument of accession, the present Covenant shall enter into force three months after the date of the deposit of its own instrument of ratification or instrument of accession.

Article 50

The provisions of the present Covenant shall extend to all parts of federal States without any limitations or exceptions.

Article 51

1. Any State Party to the present Covenant may propose an amendment and file it with the Secretary-General of the United Nations. The Secretary-General of the United Nations shall thereupon communicate any proposed amendments to the States Parties to the present Covenant with a request that they notify him whether they favour a conference of States Parties for the purpose of considering and voting

upon the proposals. In the event that at least one third of the States Parties favours such a conference, the Secretary-General shall convene the conference under the auspices of the United Nations. Any amendment adopted by a majority of the States Parties present and voting at the conference shall be submitted to the General Assembly of the United Nations for approval.

2. Amendments shall come into force when they have been approved by the General Assembly of the United Nations and accepted by a two-thirds majority of the States Parties to the present Covenant in accordance with their respective constitutional processes.

3. When amendments come into force, they shall be binding on those States Parties which have accepted them, other States Parties still being bound by the provisions of the present Covenant and any earlier amendment which they have accepted.

Article 52

Irrespective of the notifications made under article 48, paragraph 5, the Secretary-General of the United Nations shall inform all States referred to in paragraph 1 of the same article of the following particulars:

(*a*) Signatures, ratifications, and accessions under article 48;

(*b*) The date of the entry into force of the present Covenant under article 49 and the date of the entry into force of any amendments under article 51.

Article 53

1. The present Covenant, of which the Chinese, English, French, Russian, and Spanish texts are equally authentic, shall be deposited in the archives of the United Nations.

2. The Secretary-General of the United Nations shall transmit certified copies of the present Covenant to all States referred to in article 48.

APPENDIX C

Optional Protocol to the International Covenant on Civil and Political Rights

The States Parties to the present Protocol,

Considering that in order further to achieve the purposes of the Covenant on Civil and Political Rights (hereinafter referred to as the Covenant) and the implementation of its provisions it would be appropriate to enable the Human Rights Committee set up in part IV of the Covenant (hereinafter referred to as the Committee) to receive and consider, as provided in the present Protocol, communications from individuals claiming to be victims of violations of any of the rights set forth in the Covenant,

Have agreed as follows:

Article 1
A State Party to the Covenant that becomes a party to the present Protocol recognizes the competence of the Committee to receive and consider communications from individuals subject to its jurisdiction who claim to be victims of a violation by that State Party of any of the rights set forth in the Covenant. No communication shall be received by the Committee if it concerns a State Party to the Covenant which is not a party to the present Protocol.

Article 2
Subject to the provisions of article 1, individuals who claim that any of their rights enumerated in the Covenant have been violated and who have exhausted all available domestic remedies may submit a written communication to the Committee for consideration.

Article 3

The Committee shall consider inadmissible any communication under the present Protocol which is anonymous, or which it considers to be an abuse of the right of submission of such communications or to be incompatible with the provisions of the Covenant.

Article 4

1. Subject to the provisions of article 3, the Committee shall bring any communications submitted to it under the present Protocol to the attention of the State Party to the present Protocol alleged to be violating any provision of the Covenant.

2. Within six months, the receiving State shall submit to the Committee written explanations or statements clarifying the matter and the remedy, if any, that may have been taken by that State.

Article 5

1. The Committee shall consider communications received under the present Protocol in the light of all written information made available to it by the individual and by the State Party concerned.

2. The Committee shall not consider any communication from an individual unless it has ascertained that:

(*a*) The same matter is not being examined under another procedure of international investigation or settlement;

(*b*) The individual has exhausted all available domestic remedies.

This shall not be the rule where the application of the remedies is unreasonably prolonged.

3. The Committee shall hold closed meetings when examining communications under the present Protocol.

4. The Committee shall forward its views to the State Party concerned and to the individual.

Article 6

The Committee shall include in its annual report under article 45 of the Covenant a summary of its activities under the present Protocol.

Article 7

Pending the achievement of the objectives of resolution 1514 (XV) adopted by the General Assembly of the United Nations on 14 December 1960 concerning the Declaration on the Granting of Independence to Colonial Countries and Peoples, the provisions of the present Protocol shall in no way limit the right of petition granted to these peoples by the Charter of the United Nations and other international conventions and instruments under the United Nations and its specialized agencies.

Article 8

1. The present Protocol is open for signature by any State which has signed the Covenant.

2. The present Protocol is subject to ratification by any State which has ratified or acceded to the Covenant. Instruments of ratification shall be deposited with the Secretary-General of the United Nations.

3. The present Protocol shall be open to accession by any State which has ratified or acceded to the Covenant.

4. Accession shall be effected by the deposit of an instrument of accession with the Secretary-General of the United Nations.

5. The Secretary-General of the United Nations shall inform all States which have signed the present Protocol or acceded to it of the deposit of each instrument of ratification or accession.

Article 9

1. Subject to the entry into force of the Covenant, the present Protocol shall enter into force three months after the date of the deposit with the Secretary-General of the United Nations of the tenth instrument of ratification or instrument of accession.

2. For each State ratifying the present Protocol or acceding to it after the deposit of the tenth instrument of ratification or instrument of accession, the present Protocol shall enter into force three months after the date of the deposit of its own instrument of ratification or instrument of accession.

Article 10

The provisions of the present Protocol shall extend to all parts of federal States without any limitations or exceptions.

Article 11

1. Any State Party to the present Protocol may propose an amendment and file it with the Secretary-General of the United Nations. The Secretary-General shall thereupon communicate any proposed amendments to the States Parties to the present Protocol with a request that they notify him whether they favour a conference of States Parties for the purpose of considering and voting upon the proposal. In the event that at least one third of the States Parties favours such a conference, the Secretary-General shall convene the conference under the auspices of the United Nations. Any amendment adopted by a majority of the States Parties present and voting at the conference shall be submitted to the General Assembly of the United Nations for approval.

2. Amendments shall come into force when they have been approved by the General Assembly of the United Nations and accepted by a two-thirds majority of the

States Parties to the present Protocol in accordance with their respective constitutional processes.

3. When amendments come into force, they shall be binding on those States Parties which have accepted them, other States Parties still being bound by the provisions of the present Protocol and any earlier amendment which they have accepted.

Article 12

1. Any State Party may denounce the present Protocol at any time by written notification addressed to the Secretary-General of the United Nations. Denunciation shall take effect three months after the date of receipt of the notification by the Secretary-General.

2. Denunciation shall be without prejudice to the continued application of the provisions of the present Protocol to any communication submitted under article 2 before the effective date of denunciation.

Article 13

Irrespective of the notifications made under article 8, paragraph 5, of the present Protocol, the Secretary-General of the United Nations shall inform all States referred to in article 48, paragraph 1, of the Covenant of the following particulars:

(*a*) Signatures, ratifications, and accessions under article 8;

(*b*) The date of the entry into force of the present Protocol under article 9 and the date of the entry into force of any amendments under article 11;

(*c*) Denunciations under article 12.

Article 14

1. The present Protocol, of which the Chinese, English, French, Russian, and Spanish texts are equally authentic, shall be deposited in the archives of the United Nations.

2. The Secretary-General of the United Nations shall transmit certified copies of the present Protocol to all States referred to in article 48 of the Covenant.

APPENDIX D

International Covenant on Economic, Social, and Cultural Rights

PREAMBLE

The States Parties to the present Covenant,

Considering that, in accordance with the principles proclaimed in the Charter of the United Nations, recognition of the inherent dignity and of the equal and inalienable rights of all the members of the human family is the foundation of freedom, justice, and peace in the world,

Recognizing that these rights derive from the inherent dignity of the human person,

Recognizing that, in accordance with the Universal Declaration of Human Rights, the ideal of free human beings enjoying freedom from fear and want can only be achieved if conditions are created whereby everyone may enjoy his economic, social, and cultural rights, as well as his civil and political rights,

Considering the obligation of States under the Charter of the United Nations to promote universal respect for, and observance of, human rights and freedoms,

Realizing that the individual, having duties to other individuals and to the community to which he belongs, is under a responsibility to strive for the promotion and observance of the rights recognized in the present Covenant,

Agree upon the following articles:

PART I

Article 1

1. All peoples have the right of self-determination. By virtue of that right they freely determine their political status and freely pursue their economic, social, and cultural development.

2. All peoples may, for their own ends, freely dispose of their natural wealth and resources without prejudice to any obligations arising out of international economic co-operation, based upon the principle of mutual benefit, and international law. In no case may a people be deprived of its own means of subsistence.

3. The States Parties to the present Covenant, including those having responsibility for the administration of Non-Self-Governing and Trust Territories, shall promote the realization of the right of self-determination, and shall respect that right, in conformity with the provisions of the Charter of the United Nations.

PART II

Article 2

1. Each State Party to the present Covenant undertakes to take steps, individually and through international assistance and cooperation, especially economic and technical, to the maximum of its available resources, with a view to achieving progressively the full realization of the rights recognized in the present Covenant by all appropriate means, including particularly the adoption of legislative measures.

2. The States Parties to the present Covenant undertake to guarantee that the rights enunciated in the present Covenant will be exercised without discrimination of any kind as to race, colour, sex, language, religion, political or other opinion, national or social origin, property, birth, or other status.

3. Developing countries, with due regard to human rights and their national economy, may determine to what extent they would guarantee the economic rights recognized in the present Covenant to non-nationals.

Article 3

The States Parties to the present Covenant undertake to ensure the equal right of men and women to the enjoyment of all economic, social, and cultural rights set forth in the present Covenant.

Article 4

The States Parties to the present Covenant recognize that, in the enjoyment of those rights provided by the State in conformity with the present Covenant, the State may subject such rights only to such limitations as are determined by law only in so far as this may be compatible with the nature of these rights and solely for the purpose of promoting the general welfare in a democratic society.

Article 5

1. Nothing in the present Covenant may be interpreted as implying for any State, group, or person any right to engage in any activity or to perform any act aimed at the destruction of any of the rights or freedoms recognized herein, or at their limitation to a greater extent than is provided for in the present Covenant.

2. No restriction upon or derogation from any of the fundamental human rights recognized or existing in any country in virtue of law, conventions, regulations, or custom shall be admitted on the pretext that the present Covenant does not recognize such rights or that it recognizes them to a lesser extent.

PART III

Article 6

1. The States Parties to the present Covenant recognize the right to work, which includes the right of everyone to the opportunity to gain his living by work which he freely chooses or accepts, and will take appropriate steps to safeguard this right.

2. The steps to be taken by a State Party to the present Covenant to achieve the full realization of this right shall include technical and vocational guidance and training programmes, policies, and techniques to achieve steady economic, social, and cultural development and full and productive employment under conditions safeguarding fundamental political and economic freedoms to the individual.

Article 7

The States Parties to the present Covenant recognize the right of everyone to the enjoyment of just and favourable conditions of work which ensure, in particular:

(*a*) Remuneration which provides all workers, as a minimum, with:

(i) Fair wages and equal remuneration for work of equal value without distinction of any kind, in particular women being guaranteed conditions of work not inferior to those enjoyed by men, with equal pay for equal work;

(ii) A decent living for themselves and their families in accordance with the provisions of the present Covenant;

(*b*) Safe and healthy working conditions;

(*c*) Equal opportunity for everyone to be promoted in his employment to an appropriate higher level, subject to no considerations other than those of seniority and competence;

(*d*) Rest, leisure, and reasonable limitation of working hours and periodic holidays with pay, as well as remuneration for public holidays.

Article 8

1. The States Parties to the present Covenant undertake to ensure:

(*a*) The right of everyone to form trade unions and join the trade union of his choice, subject only to the rules of the organization concerned, for the promotion and protection of his economic and social interests. No restrictions may be placed on the exercise of this right other than those prescribed by law and which are necessary in a democratic society in the interests of national security or public order or for the protection of the rights and freedoms of others;

(*b*) The right of trade unions to establish national federations or confederations and the right of the latter to form or join international trade-union organizations;

(*c*) The right of trade unions to function freely subject to no limitations other than those prescribed by law and which are necessary in a democratic society in the interests of national security or public order or for the protection of the rights and freedoms of others;

(*d*) The right to strike, provided that it is exercised in conformity with the laws of the particular country.

2. This article shall not prevent the imposition of lawful restrictions on the exercise of these rights by members of the armed forces or of the police or of the administration of the State.

3. Nothing in this article shall authorize States Parties to the International Labour Organisation Convention of 1948 concerning Freedom of Association and Protection of the Right to Organise to take legislative measures which would prejudice, or apply the law in such a manner as would prejudice, the guarantees provided for in that Convention.

Article 9

The States Parties to the present Covenant recognize the right of everyone to social security, including social insurance.

Article 10

The States Parties to the present Covenant recognize that:

1. The widest possible protection and assistance should be accorded to the family, which is the natural and fundamental group unit of society, particularly for its establishment and while it is responsible for the care and education of dependent children. Marriage must be entered into with the free consent of the intending spouses.

2. Special protection should be accorded to mothers during a reasonable period before and after childbirth. During such period working mothers should be accorded paid leave or leave with adequate social security benefits.

3. Special measures of protection and assistance should be taken on behalf of all children and young persons without any discrimination for reasons of parentage or

other conditions. Children and young persons should be protected from economic and social exploitation. Their employment in work harmful to their morals or health or dangerous to life or likely to hamper their normal development should be punishable by law. States should also set age limits below which the paid employment of child labour should be prohibited and punishable by law.

Article 11

1. The States Parties to the present Covenant recognize the right of everyone to an adequate standard of living for himself and his family, including adequate food, clothing, and housing, and to the continuous improvement of living conditions. The States Parties will take appropriate steps to ensure the realization of this right, recognizing to this effect the essential importance of international co-operation based on free consent.

2. The States Parties to the present Covenant, recognizing the fundamental right of everyone to be free from hunger, shall take, individually and through international co-operation, the measures, including specific programmes, which are needed:

(*a*) To improve methods of production, conservation, and distribution of food by making full use of technical and scientific knowledge, by disseminating knowledge of the principles of nutrition, and by developing or reforming agrarian systems in such a way as to achieve the most efficient development and utilization of natural resources;

(*b*) Taking into account the problems of both food-importing and food-exporting countries, to ensure an equitable distribution of world food supplies in relation to need.

Article 12

1. The States Parties to the present Covenant recognize the right of everyone to the enjoyment of the highest attainable standard of physical and mental health.

2. The steps to be taken by the States Parties to the present Covenant to achieve the full realization of this right shall include those necessary for:

(*a*) The provision for the reduction of the stillbirth-rate and of infant mortality and for the healthy development of the child;

(*b*) The improvement of all aspects of environmental and industrial hygiene;

(*c*) The prevention, treatment, and control of epidemic, endemic, occupational, and other diseases;

(*d*) The creation of conditions which would assure to all medical service and medical attention in the event of sickness.

Article 13

1. The States Parties to the present Covenant recognize the right of everyone to ed-

ucation. They agree that education shall be directed to the full development of the human personality and the sense of its dignity, and shall strengthen the respect for human rights and fundamental freedoms. They further agree that education shall enable all persons to participate effectively in a free society, promote understanding, tolerance, and friendship among all nations and all racial, ethnic, or religious groups, and further the activities of the United Nations for the maintenance of peace.

2. The States Parties to the present Covenant recognize that, with a view to achieving the full realization of this right:

(*a*) Primary education shall be compulsory and available free to all;

(*b*) Secondary education in its different forms, including technical and vocational secondary education, shall be made generally available and accessible to all by every appropriate means, and in particular by the progressive introduction of free education;

(*c*) Higher education shall be made equally accessible to all, on the basis of capacity, by every appropriate means, and in particular by the progressive introduction of free education;

(*d*) Fundamental education shall be encouraged or intensified as far as possible for those persons who have not received or completed the whole period of their primary education;

(*e*) The development of a system of schools at all levels shall be actively pursued, an adequate fellowship system shall be established, and the material conditions of teaching staff shall be continuously improved.

3. The States Parties to the present Covenant undertake to have respect for the liberty of parents and, when applicable, legal guardians to choose for their children schools, other than those established by the public authorities, which conform to such minimum educational standards as may be laid down or approved by the State and to ensure the religious and moral education of their children in conformity with their own convictions.

4. No part of this article shall be construed so as to interfere with the liberty of individuals and bodies to establish and direct educational institutions, subject always to the observance of the principles set forth in paragraph 1 of this article and to the requirement that the education given in such institutions shall conform to such minimum standards as may be laid down by the State.

Article 14
Each State Party to the present Covenant which, at the time of becoming a Party, has not been able to secure in its metropolitan territory or other territories under its jurisdiction compulsory primary education, free of charge, undertakes, within two

years, to work out and adopt a detailed plan of action for the progressive implementation, within a reasonable number of years, to be fixed in the plan, of the principle of compulsory education free of charge for all.

Article 15

1. The States Parties to the present Covenant recognize the right of everyone:

(*a*) To take part in cultural life;

(*b*) To enjoy the benefits of scientific progress and its applications;

(*c*) To benefit from the protection of the moral and material interests resulting
from any scientific, literary, or artistic production of which he is the author.

2. The steps to be taken by the States Parties to the present Covenant to achieve
the full realization of this right shall include those necessary for the conservation, the
development, and the diffusion of science and culture.

3. The States Parties to the present Covenant undertake to respect the freedom indispensable for scientific research and creative activity.

4. The States Parties to the present Covenant recognize the benefits to be derived
from the encouragement and development of international contacts and co-operation in the scientific and cultural fields.

PART IV

Article 16

1. The States Parties to the present Covenant undertake to submit in conformity with this part of the Covenant reports on the measures which they have adopted
and the progress made in achieving the observance of the rights recognized herein.

2. (*a*) All reports shall be submitted to the Secretary-General of the United Nations, who shall transmit copies to the Economic and Social Council for consideration in accordance with the provisions of the present Covenant;

(*b*) The Secretary-General of the United Nations shall also transmit to the specialized agencies copies of the reports, or any relevant parts therefrom, from States
Parties to the present Covenant which are also members of these specialized agencies in so far as these reports, or parts therefrom, relate to any matters which fall
within the responsibilities of the said agencies in accordance with their constitutional instruments.

Article 17

1. The States Parties to the present Covenant shall furnish their reports in stages,
in accordance with a programme to be established by the Economic and Social
Council within one year of the entry into force of the present Covenant after consultation with the States Parties and the specialized agencies concerned.

2. Reports may indicate factors and difficulties affecting the degree of fulfilment of obligations under the present Covenant.

3. Where relevant information has previously been furnished to the United Nations or to any specialized agency by any State Party to the present Covenant, it will not be necessary to reproduce that information, but a precise reference to the information so furnished will suffice.

Article 18

Pursuant to its responsibilities under the Charter of the United Nations in the field of human rights and fundamental freedoms, the Economic and Social Council may make arrangements with the specialized agencies in respect of their reporting to it on the progress made in achieving the observance of the provisions of the present Covenant falling within the scope of their activities. These reports may include particulars of decisions and recommendations on such implementation adopted by their competent organs.

Article 19

The Economic and Social Council may transmit to the Commission on Human Rights for study and general recommendation or, as appropriate, for information the reports concerning human rights submitted by States in accordance with articles 16 and 17, and those concerning human rights submitted by the specialized agencies in accordance with article 18.

Article 20

The States Parties to the present Covenant and the specialized agencies concerned may submit comments to the Economic and Social Council on any general recommendation under article 19 or reference to such general recommendation in any report of the Commission on Human Rights or any documentation referred to therein.

Article 21

The Economic and Social Council may submit from time to time to the General Assembly reports with recommendations of a general nature and a summary of the information received from the States Parties to the present Covenant and the specialized agencies on the measures taken and the progress made in achieving general observance of the rights recognized in the present Covenant.

Article 22

The Economic and Social Council may bring to the attention of other organs of the United Nations, their subsidiary organs and specialized agencies concerned with furnishing technical assistance any matters arising out of the reports referred to in this part of the present Covenant which may assist such bodies in deciding, each within its field of competence, on the advisability of international measures likely to contribute to the effective progressive implementation of the present Covenant.

Article 23

The States Parties to the present Covenant agree that international action for the achievement of the rights recognized in the present Covenant includes such methods as the conclusion of conventions, the adoption of recommendations, the furnishing of technical assistance, and the holding of regional meetings and technical meetings for the purpose of consultation and study organized in conjunction with the Governments concerned.

Article 24

Nothing in the present Covenant shall be interpreted as impairing the provisions of the Charter of the United Nations and of the constitutions of the specialized agencies which define the respective responsibilities of the various organs of the United Nations and of the specialized agencies in regard to the matters dealt with in the present Covenant.

Article 25

Nothing in the present Covenant shall be interpreted as impairing the inherent right of all peoples to enjoy and utilize fully and freely their natural wealth and resources.

PART V

Article 26

1. The present Covenant is open for signature by any State Member of the United Nations or member of any of its specialized agencies, by any State Party to the Statute of the International Court of Justice, and by any other State which has been invited by the General Assembly of the United Nations to become a party to the present Covenant.

2. The present Covenant is subject to ratification. Instruments of ratification shall be deposited with the Secretary-General of the United Nations.

3. The present Covenant shall be open to accession by any State referred to in paragraph 1 of this article.

4. Accession shall be effected by the deposit of an instrument of accession with the Secretary-General of the United Nations.

5. The Secretary-General of the United Nations shall inform all States which have signed the present Covenant or acceded to it of the deposit of each instrument of ratification or accession.

Article 27

1. The present Covenant shall enter into force three months after the date of the deposit with the Secretary-General of the United Nations of the thirty-fifth instrument of ratification or instrument of accession.

2. For each State ratifying the present Covenant or acceding to it after the deposit of the thirty-fifth instrument of ratification or instrument of accession, the present Covenant shall enter into force three months after the date of the deposit of its own instrument of ratification or instrument of accession.

Article 28
The provisions of the present Covenant shall extend to all parts of federal States without any limitations or exceptions.

Article 29
1. Any State Party to the present Covenant may propose an amendment and file it with the Secretary-General of the United Nations. The Secretary-General shall thereupon communicate any proposed amendments to the States Parties to the present Covenant with a request that they notify him whether they favour a conference of States Parties for the purpose of considering and voting upon the proposals. In the event that at least one third of the States Parties favours such a conference, the Secretary-General shall convene the conference under the auspices of the United Nations. Any amendment adopted by a majority of the States Parties present and voting at the conference shall be submitted to the General Assembly of the United Nations for approval.

2. Amendments shall come into force when they have been approved by the General Assembly of the United Nations and accepted by a two-thirds majority of the States Parties to the present Covenant in accordance with their respective constitutional processes.

3. When amendments come into force they shall be binding on those States Parties which have accepted them, other States Parties still being bound by the provisions of the present Covenant and any earlier amendment which they have accepted.

Article 30
Irrespective of the notifications made under article 26, paragraph 5, the Secretary-General of the United Nations shall inform all States referred to in paragraph 1 of the same article of the following particulars:

(*a*) Signatures, ratifications, and accessions under article 26;

(*b*) The date of the entry into force of the present Covenant under article 27 and the date of the entry into force of any amendments under article 29.

Article 31
1. The present Covenant, of which the Chinese, English, French, Russian, and Spanish texts are equally authentic, shall be deposited in the archives of the United Nations.

2. The Secretary-General of the United Nations shall transmit certified copies of the present Covenant to all States referred to in article 26.

CREDITS AND PERMISSIONS

INDEX

accession, to treaty, 36
Addams, Jane, 31–33
adoption, 177–78
Afghanistan, 34, 141–42
Aristotle, 21
asylum, as human right, 60

Beijing + 5 Conference (1995), 153
Beijing Declaration. *See* Platform for
  Action
Bill of Rights: International, 85–87;
  United States, 23
bracketing of text, 154

Cassin, Rene, 28, 30
children: basic rights, 163; best interests
  of, 165; Convention on the Rights of
  the Child (1989), 163–77; cultural
  rights, 171; and the death penalty,
  173; exploitation of, 171, 172; foster
  care and adoption, 177–78; freedom
  of information, 169; freedom of

thought, 168; medical care, 170; right
  to protection, 100, 121, 178–79; separation from parents, 166–67; special
  care, 67–68; as vulnerable group,
  163
China, 3, 62–63, 76
civil and political rights: compared to
  economic rights, 129–31; as human
  right, 83–107
Code of Ethics (NASW), 7, 79, 92, 101,
  233–36, 238; application to human
  rights, 239–45; based on human
  rights principles, 79, 101; criticism of,
  234; ethical principles, 235; ethical
  responsibilities, 236, 238; respect for
  cultural diversity, 198; relevance to
  social workers, 233; self-determination, 92
collective human rights, 20, 197–98
colonial exploitation, 27, 189
Commission on Human Rights, 28–29,
  207

Communist Manifesto (1848), 23–24

community: duties, 70

convention: accession and ratification, 36; definition, 35; reservations on, 36–37

Convention on the Elimination of All Forms of Discrimination Against Women (CEDAW): provisions, 144–49; U.S. position on, 147–49

Convention on the Rights of the Child (1989): provisions, 163–77; U.S. position on, 176–77

covenant: accession or ratification of, 36; definition, 35; reservations on, 36–37. *See also* International Covenant on Civil and Political Rights; International Covenant on Economic, Social, and Cultural Rights

Cuba, 114

cultural competence, 231–32

cultural life: and children, 171; as human right, 69, 101, 122–23

cultural relativism, 62, 212–15

customary international law, 33, 37

death penalty: human rights perspective, 96; in the United States, 54–55, 97, 171, 173

declaration: as a human rights term, 34–35

Declaration of Independence (U.S.; 1776), 23

Declaration on Race and Racial Prejudice (1978), 184

Declaration on the Right to Development, 203–205

Declaration on the Rights of the Child, 163

Declaration on the Rights of Disabled Persons, 179

defamation, 59, 98

development: as human right, 201, 203–205, 208; standards of success, 205, 208

disability: persons with disabilities as a vulnerable group, 179–82; as a social construct, 179–80; UN declarations on, 180–82. *See also* Declaration on the Rights of Disabled Persons

discrimination, 53, 56–57, 93, 95–96, 136–37, 145–46, 226–27

domestic violence: as violation of human rights, 55, 73

Dred Scott case, 2

economic rights: Economic Bill of Rights, 26; compared to political rights, 129–31; as a human right, 65–66, 115–16, 121–22; publicity about, 139. *See also* International Covenant on Economic, Social, and Cultural Rights; Poor People's Economic Human Rights Campaign

education: and children, 170; as a human right, 68–69, 122

elections: as a human right, 64–65

employment: as a human right, 66–67, 116; and just conditions, 118–20; living wage, 117–18, 120; mobbing, 119–20; and trade unions, 120–21

empowerment, 229–30

Engels, Friedrich, 23, 24

equal protection, 56–57, 100–101

ethics: affect of environment on, 237; application to human rights, 239–41; case studies, 239–45. *See also* Code of *Ethics*

ethnic-sensitive practice, 231

Falun Gong (China), 63

family: definitions, 61; and human rights, 61, 100, 121

feminist practice, 231

Filartiga v. Pena-Irala, 37
foreign aid, 202–203
freedom of expression: defamation, 59, 98; as a human right, 63–64, 98, 100
French Revolution, 22

gays and lesbians, 190–91
Gandhi, Mohandas "Mahatma," 31
gender disempowerment, 135
genocide, 75
Germany: Nazi period, 45, 57–58; welfare policies, 127–28, 169
global apartheid, 201, 203, 220
globalization, 208–12

health care: as a human right, 67–68, 122; in the United States, 123
HIV–AIDS: patents on anti-HIV-AIDS drugs, 123–24, 201, 210–12; UN resolution on, 182–84
Hobbes, Thomas, 22
human rights: application to social work ethics, 239–45; civil and political rights, 83–109, appendix B, appendix C; collective rights, 20; concept of, 1, 4; economic, social, and cultural rights, 112–31, appendix D; definition, 3–4; economic development, 201–205, 208; enforcement of, 73, 75–76, 79; gender issues, 46, 135; generations of, 19–20, 69; historical development, 20–30; indivisibility of, 6; laws, 33; monitoring, 47–48, 102, 124–25; negative rights, 19; positive rights, 19–20; role in social work profession, 226; support by social workers, 8, 225–26; teaching of, 52; terminology, 34–37; third generation, 197–98; universality, 4–6, 53, 56, 71–73; women's rights, 143–44, 150–51. *See also* Universal Declaration of Human Rights

Human Rights Committee, 102–104
Human Rights Watch: human rights report (2000) on U.S., 47–48; mission statement, 47

indigenous peoples: contribution to human rights, 26–27; exploitation of, 27; forced relocation, 166; self-determination, 218–19; sovereignty in the United States, 89
Illinois Department of Human Rights, 137
indivisibility, re human rights, 6
International Association of Schools of Social Work, 32
International Bill of Rights, 85–87
International Committee of Schools of Social Work, 25
international cooperation: drug patents, 123–24, 201; scientific and cultural fields, 124
International Covenant on Civil and Political Rights (1966): provisions, 87–107, appendix B; purpose, 84; reservations by United States, 106; social work perspective, 109; submission to U.S. Senate, 36
International Covenant on Economic, Social, and Cultural Rights (1966): provisions, 112–31, appendix C; social work perspective, 126–31; submission to U.S. Senate, 36
International Federation of Social Workers, 196
International Labor Organization, 25
International Monetary Fund, 210, 211
International Permanent Secretariat of Social Workers, 25
interventions: challenging oppression, 228; cultural competence, 231–32; empowerment, 229–30;

interventions (*continued*): ethnic-sensitive practice, 231; feminist practice, 231; strengths perspective, 230–31

Israel, 91

Jebb, Eglantyne, 32

Kensington Welfare Rights Union, 139

League of Nations, 24, 26

least developed countries: foreign aid benefits (U.S.), 202–203; low income levels, 199–200; right to development, 201

leisure (as a human right), 67

living wage, 117–18

Locke, John, 22

Magna Carta, 21

marriage, 61, 121

Marx, Karl, 23, 24

mental health and illness: human rights documents on, 181–82; position of social work profession, 182

Mexico, 94–95

mobbing in the workplace, 119–20

moral relativism, 77–78

motherhood, special care, 68, 121

Nairobi Forward-Looking Strategies for the Advancement of Women (1985), 149–50

National Association of Social Workers' *Code of Ethics. See Code of Ethics*

natural law, 21

natural rights, 22

Nazi Germany, 45, 57–58. *See also* Germany

negative human rights, 19

nongovernmental organizations (NGOs),29

older persons: as a vulnerable group, 191–92; UN principles on, 191–92

Olympe de Gouges, 22

oppression, 228–29

Optional Protocol to the International Covenant on Civil and Political Rights, 107–109, appendix C

Palestinians, 91

persons with disabilities, 179–82. *See also* Declaration on the Rights of Disabled Persons

Platform for Action (1995): Beijing Declaration and the + 5 Review, 152–53; and cultural relativism, 213; 4th World Conference on Women, 151–52

Plato, 21

Poor People's Economic Human Rights Campaign, 117

positive human rights, 19–20

privacy, as a human right, 57, 98

property rights, 62

racism: position of social work profession, 189–90; slavery and colonialism as causes, 189. *See also* Declaration on Race and Racial Prejudice; World Conference Against Racism

ratification, of treaty, 36

religion, as a human right, 62–63, 98

reservation: definition, 36–37; by U.S. on covenant, 106

Roosevelt, Eleanor, 28, 44

Roosevelt, Franklin, 26

Rwanda, 75–76

Salomon, Alice, 25, 32

Scott v. Sandford. See Dred Scott case

self-determination: as a human right, 88–91, 114; international issues, 215, 218–19; social work perspective, 92–93

slavery, 2, 54, 96, 189. *See also* racism

social exclusion, 219–21

social justice: definition, 12–13; theories of, 9–11

social security, as a human right, 65–66, 121

social work profession: application of human rights, 224–27; and child protection, 178–79; importance of women's rights, 157–59; and international human rights issues, 208; international responsibility, 198; and interventions, 228–32; mission of, 232; reluctance to integrate human rights, 6–8; support of human rights, 225–26

Social Work Symposium (1995): 4th World Conference on Women, 155; and human rights, 153–57; provisions, 155–56

Socrates, 21

strengths perspective, 230–31

Taliban, 34, 141

terrorism: as excuse for violating human rights, 77–78; root causes of, 201; U.S. war on, 99

torture, as violation of human rights, 37, 54, 96

trade unions, 100, 120, 121

travel, as a human right, 60

treaty: accession and ratification, 36; definition, 35; human rights law, 33

United Nations, 28, 30, 44

United Nations Charter, 28

United Nations' system of human rights, 206

United States: Bill of Rights, 23; children's rights, 176–77; death penalty in, 97, 171, 173; Declaration of Independence, 23; foreign view of, 216–17; indigenous peoples, 89; report on human rights, 47–48; reservations regarding the Covenant on Civil and Political Rights, 106; and women's rights, 147–49

U.S. Constitution, 2, 23, 56, 63–64, 101

U.S. Supreme Court: Dred Scott decision on slavery, 2; failure to consider international law, 38–39

Universal Declaration of Human Rights (1948): adoption by United Nations, 30, 44; code of conduct, 71–72; history, 18, 29–30, 44–46; international cooperation, 197–98; provisions, 49–70, appendix A; purpose, 45–46; sexist language, 46; social work perspective, 79–80

universality, re human rights, 4–6, 53, 56, 71–73

vacation, as a human right, 67

vulnerable groups: children, 163; definition, 134; gays and lesbians, 190–91; older persons, 191–92; persons with disabilities, 179–82; persons with HIV-AIDS, 182; persons with mental illness, 181–82; victims of racism, 184–91; women, 138–39

welfare: exclusion of immigrants, 115; U.S. goal of self-sufficiency, 127–28; Welfare Reform Act (U.S.; 1996), 126

Wells-Barnett, Ida, 24

women: human rights, 143–44; NGO Forum on Women (1995), 154–55; subordination to men, 139–43; as vulnerable group, 138–39; world conference in Beijing, 151–52. See also Platform for Action; Social Work Symposium

World Bank, 211

World Conference Against Racism, 188–89

World Trade Organization, 210

World War II, 26–27, 45–46

Yugoslavia, 76